# EAST CHESHIRE
# TEXTILE MILLS

*Top left:* Silk woven to a Persian design by Cartwright and Sheldon of Macclesfield for the Wembley Exhibition of 1924.

*Top right:* A piece of 'Macclesfield stripe': silk woven by Cartwright and Sheldon of Macclesfield *c*1935.

*Bottom left:* Silk cloth woven in a garret house on Parsonage Street, Macclesfield, in the late 19th century.

*Bottom right:* A piece of Jacquard woven cloth with a traditional Paisley motif. Woven in the mid 20th century by Cartwright and Sheldon of Macclesfield using a mixture of silk and man-made fibres.

ROYAL
COMMISSION
ON THE HISTORICAL
MONUMENTS
OF ENGLAND

# EAST CHESHIRE TEXTILE MILLS

## Anthony Calladine and Jean Fricker

ROYAL COMMISSION ON THE HISTORICAL MONUMENTS OF ENGLAND

Published by the Royal Commission on the Historical Monuments of England,
Fortress House, 23 Savile Row, London W1X 2JQ

©RCHME Crown copyright 1993

First published 1993

ISBN 1 873592 13 2

*British Library Cataloguing in Publication Data*
A CIP catalogue record for this book is available from the British Library

Designed by Chuck Goodwin, 27 Artesian Road, London W2 5DA

Printed by Staples Printers St Albans Ltd

# Contents

# Chairman's Foreword

Until its decline in the mid 20th century, the east Cheshire silk industry provided silk cloth and yarn for a world-wide market. The industry played a particularly important and hitherto little regarded role in the development of early factory buildings. By the mid 18th century, the silk industry in east Cheshire was accommodated in powered factories and by the century's end the area also had a significant factory-housed cotton-spinning industry. Many of the area's textile mills, including several important 18th-century examples, were still standing in the 1980s but it was clear that the requirements of modern industry and the pressures of modern development put them under considerable threat. In response to this, the Macclesfield Sunday School Heritage Centre and Silk Museum began a survey of mills within the town of Macclesfield in 1983, and this was extended to cover the boroughs of Macclesfield and Congleton in 1986 by the East Cheshire Textile Mill Survey (ECTMS). Recognising the importance of the work being undertaken by the ECTMS, the Royal Commission on the Historical Monuments of England began the collaboration with the ECTMS which has culminated in the publication of this book.

The Royal Commission's support of the survey of east Cheshire textile mills coincided with its own study of mills in Yorkshire, and its collaboration in another survey of those in Greater Manchester. These three projects together cover the various branches of the textile industry which played such an important part in the economic and industrial development of England from the 18th to the early 20th century; this comprehensive record will assist in the understanding and appreciation of these buildings as well as stimulating further research.

The Royal Commission welcomes its association with the East Cheshire Textile Mill Survey and would like to thank R C Turner and Dr R W Brunskill, successive Chairmen of the Survey's Steering Committee, Moira Stevenson, Director of Macclesfield Museums Trust, and all the members of the Steering Committee for their co-operation. The Commissioners wish to acknowledge the work of all those involved in the survey, in particular Anthony Calladine and Jean Fricker who established the East Cheshire Textile Mill Survey and undertook the fund-raising and field investigation as well as writing the mill reports and this book. The Royal Commission would like also to thank those outside bodies who provided funding for the east Cheshire survey. Thanks are due also to the owners and occupiers of the mills surveyed who allowed access to their property and to the historical documents in their possession. Without their co-operation a survey of east Cheshire mills would not have been possible.

PARK OF MONMOUTH
*Chairman, Royal Commission on the Historical Monuments of England*

# Preface

One does not immediately think of Cheshire as a cradle of the Industrial Revolution, and certainly the clatter of machinery and the pollution of steam power appear inconsistent with the broad green acres of the Cheshire Plain. But there is another part of the county, its eastern fringe, where the mountain streams of the Pennines and the Peak District tumble down the steep slopes east of Macclesfield and Congleton. On the map these two towns may be seen to extend the arc of industrial communities running through Bolton, Bury, Rochdale and Oldham which focuses on the Cottonopolis of Manchester and its own extensions into Salford and Stockport. East Cheshire indeed has the geographical characteristics which made it potentially one of the sources of the Industrial Revolution.

Geography provided the place for such development, society provided the impetus and it was the inspiration of individuals such as Samuel Greg and Charles Roe and the enterprise of society as a whole in east Cheshire which brought about a textile industry of silk and cotton manufacture which was for a time the wonder of the commercial world. It is the development of this textile industry and its changing social, geographical and architectural consequences which is explained in this admirable volume.

After completing a survey of mills in the town of Macclesfield established by the Macclesfield Sunday School Heritage Centre and Silk Museum, Jean Fricker and Anthony Calladine realised the importance of extending the study to the whole of east Cheshire to chronicle the story of an endeavour whose physical evidence was disappearing or under threat. They set up a research unit in association with the Macclesfield Sunday School Heritage Centre and Silk Museum, financed by local contributions and guided by a Steering Committee, initially under the chairmanship of R C Turner, and began the twin tasks of recording the surviving buildings and searching for the contemporary documents which could illuminate the history of the industry and its buildings. The Royal Commission on the Historical Monuments of England, already convinced of the need to record textile mills before they disappeared, recognised the importance of the task and added its encouragement and resources, as well as photographic and graphic support, to hasten and complete the survey work. The present volume is the welcome result.

The story told by the authors is a fascinating one, whether it tells of the little boys running their fourteen miles a day up and down the 'shades', helping convert the silk filament into yarn, or of the building of the dignified Georgian mills rising by the streams whose water power was used over and over. By the mid 18th century the east Cheshire entrepreneurs began to build some of the earliest powered factory buildings in Britain to house mechanical silk-throwing machines and later spinning machinery for silk and cotton. By the mid 19th century the east Cheshire landscape, while still largely rural, was affected by the needs of the textile industry whether in weirs and dams for water power, chimneys to vent smoke from steam–power plants up the steep valley slopes, or mills to house yarn production and weavers' cottages in which yarn was converted to cloth. During the remainder of the 19th century the story was of advances in mechanisation, including powered weaving, especially with the marvellous Jacquard loom, affected however by the fluctuating fortunes of both the silk and cotton trades. The story concludes with a last spate of mill building in the 20th century before the east Cheshire textile industry was virtually eclipsed. In text, quotations, photographs and drawings the authors have told this story well and I warmly commend it to all readers.

At the same time I record the gratitude of the Steering Committee to Jean Fricker and Anthony Calladine for initiating the study and maintaining its momentum in spite of many setbacks, to all the supporters who contributed in cash and kind towards the continuation of the work, to the millowners and tenants who allowed access to property and documents, and especially to the members and staff of the Royal Commission on the Historical Monuments of England whose generous support ensured the successful completion of the task.

R W BRUNSKILL
*Chairman, East Cheshire Textile Mill Survey*
*Steering Committee*

# Acknowledgements

This study was carried out with the support of the Steering Committee of the East Cheshire Textile Mill Survey and much credit and great thanks is due to all members and to the Secretary of the Royal Commission on the Historical Monuments of England, T G Hassall. Commissioners maintained an interest, but particular thanks are due to Professor R A Buchanan who read the complete text and made valuable comments. The help of Dr John Bold, Dr R W Brunskill, Dr Jane Croom, Keith Falconer, Dr D A Farnie, Dr Ian H Goodall, Natalie Rothstein, Moira Stevenson and Dr Robin Thornes, who also read and commented upon the text, is greatly appreciated. We are grateful to Professor Claudio Zanier of the University of Pisa for information and advice concerning the Italian silk industry. Thanks are also due to Colum Giles for his advice and observations, A D Perry who took the archive and publication photographs, Roger Featherstone who took the aerial photographs, Andy Donald and Bernard Thomason who digitised the survey drawings, and Anthony Berry who prepared these and the cut-away drawings for publication. Davina Turner and Fran Brown edited the text, Jean Craven provided secretarial and clerical support and Diana Hale gave advice relating to the archive. Advice on editorial and publication issues was provided by Kate Owen, who also managed the editorial, design and production stages, and Jane Butcher.

The East Cheshire Textile Mill Survey would never have succeeded without the organisations and companies which generously provided its funding: the Royal Commission on the Historical Monuments of England, Cheshire County Council, Macclesfield Borough Council, Congleton Borough Council, English Heritage, The Countryside Commission, UK 2000, The Mersey Basin Campaign, Gradus Ltd, W H Bossons Ltd, Parkers Ltd, Slater Harrison Ltd and Derek Rose Pyjamas Ltd

Thanks are also due to Macclesfield Sunday School Heritage Centre Trust, now Macclesfield Museums Trust, for whom the survey of Macclesfield town's mills was carried out based on an initial inventory compiled by Marjorie Latham. Without the help and support of the Macclesfield Museums Trust and its staff, in particular Moira Stevenson and Louanne Collins, this publication would not have been possible. Thanks are also due to members of the Macclesfield Sunday School Heritage Centre Trust survey team; Jane Timberlake, Mark Tickner, Geoff Finch and Mark Handscombe. We would also like to thank members of the Garret Survey Team.

Particular thanks must be given to members of the ECTMS survey team: to Adele Mayer and Christopher White for draughting, to Andrew Skelhorn and Alison Taylor for research, to Sharon Marsden for typing. Thanks are also due to George Longden for special research into the mill community at Langley and to J C Wilkinson, chemist, for support in photographic processing.

The owners of all the mills that feature in this publication were never failing in their generosity and hospitality, but particular acknowledgement is due to the late J Sebire OBE of Berisfords Ltd, W R Bossons of W H Bossons Ltd, Mr Snape and Mr Booth of Gradus Ltd, Mr Adamski of Adamley Textiles Ltd, Mr Leigh, owner of Gin Clough Mill and Mr Sheldon, owner of Lumbhole Mill. A special thank you must be given to Brian Lewis who provided the Survey with accommodation.

Every effort has been made to discover and acknowledge the copyright relating to illustrative material. Any omission is regretted and information regarding copyright in any such cases is welcomed.

# Illustration Credits

# Editorial Notes

The structure of this book is outlined in the Introduction. Drawings follow the conventions outlined in *Recording Historic Buildings: a Descriptive Specification* (2nd edition, RCHME 1991), 5–8. A few conventions specific to industrial buildings have been used, namely:

upright shaft        fireproof arches

The following abbreviations have been used on some plans:

B/H Boiler house
Ch Chimney
E/H Engine house
f/p fireplace
w/w waterwheel

# INTRODUCTION

It would come as a surprise to most people to learn that the first factories to house successfully the mechanised production of textiles in this country were not those of the cotton or woollen industry but those of the silk industry. By the 1780s, the decade which saw the rapid expansion of the cotton industry, over seventy mills nationally already had been erected to produce silk. East Cheshire was an area of mechanised silk production from 1744 onwards and of mechanised cotton production from 1784. These facts, coupled with the increasing threat of demolition facing the area's textile mills, provided the stimulus for an intensive historical and architectural survey.

Initially the work was undertaken as part of a research programme for the Macclesfield Sunday School Silk Heritage Centre Trust, its aim being to produce an architectural and documentary record of all mill sites in the town of Macclesfield. On completion of this survey Jean Fricker and Anthony Calladine, who had led the Macclesfield Mill Survey, established the East Cheshire Textile Mill Survey to extend the research to include all mill sites within the boroughs of Macclesfield and Congleton, where there was a concentration of mills related to the silk industry, as well as a significant number of cotton mills. The total number of sites, 242, provided a manageable body of evidence which enabled intensive surveys to be carried out on all standing mills, whilst demolished mills were researched as far as practicable. The standing mills were recorded by means of written descriptions, photographs and measured drawings. This record was supported by searches through deeds, insurance records, maps and plans, trade directories, letters and minute books, sale catalogues, newspaper advertisements and articles, and contemporary observations. Not only did this research provide an important historical and economic background, particularly for the previously under-researched silk industry, but it also contributed significantly to the understanding of the structural development and use of mills in the region. Almost certainly, the most significant outcome of the survey has been the amount of evidence, both structural and documentary, surviving from the earliest periods of mill building during the mid and late 18th century. Unreferenced statements in the book relating to individual sites and to the development of the textile industry in east Cheshire are based on evidence gathered during the survey which is contained in the mill files which form the publicly accessible archive (see Gazetteer).

It became clear during the survey that east Cheshire's textile industry developed in fairly distinct phases, and the organisation of this publication reflects those stages of development. Chapter One provides the historical background and sets the local industry in its national context. Chapter Two examines the earliest phase of mill development in east Cheshire. It attempts to explain the housing of the silk industry before mechanisation, and details the form of factory building from the construction of the first water-powered silk-throwing mill in 1744 up to the building of the first cotton-spinning mills in the 1780s. Chapter Three covers the introduction of the cotton industry to east Cheshire from the 1780s onwards and examines how the form of mill building was affected by its needs and those of the silk industry. It also relates mill building to the developing water-power and new steam-power technology and ends with the financial crisis of 1826. This marked a watershed in the history of the region's textile industry, bringing about an almost complete cessation of mill building for almost a decade. After 1826, east Cheshire textile-mill architecture followed relatively different paths in its two branches. Chapter Four, therefore, traces the housing of the silk industry from 1826 until 1990, and deals with the growth of silk spinning in the area, the development of the Jacquard loom and the powerloom, and the effect of new technology on mill design. Chapter Five examines cotton-mill architecture over the same period and shows how developments in spinning and weaving technology encouraged large-scale production and a consequent increase in the scale of mill building and site expansion. Both Chapters Four and Five attempt to catalogue briefly the textile industry's decline during the 20th century, although a detailed economic history of this period of the textile industry is beyond the scope of this publication. Similarly, the subject of Chapter Six is worthy of a book of its own. It gives a brief view of the impact of the textile industry upon the landscape and communities of east Cheshire, and so places the mills already discussed in their geographical context.

Not all the mills recorded during the survey are highlighted in the main text, although all are listed in the gazetteer. Using this list readers will be able to consult the survey archive, which is held at the Macclesfield Museums Trust, The Heritage Centre, Roe Street, Macclesfield, Cheshire SK11 6UT. Negatives and prints of photographs taken by the Royal Commission on the Historical Monuments of England are held at the National Buildings Record at the Royal Commission's head office at Fortress House, 23 Savile Row, London W1X 2JQ.

# 1 HISTORICAL BACKGROUND OF THE SILK AND COTTON INDUSTRIES IN EAST CHESHIRE

The silk industry was the major textile industry of east Cheshire from the mid 18th to the mid 20th century. Centred on Macclesfield and Congleton, it extended as far south as Sandbach and Wheelock and as far west as Knutsford (Figure 1). Cotton spinning was established as an alternative textile industry during the late 18th and early 19th centuries, but later contracted and became concentrated towards the northern fringes of the district, in Bollington, Rainow, Wilmslow, Styal and Disley.

Macclesfield, on the banks of the River Bollin, and Congleton, by the River Dane, are situated where the Pennine hills meet the Cheshire plain. Until the building of modern road systems, both towns were on the principal route between Stockport, Manchester and the north, and Leek, Derby and the midland districts to the south. Macclesfield was also situated on an east–west cross-Pennine trading route, and was the administrative centre of Macclesfield Forest, a royal hunting ground, and the sub-district of the county known as the Macclesfield Hundred. During the medieval period, both towns flourished as trading centres for the produce from arable lowlands to the west and pastoral uplands to the east.

Expansion and industrialisation in the 18th and 19th centuries necessitated improved transport systems. The road from Macclesfield to Buxton was turnpiked in 1758 and the roads from Macclesfield to Stockport and Leek in 1762. Also in 1762, a turnpike trust was established to maintain the Congleton to Ashbourne road which connected the former to the silk industry in Derby. The road between Macclesfield and Congleton was turnpiked in 1796. The canal network encircling Cheshire was completed in 1831 with the opening of the

Macclesfield Canal which provided a link between the Trent and Mersey Canal, opened in 1777, and the Peak Forest Canal, opened in 1800. The first railway in east Cheshire was built in 1845 when the Manchester and Birmingham Railway reached Macclesfield, followed in 1849 by the North Staffordshire Railway which linked Macclesfield and Congleton to London.

In 1834 the towns of Macclesfield and Congleton were described thus:

*The principle trade of the place [Macclesfield] was formerly the making of twist buttons, but this has been superseded by the manufacture of silk in its various textures; and the magnitude and number of the factories exhibit the extent to which this important and beautiful branch of this trade is carried on in this town; there are also several cotton factories here. The River Jordan or Bollin runs through the lower part of the town, and though the stream is inconsiderable, it turns several mills. The vicinity of Macclesfield yields abundance of coal, slate and stone, and the advantages derived therefrom by the town and its neighbourhood is very considerable ... The appearance of the country around Macclesfield is agricultural, and the chain of lofty hills to the north and east give beauty and even grandeur to the situation of the town. The views from those eminances are commanding ... and, on a very clear day, even the towns of Manchester and Liverpool, with the shipping out to sea, may be discerned ...*

*The original manufactures of Congleton consisted of gloves and leather laces called 'Congleton points'; these have long since given place to a very considerable trade in the manufacture of silk, silk throwing and silk spinning etc. The first silk mill was established here in 1754, and the trade has wonderfully increased since*

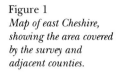

Figure 1
*Map of east Cheshire,
showing the area covered
by the survey and
adjacent counties.*

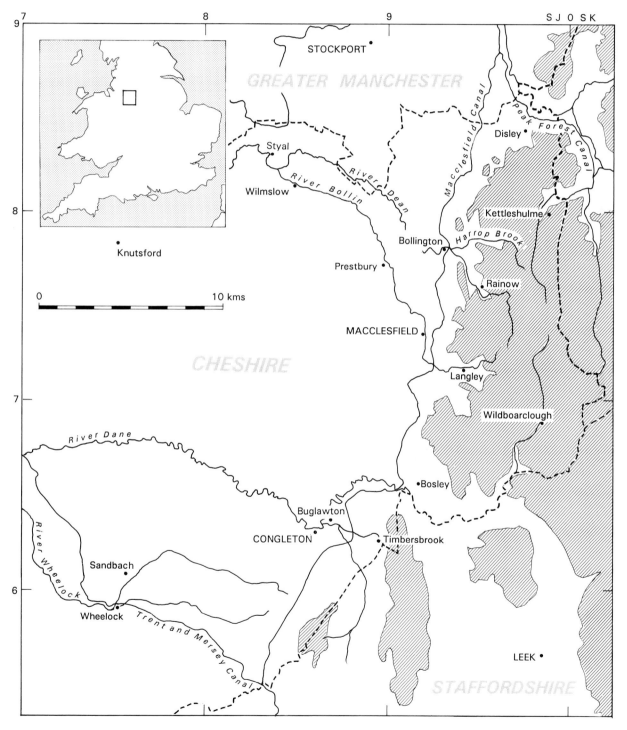

Figure 2
A c1820 view of
Macclesfield from
Windmill Brow.

*then. The ribbon branch is also of consequence here ... The appearance of the town, although ancient, is clean and respectable.*[1]
*(Figures 2 and 3)*

The reasons for the settlement and success of these industries in this area are various and complex, and should be seen as part of the wider pattern of textile production in north-west England. The old textile counties of the north-west bordered the south and west Pennine hills, and included Lancashire, Cheshire, Derbyshire and Staffordshire. Economic and industrial boundaries cannot be absolutely defined however, since there existed strong links between this region and the textile manufacturing districts further to the south and east. To the south, in the towns and hinterlands of Derby, Coventry, Nottingham and Leicester, the hosiery, lace and ribbon industries had been established since at least the 16th century. The demand for both silk and cotton yarn from these industries induced the siting of the early powered textile-spinning mills in the south-west Pennine districts and provided a continuing market for their produce. To the east, links with the Yorkshire textile industry developed in the late 18th and 19th centuries. The siting of early water-powered cotton-spinning mills spread from the Derwent and Trent valleys to the Pennine watershed valleys of Lancashire, Cheshire and Yorkshire, and particularly to the west of the range. Central to the north-west textile industry was the city of Manchester,

whose influence in the region was paramount. It was a centre for the manufacture and finishing of cloth from the 17th to the 19th century, and served as a textile market of national and ultimately of international importance.

Climatic and geographical factors were influential in both the location and specialisation of the north-west silk and cotton industries. A cool, damp climate and large areas of relatively poor land on the gritstone Pennine moors and the peat mosses to the west of Manchester were not conducive to a rich agricultural economy. Before industrialisation, in the 17th and early 18th centuries, supplementary income was found by means of processing a wide range of yarns, flax, wool, silk and cotton for example, and a variety of cloth and smallwares such as ribbons, trimmings, lace and buttons.

During the 18th century, the establishment of the newly powered textile industry in the south-west Pennines caused a dramatic reversal of the region's economy, from one of marginal agricultural subsistence to one of industrial prosperity. Ironically, the industry was attracted by those geographical factors which had hitherto determined the region's relatively poor economy. The infertile gritstone uplands were the source of fast-flowing streams for the water-powered textile mills, and of soft acidic water for processing and finishing silk and cotton yarns. The damp climate, it has been argued, was also a more suitable atmosphere in which to handle the friable cotton fibre. Additionally, rich coal beds fuelled the huge needs of the

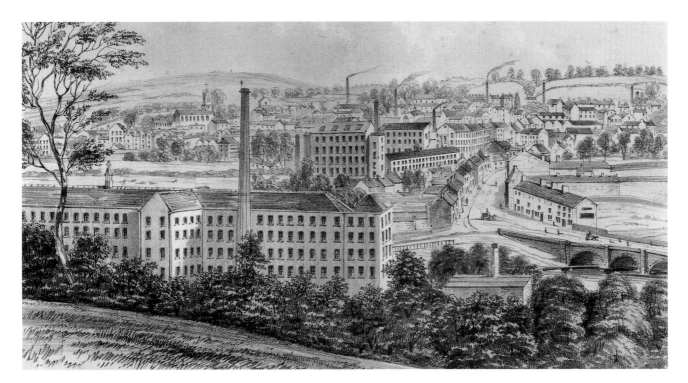

Figure 3
*A mid 19th-century view of Congleton. Old Mill stands in the foreground with Stonehouse Green Mill, Brook Mills and the other mills of the town beyond it.*

later, steam-powered factories. No less important to the new industry was the availability of a work-force familiar with the characteristics of a variety of fibres, and employable outside the influence of the craft guilds which existed in the established textile areas of the country.

In a wider geographical context, the colonisation of the Americas in the 16th and 17th centuries was a major factor in bringing about a change of emphasis in national trading patterns. Where previously only ports on the southern and eastern seaboards had been attractive to merchants and manufacturers for European trade, by the 19th century ports and their hinterlands on the west coast had become major trading centres. From overseas, through Liverpool and Manchester, came first raw cotton and then, in the 19th century, silk, both of them supplying the north-west textile industry.

## Origins of the early silk and cotton industries

Until the 18th century, the most important centres of cloth production in England were generally large towns in the south of the country. The north-west of England, by contrast, was described by John Leak in the 1570s as a region 'wher no true clothes are made'.[2] In the medieval period every main cloth-producing town had associations of weavers, cloth workers, dyers, fullers and affiliated trades, each generally related to the processing of a particular fibre. These guilds restricted entry to the trade, and this was one of the factors which encouraged textile entrepreneurs to establish themselves in areas where there were no such controls. In consequence, the early use of the imported cotton fibre, woven in union with other fibres, can be traced largely to the towns and villages of the north-west, where a variety of flax, wool and silk cloths were already in production.

Evidence indicates that in the 16th and early 17th centuries four main types of cloth were manufactured in Lancashire and Cheshire, namely linen, fustian, Manchester cotton and cotton. The production of linen cloth from flax, which was grown locally but was also imported from Ireland, was an industry of importance in the area, since it has been estimated that it occupied one-third of the labouring population of Lancashire in the 16th century.[3] In 1610 George Chetham, a Manchester textile merchant, attempted to open up markets in London for 'linen cloth, commonly called Stopport [Stockport] cloth'.[4] Fustian, which was generally a union or mixed fabric comprising a linen warp and a cotton weft, was produced in the Manchester region in this form from about the beginning of the 17th century.[5] Manchester cotton was a coarse type of woollen cloth and was recorded as early as 1551 as 'Manchester, Lancashire and Cheshire cottons'.[6]

The description of Manchester cotton of this period should not be confused with the vegetable fibre which came to be known as cotton; this was introduced into Britain in about 1600 and was then described as 'cotton wool'. It was used in fustian and as a pure weave, satisfying the demand for lighter cloth which was not fulfilled by the manufacture of native fibres. Although raw cotton, as an imported fibre, was not easily obtained, the production of cotton cloth in Manchester was described in 1641 by Lewis Roberts as an industry as significant as that of linen manufacture:

> The town of Manchester in Lancashire must also be herein remembered, and worthily, for their encouragement commended, who buy the yarn off the Irish, in great quantity, and weaving it, return the same again in linen into Ireland to sell; neither doth the industry rest here, for they buy cotton wool, in London, that comes first from Cyprus and Smyrna, and at home, work the same and persist it into Fustians, Vermillions, Dymities and other such stuffs, and then return it to London where the same is vented and sold, and not seldom sent to foreign parts, who have means at far easier terms to provide themselves of the said first materials ... It may be wished that all other parts of our Country could be so industrious.[7]

Commentators of the late 18th and 19th centuries[8] record the processing of cotton as a domestic industry in east Cheshire. However, the paucity of evidence for the early use of this fibre in the 17th and 18th centuries may indicate that it was an industry secondary to the local production of buttons, lace, ribbons and trimmings, all of which involved the use of silk yarn (or thread). Such narrow-ware was being woven in and around the towns of Manchester, Salford, Stockport, Macclesfield, Congleton, Leek and Buxton by about 1660.[9] Macclesfield in particular was known at this time for the use of silk thread in the manufacture of buttons.

## Industrialisation of processes

### The introduction of mechanised silk throwing

Silk is secreted by the silk worm and is the building material used to form the cocoon in which the worm changes into the silk moth. The silk is retrieved from the cocoons by boiling them to loosen the natural gum or sericin, thus allowing the continuous lengths of silk filaments to be unravelled. This process is known as reeling and the result is skeins of raw silk. It is in this condition that the silk arrives in Britain. In the silk mill the raw silk first needs winding, during which the silk is wound from the skeins on to bobbins whilst any knots or irregularities

in thickness are removed. It is possible for the silk to be used in this state but usually it is given a degree of twist by throwing. Thrown silk yarns can themselves be twisted together in varying multiples depending on the required result, a process known as doubling. In this way different qualities and strengths of silk thread can be produced, such as organzine,[10] which is used for the warp in weaving the finest-quality silk cloth, or tram,[11] a lesser-quality thread used for weft. Confusingly the term throwing can be used to mean not only the specific process of twisting the silk thread but also the whole process from winding through to doubling.

Silk thread can also be produced by spinning, using short lengths of silk obtained from wild silk, from those parts of the cocoon left over after reeling, or from pieces of silk thread discarded during winding and throwing. Once the silk is carded it can be spun in a fashion similar to the spinning of any short-staple fibre, such as cotton (see p 10).

Silk throwing was a well-established industry by the early 17th century.[12] In 1681 an Act of Parliament recorded that throughout the country there were 40,000 families employed in the throwing industry.[13] There is also evidence from about this time for a silk-throwing industry in east Cheshire, partly in response to the demands of the silk-button industry, and partly to supply the nation's silk weavers via the London market which controlled the merchandising of raw silk (see Chapter Two).

The machinery and organisation of the throwing industry of the 16th and 17th centuries are difficult to ascertain. Although the means of production were hand operated, the industry nationally was relatively large scale. This theory is borne out by figures given in a piece of legislation dated 1667, by which a by-law of the Company of Silk Throwsters (established in 1629), was nullified. Previously under this by-law, freemen of that Company had been prevented from working with 'above the number of 140 spindles at one time, and the assistants of the said Company with above the number of 240'.[14] This number of spindles implies that the system was not purely domestic but was a precursor of the factory system.

Production of silk thread rose during the 16th and 17th centuries as a result of an increase in demand for silk luxury and fancy woven goods. The most famous weavers' settlement of the late 17th and 18th centuries was outside the City of London at Spitalfields, where English, Flemish and French Huguenot weavers wove intricately patterned silk cloth. However, English silk-throwing methods were unable to produce the strong, fine organzine thread required for the warp in weaving the best-quality silk cloth, producing instead the coarser tram thread which was used for the weft. This situation, which constrained the development of the English silk industry, continued until the introduction of Italian throwing technology in the early 18th century. Before this time the industry remained reliant on imports from Italy for its supply of organzine. As early as the 14th century the Italians had perfected a water-powered machine on which organzine could be thrown and had developed a large and successful industry, based in Sardinia, which dominated the world market. This dominance was maintained by virtue of the intense secrecy which surrounded their throwing technology.

In Britain, efforts were made to challenge the Italian monopoly. In 1692 a petition to be incorporated as a joint-stock company was made by a group of London silk merchants and throwsters. They had been able to show 'that they and several others concerned with them have, with great expense and industry, brought to practice a certain useful and cheap way, by engines, of winding the finest raw silk which was formerly brought ready wound spun and twisted from Italy'.[15] It is not known what method of winding this company had developed, but it must be assumed to have been a failure because at the beginning of the 18th century the secret of the successful throwing of organzine was still held by the Italians. Around 1704 Thomas Cotchett, a barrister, set up a silk-throwing mill on the banks of the River Derwent in Derby (Figure 10) with the intention of producing organzine and competing with the Italians directly.[16] This building, now demolished, is thought to have been the first powered textile mill in Britain. Cotchett's venture failed because, according to the Derby historian William Hutton, 'three engines were found necessary for the whole process, he had but one'.[17]

Around 1716, John Lombe, the son of a Norwich worsted weaver, and thought to have been an apprentice of Cotchett, journeyed to Italy, risked his life in pirating the Piedmontese throwing and winding machines, and returned to England with the details of their design. In September 1718 his half-brother, Sir Thomas Lombe, a London silk merchant, received a fourteen-year patent protecting the machines and in 1721 they built a mill adjacent to Cotchett's mill in Derby. John Lombe died in 1722, but Thomas continued with the works,[18] and although he struggled to perfect the machines and to obtain silk of the right quality, it was seen by contemporaries to be a success.

Lombe's success may in part be explained by the fact that whereas Cotchett only had some form of throwing machine, Lombe had pirated not only the machine which imparted twist to the silk but also the machine with which to wind it. It may be the case, furthermore, that this winding machinery was not only of use in winding silk for the production of organzine, but could also be used for winding silk for the existing British silk industry, to be thrown on machinery already known in Britain. Evidence that a method of winding fine silk was being sought by British silk manufacturers well before Lombe's visit to Italy can be found in the 1692 London throwsters' and merchants' petition already noted. Although largely conjectural, this theory would explain the importance of Lombe's venture to the British powered throwing industry, whose rapid expansion in the mid 18th century was based on the production of tram, not organzine.

The patent on Lombe's silk-throwing machinery expired in 1732, but the difficulties in obtaining raw silk of the right quality, at the right price, caused entrepreneurs to be wary of investing in the Italian equipment. Raw silk for the production of tram was imported mainly from Persia and continued to be thrown by hand or by powered double Dutch mills, machines about which nothing precise is known. Only two silks, Italian and China, were fine enough for throwing on the Italian machinery. However, the duty on China raw silk made it expensive to import, and the Italians had banned the exportation of their raw silk in 1724 in response to the threat from the new English throwing industry. Lombe himself is reported to have said that 'if he had known before he built his mills that the King of Sardinia would have prohibited the exportation of raw silk, he should not have done it'.[19] Nevertheless he strove, albeit unsuccessfully, to retain his patent when the time came for its renewal in 1732. Moreover, within a year of its expiration, a group of entrepreneurs, together with one of Lombe's former employees, an Italian named John Guardivaglio, had established a silk-throwing enterprise at the Logwood Mill in Stockport using the methods pioneered in England by Lombe.

There is no record, however, of any investment in Italian throwing machinery having taken place in east Cheshire until 1744 when Charles Roe, a button merchant and gentleman of Macclesfield, having already 'obtained a perfect model of the machinery employed in the silk mill at Derby',[20] erected a water-powered silk-throwing mill at Park Green in Macclesfield.

In 1749 an Act of Parliament was passed which reduced the duty on China raw silk to that on Italian silk, as a result of which the importation of China silk increased. According to Nathaniel Pattison, a London silk merchant, in evidence given to a House of Commons inquiry in 1765, the Act 'encouraged many people, and him in particular, to set up silk mills in imitation of Sir Thomas Loom'.[21] In the year the Act was passed, Pattison entered into partnership with John Clayton, a silk throwster, and the Reverend Joseph Dale, both of Stockport. They were to be 'joint dealers in the art and mystery of manufacturing of raw and thrown silks for their benefit',[22] and in 1753 Clayton and Pattison built the Old Mill in Congleton for water-powered silk throwing.

These entrepreneurs were among the first exponents of the factory system and the initiators of the first factory and industrial-based economy in the world. In this context it is important to note that their activities were not entirely isolated from each other. It is possible to piece together connections between Lombe's enterprise and the setting up of Logwood Mill at Stockport, Roe's Button Mill in Macclesfield and the Old Mill in Congleton, the first four mills built in England for the throwing of organzine on Lombe's principle.

Nathaniel Pattison, in his account given to the House of Commons Committee in 1765, said that 'he lived with Sir Thomas Loom when there was no prohibition in Italy of the exportation of raw silk'.[23] This would mean that Pattison knew Lombe prior to 1724, when King Victor Amadeus II of Sardinia prohibited its exportation, and would therefore have witnessed the earliest stages of Lombe's venture.[24] Pattison was later to send his son, Nathaniel Maxey Pattison, to be apprenticed under Mr Wilson, the manager, later the owner, of the Derby mill. Pattison's partners were John Clayton, a silk throwster and mayor of Stockport in the 1730s, and the Reverend Joseph Dale, a Stockport vicar. John Clayton would have been concerned with the negotiations for the setting-up of the Logwood silk-throwing mill in Stockport in 1732, since, as mayor, he would have been involved with the leasing of the town corn mill, whose water supply was shared by Logwood Mill. Clayton later used this arrangement in leasing the Old Mill site in Congleton. A family tie connects the Stockport, Congleton and Macclesfield entrepreneurs. Dale's daughter married Samuel Lankford, who became Charles Roe's father-in-law in 1743 and subsequently his business partner.[25]

Thus, at this early stage of the industry, it appears that there was a flow of information and expertise within a confined business circle. This situation not only would have benefited those within the circle, but may, along with the large amount of capital needed to establish an organzine mill, have helped to restrict the spread of the new technology. Certainly, by 1765, over thirty years after the expiration of Lombe's patent, only seven mills had been built in imitation of that at Derby, whilst there were approximately sixty for throwing tram.[26] Of the seven built on Lombe's principle, including his own enterprise, at least four of the motivators were, as described, involved with each other at some level. The economics of the new industry, problems in obtaining raw silk of a suitable quality and the capital investment needed, would have been major factors in determining its rate of expansion. However, the influence of the business and personal links in the establishment of the factory system, paralleled by those in the early cotton-spinning industry some thirty to forty years later, should not be overlooked.

## The introduction of mechanised cotton spinning

Cotton is produced by *Gossypium* or the cotton plant, the seeds of which develop with a white, down-like covering. The down is harvested and packed into bales and it is in this form that it arrives in Britain. The raw cotton, having been extracted from the bale, is cleaned by beating and picking, known as batting, to remove seeds and dirt. The tangled cotton fibres are then combed, or carded, before being rolled into a loose rope known as slubbing. The slubbing is then slightly twisted into roving prior to being spun into yarn. Different types of yarn can be produced by varying the extent to which the roving is drawn out and the amount of twist given to it.

The invention of the flying shuttle by John Kay in 1733 vastly improved the efficiency of the loom by allowing the shuttle to be knocked through the warp threads rather than being passed from one hand to the other. The production of cloth was thereby speeded up so that the output of yarn by hand spinning became inadequate to keep pace with weavers' demands. This situation inspired several attempts in the early decades of the 18th century to invent a machine by which yarn could be spun faster. However it was not until 1767 when James Hargreaves, a Blackburn weaver, invented the spinning jenny that this was achieved successfully. Based on the principle of the spinning wheel known as the 'great wheel', on which the yarn was spun and wound on in two separate stages, the jenny was designed to operate with up to sixteen spindles. It nevertheless remained hand powered, and though primarily used in domestic workshops it also came to be used in small spinning factories.

In 1769 Richard Arkwright patented a spinning frame which combined the stages of spinning and winding-on into one mechanical process, and he followed this in 1775 by patenting a range of preparatory machines for carding and roving cotton fibres. By these means cotton spinning became mechanised and, for the first time, driven by non-human methods of motive power. Initially, the new spinning machines were housed in a mill built in Nottingham in 1769, and were driven by horse power. Two years later, at Cromford in Derbyshire, only fourteen miles from Lombe's Derby silk mill, Arkwright erected a mill in which his machines were driven by water power, and thus his invention came to be known as the water frame. The patent on Arkwright's water frame and its subsequent improvements was finally annulled in 1785. Many entrepreneurs, realising the opportunities in utilising the newly released cotton-spinning technology, invested in the building of cotton factories. These included Samuel Greg at Styal, David Dale at New Lanark and Robert Peel at Burton.

Richard Arkwright is often credited as the creator of the factory system, defined by Andrew Ure in 1835 as 'the combined operation of so many orders of work-people, adult and young, in tending with assiduous skill a system of productive machines continuously impelled by a central power'.[27] Spinning and preparatory processes were gathered together by Arkwright and organised in one building to form an integrated production process, rather than separated out in different locations and by varying levels of productivity. In the 1770s this arrangement was undeniably innovative for the cotton industry, and it introduced unprecedented levels of production. However, not only had a factory system been established for at least fifty years in the silk industry, but the building type needed to house the processes was already in existence in the form of Lombe's Mill at Derby, Roe's Button Mill and other mills in Macclesfield, and the Old Mill at Congleton, all only a relatively short distance from where Arkwright was to build his first water-powered mill at Cromford, in Derbyshire.

A further significant contribution to the spinning technology of this early period of powered mechanisation was an invention by Samuel Crompton of Bolton in Lancashire. This machine, the mule, which was originally hand powered, combined the advantages of the jenny and the water frame in order to spin yarn of a quality strong enough for warping and fine enough for weaving into muslin. The machine was perfected in 1779 and was released, without

patent, on to the market in 1780. It was adapted for driving by water power in 1792 by William Kelly at New Lanark Mills, Scotland, and was subsequently powered by steam also. Even though at this stage the mule's action was only partly powered, by 1811 it had in aggregate capacity surpassed the water frame to such an extent that 'at least 4,200,000 mule spindles were in use in the British cotton industry, as compared with only about 310,000 water frame spindles and 156,000 jenny spindles'.[28] The trend shown by these figures, and borne out by documentary evidence for the east Cheshire area, is that the majority of mills in the late 18th and early 19th centuries were housing the mule rather than the water frame.

To some extent, however, the place of the water frame was taken by the throstle, which was in effect a more highly geared metal version of the water frame. The mule was most proficient at producing fine yarns, but there was still a need for stronger, coarser yarns, either for use on their own or in combination with finer yarns, so that a variety of cloths could be produced. The throstle, by using the roller-drawing method of the water frame, was most suitable for producing these coarser yarns. Some spinning mills were devoted entirely to the throstle or the mule, but most commonly, it would seem, mills employed both machines.

In both the silk and cotton industries, the production of yarn by powered processes dominated industrial development and the design of mill buildings until the 1820s. In contrast weaving continued as a hand-operated and largely domestically housed process. In the main it was directed and controlled by merchant manufacturers, who were often not only the suppliers but also the producers of the yarn. However, in order to consolidate processes, and to supervise the weaving more closely, an increasing number of handlooms were housed within mill premises, in the later years of the 18th, but particularly the early 19th centuries. Accompanying the increased production of cloth was the growth of the finishing and dyeing industries, for which the soft acidic water of the gritstone Pennine areas was especially suited. For this reason the industry came to be located in this area and was housed in buildings of a non-specific type, either as part of a mill site or independently.

Where power was required for the process, the rate of industrial expansion relied on an increasingly sophisticated range of power systems. Initially the horse gin and the water-wheel, which had both been in use for turning of millstones and driving fulling stocks, were adapted for powering spinning mills. In this context the importance of the horse gin to early industrialisation seems to have been underestimated. Waterwheel technology developed from the use of simple and relatively inefficient wooden, undershot wheels to highly efficient and powerful iron suspension wheels, many of which continued in use and were updated throughout the 19th century. However, the full potential of the industry was only realised with the development of steam-power technology. Early steam engines were used to supplement existing power arrangements, and at sites where water supply was amply available they remained a secondary system. Nevertheless, for the enormous expansion which took place, particularly in the cotton-spinning industry, the power capacity and freedom of location provided by steam power proved to be crucial. However, although it was possibly the most important factor in the expansion of the textile industry, in that it enabled supply to meet demand, it was not the determining factor in the development of mill design.

## Economic developments in the late 18th and early 19th centuries

Britain was at war with America from 1775 until 1782 and with France from 1793 until 1815. The general effect of these hostilities was to create a boom economy. According to John Corry, writing in 1817, 'The superiority of the British navy shut up our opponents in their own ports and we commanded the commerce of the world at the cannons mouth ... Among other branches of the trade the manufacture of silk flourished in Macclesfield and experience has discovered that war is more advantageous to this town than peace'[29] (Figure 4).

With the advantages of the newly developed cotton-spinning technology, accompanied by the ready availability of capital borrowed either from individuals or a growing number of private banks, the textile industry was able to respond to and profit from this situation to such an extent that the effect upon society of the growth of these industries in the north-west textile regions has usually been described as revolutionary. Over half of the mills ever built in east Cheshire were in existence by the late 1820s, as was the infrastructure and housing to support this industry. Small communities which had previously existed as centres of agricultural economy expanded into industrial towns of overcrowded terraced dwellings which were described with horror by mid 19th-century observers. Manchester developed into the first industrialised city in the world, and became the market centre for the cotton industry, rivalling London in national importance.

The ending of the Napoleonic Wars in 1815 meant that manufacturers of those goods needed for the sustenance of the army – cloth, arms and leather – experienced a sudden drop in demand and found themselves with excess capacity. Furthermore, the lifting of wartime restrictions reopened markets to foreign

Figure 4
*A sketch, drawn in 1810, showing a view from Waters Green, Macclesfield, towards Sunderland Street. To the left is Sunderland Street Mill with its c1804 engine house, which still stands today, in front of the chimney. To the right is Waters Green Mill which was built around 1769 and was demolished to make way for the present mill in 1875. It is likely that in 1810 most of the property pictured was owned by the Pearson family.*

competition. The resulting increase in supply led to a sudden fall in prices. The Corn Law was passed in 1815 to protect farmers from the effects of the falling price of corn, but the subsequent rise in the price of bread caused considerable hardship at a time of falling wages and unemployment. The market for utilitarian cotton goods was reduced drastically, whilst in the luxury market the silk industry was affected by the influx of French silk goods. The economic slump forced weak and unprepared firms in both the silk and cotton industries into bankruptcy.

The silk industry expanded relatively slowly until 1824 when the government lifted the duty on the importation of raw silk. This resulted in a strong upturn in the industry's fortunes. A committee of Macclesfield silk throwsters and manufacturers, meeting in October 1825, concluded 'That the repeal of the duty upon raw silk has been attended with incalculably good effects in the prosperity of trade, promoting the erecting of mills and the increase of machinery and manufacture in the same ratio. That every nerve has been strained to raise the trade to the high rank it has obtained.'[30] Generally, in the period around 1825, there was marked over-expansion in all fields of industry, but this was ended by a dramatic down-turn in the health of the economy in 1826. The blame for the slump of 1826 and the subsequent depression was laid at the door of the private banks. Their liberal lending had fostered over-optimistic levels of investment at home and abroad and the resulting financial crisis led to a downturn in the economy which lasted until the early 1830s. The crisis in the silk industry was reinforced in 1826 by the government's removal of the ban on the importation of foreign woven silks, the first time they had been admitted legally into the country since their total prohibition in 1766. Without the level of protection afforded by these restrictions, the British silk industry could not compete against French and Italian imports.

## Mid 19th-century expansion and consolidation

The recovery of the silk[31] and cotton industries in the mid 1830s was, ironically, aided by the investment which had occurred immediately prior to 1826, and was characterised by the take-up of new technology and by the reorganisation of processes and resources. With these shifts in patterns of production the industry was able to withstand the regular cycles of boom and depression during this period.

Against this economic background a general rise in the output of woven silk and cotton goods can be traced.

The continuing growth in the nation's industrial economy was reflected in the expansion of the cotton industry. In its rise to dominance of the textile industry, cotton had many advantages over its competitors. Cotton fibre proved to be more adaptable to the mechanics of powered weaving than did competing yarns. Furthermore, the supply of raw and manufactured cotton proved sufficient to supply huge increases in demand and, not being a luxury commodity, the potential demand was vast, including a large export market.[32] With such a large market, distribution was vital and the gradual introduction of canals and railways efficiently connected the ports to the mills and the mills to their expanding markets.

Expansion was impeded initially by the restrictions imposed by the number of spindles which could be driven effectively, and by the necessary ratio of spinners to spinning machinery. In 1830, Richard Roberts, a Manchester engineer, succeeded in making the spinning mule self-acting so that its full spinning cycle could be performed automatically. This development presented manufacturers with the opportunities of a huge leap in production without an increase in labour costs. Consequently there was a desire to house more spindles by building bigger mills.[33]

In contrast, the mechanised silk-throwing industry, having provided the impetus for future technological advance in all textile-spinning industries, progressed only slowly during this phase, with no basic alteration to machinery. The silk-spinning industry, however, as a complementary industry to silk throwing, was in the formative stages of its mechanisation. In the production of thrown silk, from the beginning of the process to the end, a great quantity of waste silk was produced and the high cost of silk made it desirable that this waste should be used. Problems in dealing with the unequal fibre lengths and in maintaining the lustre of the silk were overcome by a series of mechanical developments during the mid 19th century. In 1836 Gibson and Campbell of Glasgow patented a machine which successfully adapted the principle of the throstle spinning machine, and in 1877 Lister's invention of the self-acting dressing machine finally resolved the difficulties inherent in the preparatory stages. Although the powered spinning of silk had been established at Galgate in Lancashire in 1792, it was not until the 1830s that, as a result of technological progress, silk spinning became an industry of importance in Yorkshire, Lancashire and Cheshire.

A significant advance was made for the silk industry by the introduction of Jacquard weaving, during the 1820s and 1830s. This type of hand-weaving mechanism, using punched cards, enabled the weaver to control the whole process by which the most intricate designs of cloth were produced. The development of powered weaving was arguably the most significant advance for the textile industry as a whole at this time. The first patents for powered broadloom weaving had been taken out by Edmund Cartwright in the 1780s, but the machine was not perfected and did not come into widespread use until the 1820s and 1830s. The loom was intended originally for cotton weaving but was also brought into use for silk. Although the take-up of this technology was slow in the silk industry where the loom was only suitable for coarse silks, increasing prosperity for both the cotton and silk industries was dependent ultimately upon the cheap and efficient manufacture of cloth as well as yarn. Developments in mill architecture were strongly influenced by the need to accommodate the new technological advances in both spinning and weaving and the increasingly complicated organisation of processes.

Firms which came to dominate both the silk and cotton industries in the mid to late 19th centuries were those which integrated spinning and weaving and were able to control the processes of production from the raw fibre to the finished cloth. In the silk industry, numbers of new firms and many of those firms which had survived the depression of the late 1820s and early 1830s expanded into Jacquard weaving, powerloom weaving, silk spinning or combinations of these processes. Although there is evidence from the early days of the industry for the investment by firms in more than one process, it was not until the mid 19th century that a substantial level of production was reached by firms involved in both throwing and weaving, to the extent that this general reorganisation of the industry contributed significantly to its survival.

Although still subject to cyclical booms and slumps, the silk industry flourished during the 1840s, benefiting in particular from political disturbances in Europe in 1848 which disrupted the French industry. The Great Exhibition of 1851 both celebrated and stimulated production in the English silk industry, but by the late 1850s a general commercial depression and the restoration of the industry in Europe adversely affected the home industry, as a prelude to a major depression in the 1860s.

# The industry in the late 19th and early 20th centuries

The closing decades of the 19th century and the opening decades of the 20th century saw a marked decrease in the rate of industrial expansion. In the 1860s the effect of the American Civil War on the cotton industry was not only to cause widespread insolvency in the short term, but, more importantly, to send a ripple of depressions throughout the decade and begin a decline in cotton prices which lasted until the end of the 19th century. For the silk industry, the loss of the American market for its goods during the Civil War led French manufacturers to flood a British market laid open by the 1860 Cobden Chevalier treaty with France. Under the terms of this treaty Britain pursued a policy of free trade whilst France retained protective duties on British silk goods entering the French market. This removal of protection for British silk manufacture precipitated a serious slump which the industry initially seemed to survive, but which in reality marked the beginning of an erratic decline. Nevertheless, the textile industry as a whole increased its output dramatically in the later years of the 19th century to satisfy an export market of an unprecedented scale. Capital investment and the size of individual firms increased, encouraged by the limited liability statutes of 1856 and 1862[34] and the trend towards raising money on the stock exchange.[35]

The effect of these developments led to the organisation of both the silk and cotton industries of the late 19th century on a specialised basis, with firms generally concentrating on either spinning processes (including silk throwing) or weaving. The cotton industry had become concentrated in Lancashire, with weaving in the north and spinning in the south. The silk industry was centred in east Cheshire, with Macclesfield dominating the silk-throwing and hand-weaving market. The silk-spinning and powered-weaving industries were more widespread. Although Congleton was a centre of silk spinning, this industry also became located, under the influence of Samuel Lister, in Yorkshire. Similarly, powered weaving was carried out both in Macclesfield and in Lancashire. Specialisation of firms engendered problems in itself, in that spinners became ignorant of the needs of the woven-cloth market and the industries became reliant on the action of middlemen and agents to transport and deal between companies. Because exports continued to expand, the overall result was that the industries became blinkered, short sighted and complacent.[36]

The effects of such a huge dependence on the export market backfired in the face of increasing foreign competition. Economic and technological development abroad was growing rapidly, aided in part by British international investment, so that when the First World War cut Britain's overseas links and plunged the country deeply into debt, competitors were quick to take advantage. The American, German and Swiss cotton industries were competing directly with British cotton spinners by means of the quicker, cheaper and more efficient ring-spinning frame, which only slowly replaced the mule in Britain, and was used initially only for coarse spinning. The market for cotton cloth was taken over by cheaper produce from countries such as India, and later Japan. As a result, the worth of British textile exports fell from £288,900,000 in the period 1920–9 to £106,000,000 in the following decade.[37]

For the silk industry a brief recovery in the early decades of the 20th century did not enable it to compete with the increasing use of artificial silk or rayon, the main production centres of which lay abroad in America, Japan and Germany. The late revival of the industry occurred during the 1920s and 1930s, partly as a result of the government's reimposition of protective duties, and partly as a result of the fashion for short, washable silk dresses, particularly in 'Macclesfield stripe'. The Second World War produced the last major boost for the industry. Parachutes, badges and neckwear were supplied to the armed forces. Several mills and all available silk were requisitioned by the Ministry of Supply.[38]

This wartime boost to the industry failed to halt its ultimate decline. The introduction of man-made fibres finally brought about the end of the silk industry on any large scale, but sustained the presence of a textile industry in Macclesfield. A small number of firms are still in production in Macclesfield, processing silk, although hand weaving was finally abandoned in 1981. Ribbon manufacture is still an industry of significance in Congleton, albeit in the hands of one company. Cotton manufacture no longer takes place in east Cheshire, although the dyeing and finishing industries for all textiles still survive.

# 2 HOUSING THE SILK INDUSTRY *c*1700–*c*1780

Various cloths and smallwares were produced in east Cheshire during the 17th and 18th centuries, with local districts specialising in particular kinds of manufacture. Ribbon weaving was the predominant manufacture in the south of the region, centred on Congleton, whereas in the north, around Bollington, Rainow, Wilmslow and Disley, the spinning and weaving of cotton and linen were carried out. In Macclesfield and neighbouring villages, the manufacture of silk buttons and the throwing and weaving of silk were characteristic local industries. Woollen cloth was manufactured in Cheshire and regular fairs were held in Macclesfield for the sale of wool.[1] The cloth was fulled (felted) in mills known to have existed at Macclesfield, Rainow and Congleton, and there is some evidence for the existence of bleaching and dyeing industries in the area.

Macclesfield buttons, produced as early as the 16th and 17th centuries, were made from wooden or horn moulds which were padded and embroidered with combinations of silk or linen thread, horsehair, ox hair and mohair (Figure 5). In 1574 a debt was entered into the Macclesfield town accounts for 'buttonz and for making buttonz of ye value of 15*s*.2*d*'.[2] In 1631, the inventory of Richard Turton, a Buttonman of Rainow, included, '13 great grosse of silke buttons ... 1 pound weight of untwisted silke ... twisted silke' as well as '20 sheepe and 4 lambs ... 2 bullorks'.[3] By the mid 17th century, the industry had become so well established that in 1655 the Corporation of Macclesfield considered that owing to 'the trade and manufacture of the skilful and well making of buttons here and the blessing of God thereupon the inhabitants thereof and places adjacent are much bettered in their livelihood and estates than heretofore'.[4]

It seems to have been usual for button merchants to have supplied the button makers with the materials, returning later to collect the completed article. Stephen Rowe, a Macclesfield button merchant, organised his business on this putting-out system. In 1617, the contents of his house included amounts of raw materials, namely hair, thread, linen, yarn and silk, moulds for the bases of buttons and quantities of finished buttons amongst which were '4 great gr [gross] of 4 courst sylk buttons'. Goods to the value of £3 9*s* 0*d* were assessed in work 'put forth', that is to say put out to button makers. His will provides evidence of trade links with Flushing in Belgium, and London, whilst his home interests also included agriculture, with cattle and arable farming.[5] Joseph Street, who described himself in his will of 1781 as a 'button maker',[6] was in fact a button merchant and a partner of John Acton. According to Samuel Finney, writing in the late 18th century, Street frequently paid out £12 to £18 a week to the Wilmslow button makers he supplied. Finney himself knew that 'a good diligent button maker would have earned about three shillings and sixpence a week' and this would mean that Acton and Street were supplying between sixty and a hundred button makers in Wilmslow alone.[7]

There appear to have been a number of different outlets for the sale of buttons, including local shops and market stalls.[8] Richard Pownall was described in his will as a Congleton 'button man' and seems from an inventory also to have been a haberdasher. At his death in 1739 his stock included silk cloth, metal buttons, silver buttons, button moulds and whalebone to the value of £854.[9] Chapmen on horseback hawked silk goods and other items around the villages. Not all, however, were poor pedlars; some

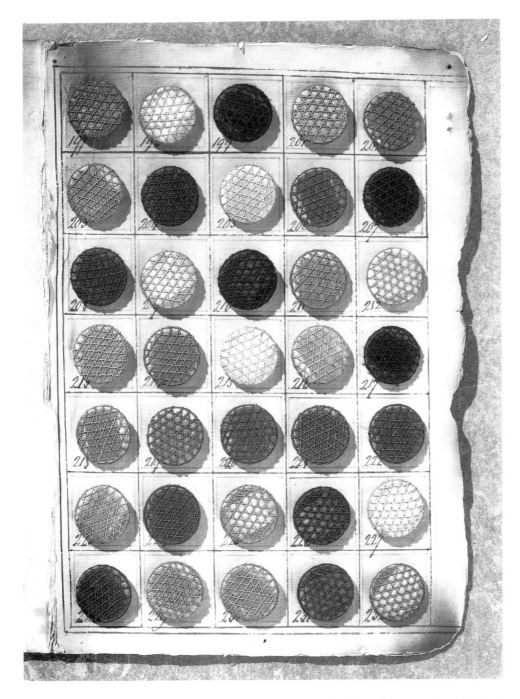

Figure 5
*A sample card of silk-covered and embroidered buttons made by the firm of Brocklehursts around 1800.*

managed to accumulate large amounts of capital. Samuel Braddock, a Macclesfield chapman, had 'silk mohair buttons and good debts' to the value £342 14*s* 5*d* when he made out his will in December 1736.[10] William Brocklehurst was also described as a chapman, but the Brocklehursts had owned land in Hurdsfield, near Macclesfield, since the 16th century and were a wealthy family.[11]

The organisation of the button-making industry had close associations with the early silk-throwing industry in east Cheshire, and as such

was a stimulus and source of capital for the early industrialisation of that industry. The button industry provided a ready-made infrastructure, including important investment and trading links with London. The raw silk was imported through London, the only legal port of entry for silk,[12] and was accompanied on its journey by London merchants. Owing to local restrictions on who could trade in Macclesfield in the 17th century, a number of London merchants became freemen of the town in order to bypass the legislation. In 1686 James Nixon, a

**Figure 6**
*The hand throwing of silk involved running lengths of silk thread from the throwing 'wheel', or gate, to a fixed rail. By turning a handle on the throwing 'wheel' the silk was twisted.*

Macclesfield chapman, nominated John Whiteman, a London silkman, as a freeman of Macclesfield. The mayor and burgesses accepted the nomination in return for the payment of £40.[13] These merchants sometimes retained local agents or 'factors' who would buy and sell goods on their behalf. In 1700, for example, Samuel Wood, a Macclesfield 'dealer in silk and mohaire', was a factor on behalf of Mr John Dubourg and Mrs Van Nypens, merchants of London.[14] The importance of London capital to the local silk and button industry is difficult to assess from the small amount of evidence that has come to light. London provided a large market for both silk yarn and silk buttons, but to what extent London merchants were involved with the east Cheshire hand-throwing industry is not known, nor to what extent capital generated by local enterprise was tied up in credit to the London suppliers of raw silk.

There is evidence for the existence of hand throwing in east Cheshire from about the mid 17th century. In 1681, for example, John Massey of Rainow, yeoman, owned one black cow, two little sheep and three calves worth £8, as well as a silk-twisting wheel and three old ladders worth 5s.[15] In 1732, six throwsters, listed as 'twisters', rented stalls on Macclesfield market,[16] and a number are recorded in mid 18th-century wills, inventories and rate books.

There is evidence for silk weaving in the south-west Pennine region from the mid 17th century. In Manchester and Salford, between 1648 and 1691, eleven testators were described as silk weavers,[17] and around 1660 parchmentary (lace) weaving was being carried out in and around the towns of Stockport, Macclesfield, Congleton, Leek and Buxton.[18] Samuel Yates affirms in his *History of Congleton* that in Congleton the 'manufacture of ribbons for the

Coventry merchants was established in the year 1755'.[19] In 1759, members of the Manchester Methodist Circuit included thirteen from Congleton. Amongst these were named a sieve maker and a silk weaver, two button makers, three spinners and six ribbon weavers.[20] The latter were all women, living on Dog Lane (now Canal Street).

Congleton ribbon weavers were supplied with silk yarn by Coventry merchants who collected the finished ribbons. However, by 1789 two firms of Congleton ribbon merchants had been established. A trade directory of that year lists W Davenport and Widow Jackson and Son as ribbon merchants on Lawton Street.[21]

There is evidence of narrow-silk weaving in Macclesfield from the late 17th century. In 1696 the household goods of Francis Dale, who manufactured the best silk and tinsel galloons, statute braids and perriwig ribbon, were worth almost £530.[22] John Prout, writing in 1829, dated the introduction of broad-silk weaving in the town to the year 1756, when it was confined to the manufacture of black fringes as well as culgee,[23] later called bandanna. The production of bandanna handkerchiefs came to be a staple of the Macclesfield hand-weaving industry.[24] As they were patterned by printing, the quality of both the silk and the weaving did not have to be high.

## The hand-throwing industry

There appear to have been two principal methods of hand throwing. The more technologically advanced method used a hand-powered version of the large, water-powered, Italian, cylindrical throwing machine (see p 9). Although this hand-powered machine was used in France and

Italy, it seems not to have been widely used in Britain.[25] The method of hand throwing which seems to have been most commonly used was described to the 1841 Parliamentary Committee of Inquiry into the Employment of Children (Figures 6 and 7):

> *For twisting it is necessary to have what are designated 'shades' which are buildings of at least 30 or 35 yards in length, of two or more rooms, rented separately by one, two or four men, having one 'gate' and a boy called a helper … The upper storey is generally occupied by children, young persons or grown women as 'piecers', 'winders' and 'doublers', attending to their reels and bobbins, driven by the exertions of one man … He (the boy) takes first a rod containing four bobbins of silk from the twister who stands at his 'gate' or wheel, and having fastened the ends, runs to the 'cross' at the extreme end of the room, round which he passes the threads of each bobbin and returns to the 'gate'. He is despatched on a second expedition of the same kind, and returns as before, he then runs up to the 'cross' and detaches the threads and comes to the roller. Supposing the master to make twelve rolls a day, the boy necessarily runs fourteen miles, and this is barefooted.*[26]

Turning the wheel twisted the threads of silk, and the twisted threads were then wound on to a bobbin or roller. Estimates of the minimum required length of the room, or run, given to the 1841 Parliamentary Committee of Inquiry into children's working conditions, vary from '25 yards' (23 m) to the above '35 yards' (32 m). One account given to an 1863 Parliamentary Commission describes a shade as being 'usually on the lowest storey of the building ... frequently dark and damp'. Another account refers to a shade in an upstairs room, but all those who gave evidence to the Inquiry were agreed on the basic principles of the twisting and related processes, and on the need for these processes to be housed in a long shade of a minimum of 23 m in length.[27] A system of production which is likely to have existed for at least as long as the process it housed was described in 1841 by Hannah Hastel:

> *I am the wife of Josiah Hastel, belonging to this factory or 'shade'. My husband was brought up as a helper from his youth; he then became twister [throwster], and put by enough money in the last fifteen years to enable him to build this factory, our private house we live in, and four private houses*

**Figure 7**
*The hand throwing of silk survived in Leek, Staffordshire, until the 1940s. This photograph of a shade was taken in the 1930s.*

*below. He had nothing to start with but what I saved out of service, which was about £90. We now employ ten 'piecers', and three 'doublers' in the upstairs rooms; one is a twisting room, the other a winding room. The lower shade we set to four twisters, who pay us rent, and work for whom they like. We pay the twisters 7sh. 6d. for 42 rolls per week; if they make more than 42 rolls we give for each additional roll 3d. An active man makes 15 rolls a day. I know that my husband, when he worked, could make 18; but then the silk was better and smoother. A man, now-a-days, thinks he has done a good day's work if he makes 12 or 14 rolls. The twisters are not regular in their work. Today they are all gone a-drinking; but then they must work faster and harder to-morrow to make up for it.*[28]

The amount of capital required for setting up a throwing business is difficult to ascertain. An inventory of 1727 attached to the will of Edward Mottershead lists his barn as containing 'a twisting wheel and spindles and two crosses' valued at 4s. When compared with the valuation of his 'table and a form' at 4s and a bed at 15s it can be seen that the purchase of silk-throwing equipment of this nature was not an investment requiring a large source of capital.[29] Initially, the major expense in setting up a silk-throwing business would have been the cost of building or acquiring premises. Evidence for the cost of buying comes from a lease dated 15 October 1770 which details the purchase of a 'shade standing in Jordangate [Macclesfield] with a garden, stretching yard, croft or twisting yard' from Jonathon Forrest, threadmaker. The property cost Jonathon Clulow £80, probably money he had raised from his trade as a baker.[30] In January 1771, James Smale, a Stockport twister, insured his Macclesfield 'workshop rooms' in the tenure of a throwster, for £300.[31] Whilst neither of these amounts represents the actual cost of building a shade, they give some idea of the value the owners themselves placed on the buildings, and certainly the latter figure would have related to the cost of rebuilding the premises.

### Throwing shades

The difference between the above two costings may possibly be related to the differing types of structure which seem to have been used for silk throwing. The term shade was probably first used to describe the type of structure illustrated in a 12th-century manuscript, which shows weaving being carried out under a canopy carried on four corner posts.[32] This arrangement is probably similar to the 'long sheds on posts' described in a mid 17th-century survey of the Commonwealth as being newly erected in various parts of Macclesfield.[33] Moreover, the 18th-century name for silk-throwing premises, 'shades', later called sheds, can be linked with the name 'screona', meaning shade or shelter, given in the Germanic Laws (early medieval texts) to premises used by women for textile production.[34] It is possible that these types of shades may have been similar to the rope walks used for twine making which survive in south Somerset.

The workshop owned by James Smale, described as 'rooms', would probably have been a more substantial structure for the housing of hand throwing, similar to that described to the 1841 Parliamentary Committee of Inquiry. The layout of a building for this purpose needed to incorporate an unrestricted throwing floor measuring at least 23 m long, being sufficiently narrow for evenly spaced windows to illuminate the process with maximum daylight. Ideally a minimum of two storeys was required, one to house the throwing, the other to house the associated processes and storage.

Documentary evidence for the existence of such buildings is sparse, although several are noted in the 1784 Tax Assessment and the Schedule to the 1804 Enclosure Award Map.[35] A shade is known to have stood on the site purchased by Charles Roe in 1743 for building the first water-powered throwing mill in Macclesfield. The dimensions of the plot, 23·8 m by 10 m,[36] would have accommodated exactly the length of a twisting shade. A now untraceable counterpart lease[37] dated 1771 records Thomas Varden as occupying 'three houses and a twisters' shade' in Macclesfield. It is possible that this is the site described in the 1784 Tax Assessment for Macclesfield as a shade on Chestergate, occupied by James Verdan, and that both these documents refer to a building known as Chestergate Mill. If this is the case, Chestergate Mill (Figure 8) was the only known complete example of this type of building still standing at the time of the survey.

The mill, recently demolished, was situated towards the west end of Chestergate and was roughly rectangular on plan. Its original length was 25·1 m — sufficient for the hand-throwing process described — and its upper storey formed one undivided room. The building was three-storeyed, with floor to ceiling heights averaging 2·2 m, at least 0·3 m lower than the 18th-century mill buildings which are known to have housed machines for mechanised silk throwing. Its width of 6·1 m was also 0·6 m less than the narrowest width in mills built for this process. The scale of this building was, however, compatible with the requirements of the hand-powered silk-throwing process as described by Hannah Hastel (see above).

Architecturally, Chestergate Mill incorporates features which can be seen as characteristic of local building styles. Built of brick with a stone-flagged roof, the building typifies the use of materials from both highland and lowland Cheshire. In Macclesfield, gritstone, obtained in abundance from the quarries in the Pennine hills to the east of the district, was used for roofing until about 1831, when the opening of the Macclesfield Canal introduced slate from Wales and the Lake District as a common roofing material. The walls of Chestergate Mill were built of handmade brick which generally replaced stone or timber framing as a walling material during the 18th century. In 1792 John Byng wrote of Macclesfield that 'one knows a place to be enriching and increasing when it is surrounded by brick kilns'.[38] Local clay deposits made bricks of a warm reddish-brown colour. Variations in tone produced in firing enabled bricklayers to create simple decorative effects by

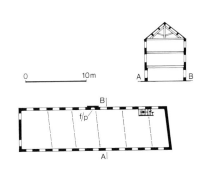

Figure 8
*Chestergate Mill, Chestergate, Macclesfield. Built in the early to mid 18th century, there is some evidence to indicate that Chestergate Mill was erected as a shade for silk throwing. The left end of the mill was altered and refaced in the 19th century. The second-floor plan shows that the floors were heated by open fires.*

contrasting the colours of header and stretcher bricks in Flemish bond brickwork.[39] The brickwork of Chestergate Mill, however, was laid to English Garden Wall bond. Internally, the use of hewn oak for the heavy king-post roof truss

21

*a*

Figure 9
*Chestergate Mill,*
*Macclesfield:*
*a) heavy, oak king-post*
*truss;*
*b) timbers engraved with*
*arabic-numeral assembly*
*marks.*

(Figure 9a) is a representative feature of industrial buildings from the mid to late 18th century, when builders were yet able to rely on the supply of native materials. The roof members of Chestergate Mill were incised with rare, arabic-numeral assembly marks (Figure 9b) and held in place with pegged mortice and tenon joints.

Small, segmental brick-arched window openings placed at regular intervals on the front and rear elevations light each storey. They are similar to those of the Button Mill, Macclesfield, built in 1744, and of the Old Mill, Congleton, built in 1753, although the style continued in use throughout the early 19th century. At top-floor level on the rear, north elevation, a bricked-up doorway may indicate the provision of separate access to this floor at an early period of its use. This arrangement was common in garret (upper-storey workshop) houses to allow entry to the working premises by avoiding passage through the living accommodation.[40]

In east Cheshire one other building, Croft Mill, Macclesfield, which was demolished in

1988, appeared from its structure to have been built as a shade. Although its date of construction is unknown, Croft Mill can be seen in plan on the 1804 Enclosure Award Map[41] of Macclesfield and is located, like Chestergate Mill, well away from the known sources of water power. Built as a three-storeyed building measuring 6·5 m wide by 25 m long, the floor to ceiling heights were low, averaging just 2 m. The original roof timbers were of similar cut and construction to the Chestergate Mill timbers. Walls were constructed of handmade brick, laid to English Garden Wall bond, while windows were elongated with segmental brick arches and were arranged at regular intervals along the front and rear elevations at each floor level.

Although from the structural and documentary evidence both Chestergate Mill and Croft Mill were almost certainly built for hand processes, and probably for hand-powered throwing, they have the essential elements characteristic of all factory building: a well-lit, uncluttered floor area large enough for the efficient accommodation of processes, and adequate accommodation for ancillary processes and storage. Architectural embellishment and amenities for employees did not feature in these buildings. The new throwing technology, however, which was powered either by water or by horses, greatly increased the scale of operations and thereby extended both building specifications and design.

*b*

## The mechanisation of the silk-throwing industry

The introduction of mechanised silk throwing into east Cheshire in the mid 18th century gave rise to the construction of a group of horse-powered and water-powered mills which are of great significance in the chronology of mill development throughout the country. The implications of the construction of these mills, predating Arkwright's developments at Cromford by a generation, have not hitherto been fully recognised, nor has the significance of the concentration of the mills in Cheshire. By 1765, four of the seven mills in England housing powered Italian silk-throwing machinery were located in the north-east of the county, while in Macclesfield alone, in 1761, the seven largest silk firms employed some 2,500 hands between them.

The first attempt to establish a silk-throwing mill in Britain was made by Thomas Cotchett around 1704. His mill in Derby (Figure 10) was intended to house the double Dutch machine (see below) and was described in 1739:

*[the mill] is 62 feet long, 28 feet 5 inches broad, and 35 feet high, contains three storeys, the upper of which is a garret made use of as a lumber room,*
*has 6 dormant windows in the roof, in the other 2 storeys are 8 double Dutch mills, four in each storey ... The west front of this building is brick, and has 12 handsome windows, 6 in each storey; the east front is a studded wall covered with plaster work, and windows in two rows, and the whole length of the building.*[42]

The mill was powered by a 4·1 m diameter waterwheel constructed by the engineer George Sorocold. It is not known whether the mill was built by Cotchett or reused, but in either case it was not a success. Moreover, it was dwarfed in size and scale by a mill erected on an adjacent site by John Lombe around seven years later.

In 1718 John Lombe brought to England Italian methods of winding and throwing organzine, the fine silk yarn used for warp, and in 1721 he built a silk mill in Derby for these processes (see p 9) (Figure 10). Lombe's mill was a five-storeyed building, 33·5 m long, 12 m wide and 17 m high. It was driven by an undershot waterwheel 7 m in diameter, constructed, like the wheel of Cotchett's mill, by George Sorocold. The three upper storeys of the mill contained seventy-eight winding engines, of the design which John Lombe had brought from Italy, whilst the two lower floors contained twelve of the Italian throwing machines. Next to

Figure 10
*A 19th-century engraving of Lombe's Mill, Derby, which was erected in 1721 on the banks of the River Derwent, also shows Cotchett's silk mill of c1704 to the right. Only the basement arches of Lombe's Mill now survive.*

the mill stood a T-shaped building, three storeys high, which was used for doubling, then still a hand process, and which also contained a counting house. Across a courtyard from the doublers' shop stood the warehouse with its bell tower. The site also contained another counting house and a seven-roomed dwelling house for the mill manager.[43]

The importance of Lombe's mill lies not only in that it housed the first production of British organzine silk but in that it was the first successful textile-factory building to be erected in this country and as such can be said to be of pre-eminent importance in British industrial history. The building of this mill marked the realisation of the factory system in England, by which the processes of production were carried out consecutively within a single building, performed by mechanically powered machines which were not reliant on attendants for speed of production or hours of operation. After the expiration of Lombe's patent in 1732 several silk mills were built in imitation of that at Derby. The first in Cheshire were Logwood Mill at Stockport,[44] initiated in 1732, the Button Mill in Macclesfield, built by Charles Roe in 1744, and an unknown mill, possibly Townley Street Mill, erected by 1769 in Macclesfield and occupied by Glover and Co. In Congleton, the Old Mill, built by John Clayton, a former Mayor of Stockport, and Nathaniel Pattison, a London throwster, was erected in 1753. Thus, by the mid 18th century, silk throwing in Britain was factory based, well before the introduction of powered cotton spinning.

## Silk firms and sources of finance of the early powered silk industry

In 1765, in response to the post-war slump, the House of Commons carried out an inquiry into the state of the silk industry. Nathaniel Pattison gave evidence that there are seven mills in England that work Organzine on Sir Thomas Lombe's principle and that such mills can also work Tram'. Mr Blackstone, a throwster, said on being examined, 'that the number of mills in England for throwing Tram are upwards of 60'.[45] Of the seven mills erected in England by 1765 and housing Italian-style throwing machinery of the type pirated by Lombe, four were in Cheshire (see above). In Macclesfield seven major silk-throwing firms, including the two firms using Italian machinery, were listed, together with twelve mills of 'inferior note'. Already, therefore, by 1765, east Cheshire mills formed around one-third of the mill capacity of the English silk-throwing industry as described in the Parliamentary record.[46]

The seven major silk-throwing firms in Macclesfield, based on the number of hands employed in 1761 (figures in brackets) were: Philip Clowes (720), Glover and Co (400), Braddock and Hall (360), Langford, Robinson and Co (359), Bradburn and Gosling (271), Swain and Gosling (229) and William Hall (140).[47] John Corry, a local historian, wrote in 1817 that:

> In a short time [after 1756] no less than twelve Silk Mills were established in Macclesfield in the following order: Roe, Robinson and Stafford, Mill Street; Greaves and Huxley, Waters; Jonas Hall, Chestergate; Braddock and Hall, Churchside; William Hall, Chestergate; Thomas Hall, Barn Street; John and John Rowbotham, Waters; Philip Clewes, Barn Street; Greaves and Johnson, Newgate; James Rowson, Dog Lane; Joseph Simpson, Waters; James Mayson, Back Street.[48]

The two lists contain many names which were common in the town prior to the introduction of the new throwing technology in 1744 at the Button Mill, thus confirming the predominance of local investment. The Macclesfield Land Tax Assessment of 1743 lists William Greaves as Mayor, and Samuel Huxley, John Stafford, Thomas Braddock, John Glover and Samuel Glover, amongst others, as principal owners of land and property in the town.[49] The names Hall, Johnson, Clewes and Rowson are also given, together with the names of several other families who became prominent in the Macclesfield silk industry. This suggests that the main sources of financial input and initiative came from local land and property owners, a number of whom had made capital from the silk-button, hand-throwing and ancillary industries. The Hall family, for example, was involved in the silk industry by 1726, when Jonah Hall was described in his will as a twister.[50] Samuel Braddock was a chapman in 1738,[51] James Braddock was a dyer at Henbury in 1758[52] and Nathaniel Braddock made his money as a button merchant before building Gutters Mill, Macclesfield, in 1750.[53] The Glovers, who built Pear Tree House (Figure 148) in Macclesfield in 1728[54] were silk merchants, and may have had some connection with the firm of Glover and Unwin, Lombe's silk-purchasing agents.[55]

Charles Roe was described in 1744 as a button merchant (Figure 11). He came to Macclesfield at least two years before building the first water-powered silk-throwing mill in the town and east Cheshire, and was in a sufficiently sound financial position to be made a freeman of the borough in October 1742.[56] It is, however, not clear how Roe acquired his capital. It is possible that his marriage in 1743 to the daughter of Samuel Lankford, a silk merchant,[57] provided

Figure 11
*Charles Roe (1715–81), the builder of the Button Mill, Macclesfield, the first water-powered silk-throwing mill in east Cheshire.*

one source of capital, although the will of his father, the Reverend Thomas Roe of Castleton, refers to interests in 'mines and shares of mines'[58] and may account for another source. When, after Roe's liquidation of his assets in the company in 1764, Lankford, Robinson and Co were declared bankrupt in 1773, amongst the assigners in bankruptcy were Samuel Glover and William Greaves, described at this time as London merchants.

One firm not on the above lists is that of George Pearson and George Hordern who built Sunderland Street Mill, Macclesfield, in 1769 for silk throwing, possibly for the use of Lombe's machinery. The Pearsons were not a wealthy family. George Pearson's father was a tailor but by the investment of capital pooled in partnership his firm became one of the largest firms in the town. By 1810 the Pearsons owned three mills on Waters Green (Figure 4).[59]

As well as local investment there is also evidence for some investment from London silk merchants in a limited number of companies,

notably Nathaniel Pattison's investment in the Old Mill at Congleton. In Stockport in 1732 a consortium of investors was formed for the purpose of throwing silk at Logwood Mill by means of Lombe's machinery. These included Thomas Eyre and Talbot Warren of Stockport, Thomas Hadfield and George Nicholson of Heaton Norris, near Stockport, and John Gurnell of the City of London, merchant.[60] However, the main sources of finance for the mid to late 18th-century provincial silk industry can be seen to have been capital accumulated by the middlemen of the silk smallware trade and other industries and capital from local land and property-owning families.

The approximate cost of mill building in the early period is known in some instances. The Old Mill, Congleton, was completed in 1753, and cost in excess of £5,000.[61] This sum was almost double the value of Roe's Button Mill in Macclesfield, whose 'silk mills, buildings, premises, machinery and utensils alone' were valued at £2,800 in 1762.[62] However, the Old Mill was much larger than the Button Mill, and was funded by London capital.

### Processes in relation to the design of mill building

Of the seven major Macclesfield silk-throwing firms listed in the *Journals of the House of Commons* for 1765, only two, Lankford, Robinson and Co and Glover and Co, are noted as using machinery on the Italian principle and were therefore producing organzine. The five remaining firms were presumably using the double Dutch machine, about which very little is known, for the production of tram. Unfortunately, since no description of the 'Dutch mill' can be found, the relationship between the machinery and the building specifications cannot be fully examined. Some details can be gleaned from a 1739 description of Cotchett's c1704 silk mill in Derby, which at that time was occupied by Thomas Lombe. It was described as containing on its two lower floors, '8 double Dutch mills, four in each storey, all in complete working order with 148 spindles in each mill'.[63] The building was of three storeys, 18·9 m long and 8·6 m wide. It is not clear whether the mill was working to capacity or whether it could have housed a larger number of spindles.[64]

By contrast, contemporary accounts of the Italian throwing machinery (Figure 12), and descriptions of the organisation of related processes within Lombe's mill, are detailed in their observations and are in general agreement on specifications, although there is some variation in the exact dimensions. In his *Tour through* the *Whole Island of Great Britain*, Daniel Defoe commented of Lombe's enterprise:

> *Here is a curiosity in trade worth observing as being the only one of its kind in England namely a throwing or throwsters Mill which performs by a wheel turned by the water; and though it cannot perform the doubling part of a throwster's work, which can only be done by a handwheel, yet it turns the other work and performs the Labour of many hands. Whether it answers the expense or not, that is not my business.*[65]

In the mill, winding was carried out on the three upper floors, whilst throwing was carried out on the two lower floors. The throwing machines were 5·8 m high,[66] and were accommodated in the two lower storeys of the mill. Assuming that the story of John Lombe's visit to Italy is true, he would have seen the circular throwing machine accommodated in Italian mills in the same way, 'tended by four groups of operatives working on two floors of a building, some at floor level, others on platforms'[67] as is shown in historical illustrations. Lombe's Mill is said to have contained twelve circular throwing machines. However, if the mill was 33 m in length[68] it could not have accommodated twelve of the machines in line, since the diameter of each of Lombe's machines was around 3·9 m.[69] As the mill was 12 m wide they could have been arranged in pairs down its length.

The floor-by-floor arrangement of processes in Lombe's mill was probably repeated in Clayton and Pattison's silk mill, the Old Mill, built in Congleton in 1753. Certainly by 1822 the arrangement of processes was the same, and the implication of Yates's description of the mill at this time is that the original, circular throwing machines had been positioned on the two lower floors, as in Lombe's mill:

> *Three of the rooms contain seventy-five winding engines, which perform 32,850 movements. Their office is to draw off or wind upon a small cylindrical block of wood, or bobbin, the raw silk, which is placed upon a hexagonal wheel called the swift. The other two rooms contain the cleaning engines and the spinning, doubling and throwing mills. The cleaning engine winds the silk from the first set of bobbins onto another; in this part of the process many children are employed, whose nimble fingers are kept in constant exercise by tying threads that break. The cleaning engines are twenty-one in number, and perform 3,150 movements. The spinning and throwing mills were originally of a circular form and turned by upright shafts, passing through their centres, and communicating with shafts from the water-wheel; their*

*diameter between twelve and fourteen feet, and their height about nineteen feet.*[70]

## Powered silk-throwing mills

Seven mills built to house early powered silk throwing in east Cheshire prior to the 1780s have been identified. In Macclesfield these are the Button Mill, built in 1744, Gutters Mill of 1750, Townley Street Mill, built before 1769, Sunderland Street Mill, built in 1769, and Rowbotham's Mill, pre 1784; in Congleton they are the Old Mill, built in 1753, and Slate's Dane Mill, pre 1775.[71] Only two of these remain standing: the Old Mill, reduced from five to two storeys in 1939, and Sunderland Street Mill, reduced from five to three storeys by 1935. In addition to these standing buildings, there is evidence from other sources for the structures of the now demolished Button Mill, Gutters Mill and Slate's Dane Mill.

Figure 12
*A one-third scale model of an Italian circular silk-throwing machine of the design used by John Lombe in his Derby silk mill. This model forms part of the exhibition in the Macclesfield Heritage Centre, Silk Museum.*

From what is known of the structure of these buildings, which are amongst the earliest powered factory buildings in Britain, an indication can be given of their form and construction. Two of the mills, the Old Mill and Sunderland Street Mill, were five storeyed, whilst the Button Mill, Gutters Mill and Slate's Dane Mill were four storeyed. Four storeys would seem to have been the minimum required to house efficiently all the processes of silk throwing using Italian machinery. Floor to ceiling heights of 2·3 m to 2·4 m are common, although 3·3 m and 3·4 m are recorded at Slate's Dane Mill and the Old Mill respectively. In plan the buildings were narrow, with external widths of between 7 m and 8 m. This dimension was based on the requirements of the machinery and the need to provide adequate light to the floor area, and was limited by the span achievable by an unsupported timber beam. Internal supports would have restricted the use of floor space, and since they were not necessary for this span, props or columns were not a feature in mills of this period. The length of the mills was variable, but the dimensions of between 25·6 m and 29·3 m appear to be the maximum building distance away from the waterwheel in early, east Cheshire, water-powered mills, with the exception of the Old Mill, Congleton. Gutters Mill measured only 16·2 m in length[72] but was horse powered and had no known association with the Italian machinery.

Most of these mills were rectangular in plan, but the Old Mill and the Button Mill each had wings which were almost certainly used as offices and warehousing. At the Button Mill the wing produced the L-shaped plan which was to become relatively common for east Cheshire mills during the early period of their development. No toilet blocks or external hoist towers have been identified in this early phase of mill building.

At least three of the mills, and probably all five, were built of brick. The brickwork of the Old Mill is particularly fine, using Flemish bond on all elevations and with a decorative, chequered effect achieved on the gable elevations by alternating dark stretcher bricks with light header bricks. This treatment was rarely used on industrial buildings, and the type of bonding on return and rear elevations was almost invariably English Garden Wall bond. However, the style of these mills was generally restrained and essentially vernacular, with the exception of the Old Mill with its pedimented centre, cupola and end pavilions (all other pedimented mill buildings in the district date from the early to mid 19th century). Doorways do not appear to have been singled out for architectural ornamentation. Windows were arranged at regular intervals of about 1 m apart, and were domestic in scale and design, with either flat, cambered or segmental brick arches. Fixed, small panes were held in wooden frames with only occasional single-pane

**Figure 13**
*Plan and elevation of the Old Mill, Congleton, built in 1753. Areas which remain as originally built are shaded black on the plan; the elevation is a reconstruction of its likely initial appearance.*

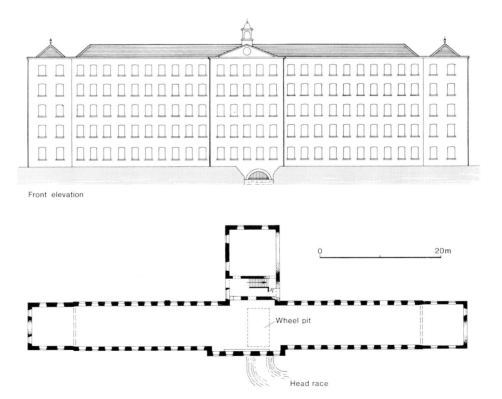

Front elevation

0           20m

Wheel pit

Head race

opening lights. This fenestration pattern created the characteristic regularity and uniformity of early factory architecture which has a pleasing harmony of scale and functional propriety.

In east Cheshire, only the Old Mill and the Button Mill are known with certainty to have been built to house Italian throwing machinery. The two remaining storeys of the Old Mill, which was built in 1753, are the earliest standing remains of a textile mill in Britain, and they give valuable evidence of early industrial architecture designed to house Lombe's Italian silk machinery. The deeds recite that the building was to be used 'as a silk mill with engines of various kinds for the winding, doubling, twisting and working of silk or other goods with a waterwheel for the turning or working of such mill and engines as there is'.[73] The 'engines of vari-

ous kinds' included eleven Italian-design throwing mills.[74]

The mill is situated on the north bank of the River Dane and was described by Samuel Yates in 1822 thus: 'The first silk mill which is the largest and most conspicuous structure in Congleton, is built of brick, with a pediment, containing the dial plate of the clock in the centre. It is 240 feet long, 24 feet wide, and 48 feet high, consisting of five stories; and is lighted by 390 windows.'[75] Only the ground and first floors of the five-storeyed mill survive, but its original form is known from earlier drawings, photographs and plans. The mill (Figures 3, 13, 14, 15) was twenty-nine bays long with a five-bay-wide centre, breaking forward under a pediment, flanked by ten-bay-long ranges which terminated in recessed, two-bay-long ends. A

Figure 14
*Reconstruction of the possible original arrangement of machinery in the Old Mill, Congleton. Eleven circular throwing machines were housed on the ground floor with winding machines above.*

29

**Figure 15**
*This aerial view of the Old Mill, Congleton, taken c1930, shows the thirty bays and five storeys of the original mill to the left and the substantial extension of c1830 to the right. Behind the mill extension is the town corn mill, since demolished.*

cupola surmounted the centre of the building, and the end bays had pyramidal roofs. To the rear a centrally placed wing rose the full height of the mill. It probably served as a warehouse, perhaps with a counting house next to the main entrance on the ground floor, and it also housed the mill's staircase which has cast-iron newel posts, a close string and timber balusters. The internal width of the building, 6·6 m, is almost exactly that of the Button Mill, but the length, 73·1 m, is exceptional for an 18th-century east Cheshire mill. The Old Mill housed eleven circular throwing machines in 1765,[76] each at least 3·6 m in diameter,[77] and the length of room needed for these machines alone, without allowing for working space between them and that taken by the waterwheel, would have been 40·6 m. The position of the wheel, slightly off-centre behind the central pedimented bays, implies that six machines were set to its west and five to its east. It is possible that these eleven machines were set in the main body of the mill, and that the two recessed end bays were divided off by cross walls, since removed. Scars on the inner wall face, and the fact that these end bays were separately roofed, are both evidence for cross walls. These areas may well have been used for storage.

Dimensions of the demolished Slate's Dane Mill at Congleton come from an auction sales notice of 1811, and are comparable to those of the Button Mill, except for the ground floor to ceiling height:

*All that extensive FACTORY for throwing silk with machinery fixed to the building, and 136 dozen of spinning spindles, 119 dozen of tram, and 2500 swifts, near Congleton Bridge on the River Dane, (and worked thereby), in the possession of Mr Thomas Slate, the same is four stories high, each of the rooms or storeys 84 feet in length by 27 feet in width, the mill room 11 feet in height, 1st engine room 7 feet 2 inches in height, the 2nd engine room 7 feet 4 inches in height, and the uppermost or Doublers Room 8 feet in height; with a good piece of building adjoining, which has been used for two weaving rooms.[78]*

The puzzling statistic is the height of 3·3 m for the mill room, which is difficult to explain in terms of housing machinery in a mid 18th-century mill, but which relates to the ground floor of the Old Mill.

The machinery of the now demolished Button Mill, which included double Dutch machines as well as the Italian throwing machine, was recorded in 1765 along with the number of hands employed:[79]

A state of the silk mills belonging to Lankford, Robinson and Stafford, of Macclesfield, for four years past, on Sir Thomas Loom's construction

| Year | | Dutch mills | No of hands |
|------|------|-------------|-------------|
| 1761 | 6 mills | 2 Pair | 350 |
| 1762 | 6 mills | 2 Pair | 350 |
| 1763 | 5 mills | 1 Pair | 280 |
| 1764 | 3 mills | 1 Pair | 180 |

The Button Mill was situated at the south end of Mill Street (Figure 16). The main block extended in a north-easterly direction from Mill Street, and a smaller wing, wedge-shaped in plan, ran from its western end to form a continuous elevation with the gable of the main block along Mill Street. The irregular wedge-shaped plan must have been caused by land boundaries. Roe's Monument (Figure 17), erected in Christ Church, Macclesfield after his death in

1781, depicts the mill being turned by a single waterwheel. This source, together with historical maps and plans, shows the wheel to have been positioned close to the junction of what appears to be the original block and an extension in line. Although the total length of this range was 43·5 m, the original block to which

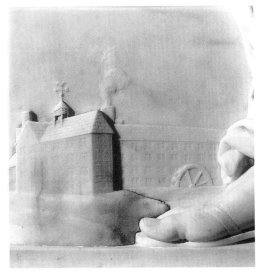

Figure 16
*The Button Mill, Macclesfield (right), was built in 1744 by Charles Roe to house Italian circular silk-throwing machinery. Depot Mill (left) was built in 1810, possibly for cotton spinning.*

Figure 17
*This relief of the Button Mill forms part of the memorial to Charles Roe which was erected after his death in 1781 in Christ Church, Macclesfield (Figure 158). It depicts the main range of the mill and its undershot waterwheel.*

the wheel related measured 22 m and had an internal ground-floor width of 6·7 m. The diameter of the circular throwing machines which Roe used is not known, but since from other evidence it is likely that it was between 3·6 m and 4·5 m,[80] the width of the mill would have comfortably accommodated such machines with adequate room on either side for access. The housing of these machines within the length of the building is more difficult to explain because the six circular throwing machines known to have been in the mill in 1761 (see above) would not have fitted within the length of what appears to have been the original mill. The explanation for this is not clear, but it is possible either that the mill was originally longer than 22 m, or that it had been extended by 1761 so as to house more machinery.

The Button Mill was four storeys high, and from the arrangement of processes described in both Lombe's mill, Derby, and the Old Mill, Congleton, this would seem to have been the minimum desirable number of storeys needed to accommodate the throwing and ancillary processes. The original floor to ceiling heights were 2·3 m. The Italian throwing machine, which measured up to 5·8 m in height, must therefore, as in Lombe's Mill and the Old Mill, have passed through the first floor, the whole of the machine being turned by a continuous upright shaft. Floor to ceiling heights on upper levels where the winding and cleaning processes were carried out are not thought to have been significant since the machinery was small scale and lightweight.

The Button Mill was built of handmade bricks laid to English Garden Wall bond. Loadbearing walls supported a hipped and stone-flagged roof which was carried on oak king-post trusses. The windows, which were square with segmental, header-brick arches, were arranged at a distance of 1·5 m apart. The distance between the windows is wide in relation to the average width of 0·9 m to 1·2 m in 18th-century mills. Windows on the south-east gable elevation of the Mill Street wing featured prominent stone voussoirs with keystones. The roof ridge was surmounted by a bell tower and weather vane close to the intersection of the two wings.[81] The basic layout and design, scale and construction of this mill provided a model for the housing of the textile industry in east Cheshire for almost the next 100 years.

Sunderland Street Mill (Figure 18), the only surviving mill building in Macclesfield from this early period, was erected in 1769[82] and formed part of an intense industrial development around the Pickford Street, Sunderland Street and Waters Green area, the first industrialised area in Macclesfield. There is no direct evidence that Italian throwing machinery was housed in the mill, but since Pearson and Hordern, its builders and occupants, had previously owned machinery in Townley Street Mill,[83] in which this technology was used,[84] it is possible that Sunderland Street Mill was built to house such machinery. The mill is comparable in style, construction and layout to Roe's Button Mill, and is situated on the west bank of the River Bollin, exactly at the point where the Dams Brook flows into the Bollin. The original mill appears to have measured 20·3 m in length[85] and was powered by an external waterwheel. The internal width of the ground floor is 7·1 m, just 0·3 m wider than the Button Mill, and it would have allowed for the accommodation of the Italian machinery. Although the mill is now three storeyed, it was originally five storeyed, with a hipped and stone-flagged roof. Evidence indicates an original floor-to-ceiling height of 2·4 m, which is again comparable to the Button Mill at 2·5 m. The mill was built of handmade brick laid to Flemish bond on its west (public) elevation, and to irregular English Garden Wall bond on its east (rear) elevation. Windows are segmental brick-arched and spaced at 1 m apart.

By 1804 Sunderland Street Mill had been extended southwards by about 28·5 m, and had become T-shaped in plan with the addition of the engine and boiler houses[86] (see p 67). A break in bonding is apparent between the earliest phase of building and a further extension to the north, shown on Cawley's map of Macclesfield in 1838.[87] The style and construc-

Figure 18
*Sunderland Street Mill, Sunderland Street, Macclesfield, was built in 1769. The mill, which was extended to the right in the early 19th century, and had a privy tower added, was reduced from five to three storeys in the early 20th century. The ground-floor plan shows it as it might have been when first built.*

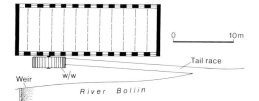

tion of the original mill and the north extension are almost identical. Modern alterations have unfortunately obscured any evidence of power transmission or other internal fittings, and the only remaining evidence for the water-power system is the weir and ashlar masonry blocks in the east wall of the mill.

From the dimensions of the early silk mills, including Townley Street Mill which measured 29 m by 8 m,[88] together with historical and structural evidence, there emerge a number of constants in the specifications of early mill buildings, although it is not always possible to know precisely how the various machines were arranged within them. Building to these specifications, using local building materials, generally with little architectural pretension, produced a building type so successful for the purpose of housing a range of textile processes that it was repeated in essence throughout the 19th century, and is typical of the period from 1780 to 1826 when the majority of the textile mills in east Cheshire were built.

## Power systems in relation to the design of mill building

The sources of power for the major silk-throwing enterprises were water power and horse power. It is probable that the importance of horse power as a motive source during the formative stages of industrialisation has been underestimated and that the source of power for mills which housed mechanised processes but were not located near to watercourses may be explained by the use of horse power. This may, for example, apply to mills on Back Street (now King Edward Street), Newgate and Dog Lane (now Stanley Street) in Macclesfield.[89] Gutters Mill, Macclesfield, now demolished, was another such mill, built in 1750 and situated on a spur of land high above the river valley. It was advertised in 1812: 'To be let and entered upon immediately, a silk factory situate on Bunkers Hill, in the centre of the town of Macclesfield, four storeys high, eighteen yards long by seven yards wide, with a good horse-wheel attached'[90] (see p 56).

Water was the most significant source of power for the early silk mills. The Italian silk industry was turning its throwing machinery by means of waterwheels as early as the 13th century.[91] An early 17th-century Italian illustration of the circular, silk-throwing machine shows it being driven by a single undershot waterwheel positioned outside the mill[92] (Figure 19). A 19th-century Italian publication appears to illustrate the machine being driven by a waterwheel

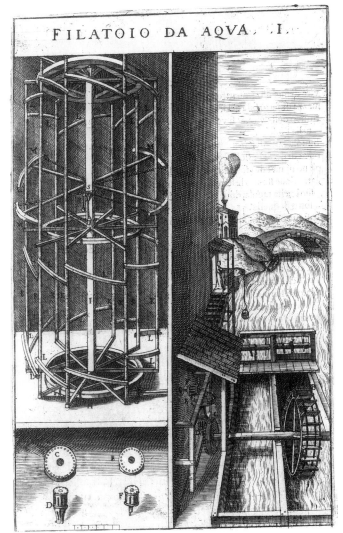

attached directly to the upright shaft of each machine.[93] However there is no evidence, either structural or documentary, that any of the early British silk mills used this type of multiple water-wheel system. It is clear from the surviving evidence that both Cotchett's mill[94] and Lombe's Mill in Derby were driven by a single waterwheel, and this would also appear to be true of all the east Cheshire mills of this early period. Waterwheels at this time would almost certainly have been undershot and constructed of wood, with drive carried via lengths of timber shafting to the machinery.

Evidence for the use of water power is known for five of the textile mills built in east Cheshire for mechanised silk throwing before the 1780s, namely the Button Mill, Sunderland Street Mill and Townley Street Mill in Macclesfield, and Slate's Dane Mill and the Old Mill in Congleton. The leases for all the Macclesfield sites were purchased from Joseph Pickford of Althill, Lancashire, who owned large

Figure 19
*An illustration, published in Zonca 1607, shows the driving mechanism of the Italian circular throwing machine (by permission of the British Library, 537M8).*

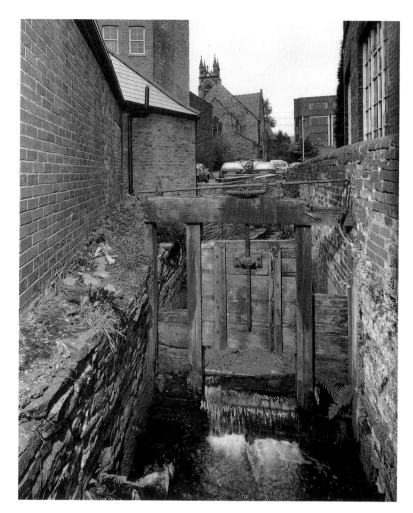

**Figure 20**
*Sluice-gates were used to control the flow of water to waterwheels. This sluice-gate on the Dams Brook near Pickford Street, Macclesfield, is in the same position as a sluice-gate which regulated the flow of water to Pickford Street 'B' Mill in the late 18th century.*

tracts of prime development land near the confluence of the River Bollin and the Dams Brook. The details of these indentures show how important secure water rights were to those involved. The Dams Brook did not have the capacity to provide enough head of water for the more efficient breastshot and overshot wheels. Even to provide adequate power for undershot wheels, arrangements had to be made for the damming of the brook. A sluice-gate (Figure 20), much renewed, still exists on the Dams Brook to the south of Pickford Street, at a control point for Pickford Street 'B' Mill, Macclesfield (a cotton mill now demolished). The River Bollin, although more powerful than the Dams Brook, was restricted in its use because of existing water rights, the most ancient being those of the corn and fulling mills in Sutton.

In 1743, together with the land for building the Button Mill, Charles Roe secured water rights in the Dams Brook.[95] By 1750, it seems that this source was already insufficient since Roe and his partner, Samuel Lankford, leased the Sutton corn mills from Lord Lucan,

together with the right to divert 'waste and useless' water from the Sutton mills to their Macclesfield mill.[96] In April 1769, Pickford let land by the River Bollin to Pearson and Hordern for the purpose of building Sunderland Street Mill, demising also the right to 'impound and raise the water of the said brook by any weirs, locks or other devises, and to convey the same by any soughs or trenches to the waterwheel or waterwheels to be used at the silk mills intended to be erected on the said plot'.[97] A month later Pickford re-let Townley Street Mill, 200 m upstream of Pearson's mill, to the firm of Glover, Greaves and Huxley, by an indenture in which the water rights of Pearson and Hordern were carefully ensured. For these rights they paid Pickford £22 2s 0d above the annual rent of £3 14s 9d.[98] The struggle for water rights in Macclesfield meant that the long-term use of water power there was obviously not practicable, and the proportion of mills known to have used water power in the town after 1780 is small in spite of distribution patterns which show a large number of sites following water-courses.

In Macclesfield, evidence for the structure of waterwheels in this period relates to two sites only, the Button Mill and Sunderland Street Mill. The Button Mill's waterwheel is clearly shown on Roe's monument in Christ Church, Macclesfield (see Figure 17). Sited externally, at the centre of the north-east wing, the wheel is estimated to have been about 9.23 m in diameter, and appears to have been undershot. The wheel of Sunderland Street Mill was also positioned externally, against the east wall of the mill.[99] Possibly low breastshot, to judge from the position of the weir adjacent to the mill, the wheel seems to have been housed on low supporting walls.[100] This arrangement may be a later modification of an earlier arrangement.

In Congleton, the powerful River Dane and its several tributaries provided greater capacity for water power. Both the Old Mill and Slate's Dane Mill were turned by the River Dane. Clayton and Pattison's Old Mill was built adjacent to the town corn mill on land leased from the burgesses of Congleton. By virtue of a lease of November 1752[101] the burgesses allowed water to be diverted from the Dane to the silk mill by means of the same weir (Figure 21), sluice and culvert as was used for the corn mill. However, because this reduced the flow of water to the town mill, Clayton and Pattison, at their own expense, had to replace the corn mill's gearing so that it would grind the same quantity of corn, using less water. Later, in March 1754, Clayton and Pattison leased the corn mill, which gave them greater control over the flow of water.[102]

Of the 18th-century silk-throwing mills, the Old Mill is the only mill in east Cheshire known to have had its waterwheel positioned centrally within the building. Samuel Yates described the system in 1822: 'The whole of this elaborate machine ... is put in motion by a single water wheel 19 feet 6 inches in diameter and 5 feet 6 inches broad, situated in the centre of the building.'[103]

Yates's evidence that the mill was powered by a single waterwheel is supported by the 1752 indenture of lease which states that the drive was to be supplied by 'a waterwheel for the turning or working of such mill and engines as there is'.[104] There is no apparent structural evidence that there was another wheel elsewhere in the mill or of a dual wheel system in the central wheel pit. The earliest evidence that the wheel was positioned at the centre of the mill is contained in a sketch plan of Congleton drawn between 1775 and 1803.[105] Having being drawn at least twenty-three years after the building of the mill the plan does not provide conclusive evidence that this was the wheel's original position. However, there is no structural evidence of any other wheel positions or of any alteration in the course of the mill race. Moreover, the existing mill race utilised water diverted from the corn mill and discharged into the corn mill's tail race, the arrangement laid down by the 1752 lease.

In spite of this evidence it is remarkable that a mill of this length was powered by a single waterwheel driving, via timber shafts, two rows of silk-throwing machines extending over 30 m on each side of it on two floors, as well as winding and cleaning machinery on the three upper floors. It is, of course, possible that the original power system was different from that for which there is evidence. However, it must be borne in mind that the circular silk-throwing machine needed relatively little power to drive it, being made almost entirely of wood, and that its spindles turned at only approximately 320 revolutions per minute.[106] Furthermore, although the horizontal shafting carrying the drive from the wheel was most probably timber, each shaft would not have been of any great length, but rather a series of short shafts linking the upright shafts of each throwing machine and would therefore have been able to cope with the torque. The stress on these shafts and the waterwheel may have been lessened by not starting the Italian throwing and winding machines all at once. James Brindley, initially engaged by Nathaniel Pattison to construct the waterwheel, also made 'many new and useful improvements particularly one ... for stopping, in an instant, not only the whole of this extensive system

throughout its various apartments, but any part of it individually'.[107] The significance of Brindley's improvement may have been not so much in stopping the machinery but in being able to start it gradually, introducing one or two machines at a time.

The position of a waterwheel may have been one of the factors determining the length of a mill and the evidence from east Cheshire points to this having been the case. The dimensions of between 25·6 m and 29·3 m appear to be the maximum building distance away from the wheel in early water-powered mills in east Cheshire (the Button Mill 1744, Sunderland Street Mill 1769 and Park Green Mill 1785). If the wheel was positioned centrally, the maximum length would be in the region of between 51 m and 58 m, plus the width of the wheel pit. Interior housing enabled the gearing to be taken more efficiently from each side of the wheel, but used up a large proportion of space in the building. Evidence for water systems from this period suggests that, as in the later period, the availability of water sources, their fall and velocity, the demands made by processes which were in themselves affected by economic considerations, resulted in a variety of systems, each of which was a unique response to these factors.

By 1780, the form and organisation of a flourishing, mechanised silk-throwing industry, with attendant ancillary processes, was well established in east Cheshire, housed in a proven and successful building form. This framework successfully housed the growing silk-throwing industry and was easily adapted for the newly mechanised cotton-spinning industry which was introduced to the area during the late 18th and early 19th centuries.

Figure 21
*This weir across the River Dane, Congleton, dammed the river for the town corn mill. When Clayton and Pattison leased the site of the Old Mill in 1752 they agreed to raise the weir in order to ensure sufficient water both for their silk mill and the corn mill.*

# 3  HOUSING THE SILK AND COTTON INDUSTRIES *c*1780–1826

*The habits of the people employed in the silk mills and twister's sheds, were ...
tolerably decent and regular; their wages moderate, but proportionate to the price
of provisions; and general contentment was the consequence ... but the time was
approaching when this moderation was to be subverted by excess. In 1785 some
Lancashire men came to Macclesfield and erected a Manufactory for spinning
cotton on the banks of the Bollin in that part of town called the Waters.*[1]

Between 1743 and 1783, when textile mills in east Cheshire were built exclusively to accommodate the processes of the silk-throwing industry, at least twelve mills were erected in the area. The period 1784 to 1826 was generally one of great prosperity for the textile industry, owing partly to the effect of the wars with America and France and partly to the protection provided by embargoes upon the importation of foreign silk goods. During this period at least 119 silk and cotton mills were erected.

This expansion in mill building accelerated after the annulment of the patent on Arkwright's water frame in the early 1780s, and together with increased supplies of raw cotton it resulted in an unprecedented rise in the output of manufactured cotton. This rise enabled manufacturers to satisfy the growing demand for cotton cloth from both domestic and foreign markets. The consequence in east Cheshire was the construction of a large number of new cotton-spinning mills. Lower Heyes Mill, Lower Beech Mill, Johnson's Mill and Pickford Street 'B' Mill in Macclesfield, Cow Lane Mill and Millbrook Mill in Rainow, Oak Bank Mill in Bollington, the Daneinshaw and Stonehouse Green Mills in Congleton and Quarry Bank Mill at Styal were all built in the mid to late 1780s for spinning cotton.

In contrast, new mills in the early 19th century were built mainly to house the growing silk-throwing industry. The favourable economic climate which existed between the commencement of hostilities with France in 1793 and the financial crisis of 1826, together with the wide-spread introduction of steam as the primary source of power, stimulated the construction, during the first twenty-five years of the 19th century, of about seventy of the 246 mills built in east Cheshire. Some forty-two of these mills were in Macclesfield, and thirteen in Congleton.[2] It appears that almost all of them were built for silk processing, representing the consolidation of the silk industry and a contraction of investment in the cotton industry in this area. Only nine of the seventy mills have been identified as being built for cotton spinning and of these at least five had been converted for silk processing by 1826. A number of 18th-century cotton mills were also converted to silk at this time. In 1825, at the height of the expansion of the silk industry, twelve mills were erected in Macclesfield alone in a single year.[3]

The building expansion of east Cheshire's textile industries in the late 18th and early 19th centuries greatly increased reliance on borrowed capital. The sources of this capital now extended beyond close family and partners to those members of the gentry and landowning classes with whom it was known loans could be raised in the form of mortgages. In 1806, for example, John Lowe, the builder of Gin Clough Mill, Rainow, borrowed £2,100 from John Brocklehurst, a Macclesfield silk manufacturer and landowner.[4] Capital was also made available by an increasing number of private banks whose links with the textile industry were very close. They supplied capital for the building of mills and the establishment of textile firms. For example the Hawkins, Mills and Company Bank provided

Edward Maddock and Thomas Cockson with a mortgage on Lower Heyes Mill, Macclesfield, in 1784.[5] Moreover, banks were themselves established and financed by textile manufacturers. In Macclesfield, Daintry and Ryle, cotton spinners and silk throwsters, took over the Hawkins, Mills and Company Bank in 1800 (Figure 22), and in 1802 Thomas Critchley, a Macclesfield silk manufacturer, established the Critchley and Turner Bank. When this bank failed in 1816 it was taken over by the Brocklehurst family, also silk manufacturers.[6] In Congleton, the bank of Johnson and Son, silk manufacturers, had been founded by 1811. The establishment of these credit systems facilitated the expansion of existing firms and the entry of new firms into the textile industry, and provided the capital necessary to take advantage of new technology.

## The establishment of the cotton industry in east Cheshire and its effect on the silk industry

There is relatively little evidence for hand-powered cotton processing in east Cheshire until the 1780s when, in Wilmslow, the spinning of cotton yarn on hand-operated jennies began to replace the manufacture of buttons and the spinning of jersey wool as the staple domestic industry. Spinners were supplied with raw cotton by masters who also provided them with jennys, and were paid by the pound of finished yarn.[7] The preparatory processes of cleaning, carding and slubbing were performed by hand by the spinners themselves. In about 1780, however, at least one mill was built in east Cheshire solely for powered carding and slubbing: 'Mr Bower,

Figure 22
*An 1841 five-pound note issued for the Daintry Ryle and Company Bank of Macclesfield. Daintry and Ryle were cotton spinners and silk throwsters who took over the Hawkins, Mills and Company Bank in 1800.*

37

Figure 23
*Samuel Greg
(1758–1834), a wealthy
merchant-manufacturer of
Manchester, who built
Quarry Bank Mill at
Styal in 1784.*

one of the most capital masters in this branch, has lately erected a building ... near Wilmslow Bridge, with a water wheel which cards and slubs his cotton, and so prepares it for his Jennys.'[8] The gradual mechanisation of these preparatory processes was completed around 1810, bringing about the increase in production essential to supply the demands of mechanised spinning.

Quarry Bank Mill at Styal, near Wilmslow, was one of the first mills built for housing as many elements of mechanised production as were available, including the preparatory processes. It was built in 1784 by Samuel Greg, already a wealthy merchant-manufacturer of Manchester, who was attracted to Wilmslow by the ready availability of skilled spinners and by the potential of the River Bollin to provide water power. Initially, although the mill was not worked to full capacity, 150 workers, mostly children, were employed on water frames to produce 1,000 lbs of cotton yarn per week. The

finest was spun from Brazilian cotton and was sent to Greg's hand loomshops at Eyam in Derbyshire[9] to be woven into muslin.[10]

It is highly probable that the cotton yarn produced by the east Cheshire spinning factories was put out to handloom weavers in the neighbouring towns and villages. However, the first evidence for the weaving of cotton cloth is not until 1789, when Philip Antrobus was described as a Bollington 'check manufacturer'.[11] As the Antrobus family were spinning cotton in Bollington, building Higher and Lower Mills for this purpose in the 1790s and Lowerhouse Mill in 1818, it is probable that Philip Antrobus was putting out the yarn to cottage weavers in the area. Samuel Oldknow, a cotton spinner of Stockport, historically part of Cheshire, employed 300 trained weavers by 1786. They journeyed to his warehouse to collect the cotton warps and weft which they wove at home. Sometimes they were supplied with raw cotton, for the spinning of which they were paid extra.[12]

Similarly, there is little evidence for handloom weaving on cotton-mill sites. Although Lumbhole Mill, Kettleshulme, was described in 1815 as 'a building two-storeys high ... lately used as a loomshop',[13] and was later used as a cotton mill, it is not clear whether the site was at this date being used for the production of cotton. Generally, there is no evidence in east Cheshire that hand-powered looms were housed in the cotton mills, and it would seem that, unlike the area's silk industry, it was not until the introduction of the powerloom that weaving was carried out on cotton-mill sites to any great extent.

The main markets for cotton yarn were Manchester and Glasgow where the yarn was sent in batches to be sold by agents. Much of the yarn spun in Wilmslow was sent to Glasgow 'where it is manufactured and perhaps finds it way back again into this country in the travelling Scotchmen's packs'.[14] Richard Martin, who built Daneinshaw Mill in 1784, Congleton's first cotton mill,[15] seems to have sold much of his produce in both markets. Not only did he retain an agent in Glasgow, but on New Year's Day 1788 he entered into a partnership with Thomas and John Whitfield, Manchester merchants. The partners agreed that Thomas Whitfield would sell the cotton twist in Manchester whilst Richard Martin and John Whitfield would superintend the work in the factories.[16] Manchester rapidly became the trading centre for the cotton industry, and many firms maintained a presence in the city. In 1788, for example, Aaron Clulow, a cotton spinner with a mill in Macclesfield and another in Bollington, also had a warehouse in Parsonage Lane, Manchester,[17] and in the early years of Quarry Bank Mill, Samuel Greg (Figure 23) marketed his cotton in Manchester and, indeed, lived there until 1797.[18]

The introduction of cotton spinning initially caused problems for the east Cheshire silk industry. The cotton industry paid higher wages and consequently drew workers from throwing silk into spinning cotton. 'In a short time after cotton spinning was established' in the area, the silk-throwing firms were forced to raise the wages of silk 'millmen' from 7*s* per week in 1776, to an average of 16*s* per week.[19] Nevertheless, the silk industry was generally very prosperous with the result that, in the view of John Corry writing in 1817, 'wealth flowed into the coffers of the principal throwsters'.[20] Moreover, the industry received a boost with the commencement of the hostilities with France in 1793, and with the general introduction of the hand-powered broadloom[21] in the late 18th century.

The hand broadloom weaving of silk was largely carried on away from the mills by weavers working in the purpose-built, top-floor garrets of three-storey houses (see p 54). Weavers worked either independently or under the control of millowners who employed them as outworkers. Those millowners who produced both silk yarn and woven cloth seem to have been known as manufacturers, but the term manufacture could be interpreted in two ways, meaning either the weaving of yarn, or, according to John Brocklehurst, the 'manufacture of raw silk through all its processes of throwing, dyeing and weaving into goods'.[22]

During the early part of the 19th century, particularly as the silk industry recovered from the depression following the Napoleonic Wars, throwsters began increasingly to turn to manufacturing and to house handlooms within their mills. The *Macclesfield Courier and Herald* commented in 1821: 'It is but lately that great weaving establishments have been set up at Macclesfield and Manchester and other places, but several branches [of weaving] are now carried on in these places, which have in consequence been entirely discontinued in Spitalfields',[23] and in 1822 Sandbach was described as having 'several manufactories established in the town and its immediate neighbourhood for the throwing of silk and weaving it into various textures'.[24]

Both broadlooms and ribbon looms were housed in established mill premises. In 1817 Gutters Mill, Macclesfield, was advertised as being 'well calculated for weavers, being well lighted'[25] and by the late 1820s Bank Top Mill, Catherine Street Mill, Chester Road Mill, Exchange Mill and possibly Alma Mill in Pickford Street, Macclesfield, all accommodated looms and were integrated sites. William Bayley was manufacturing in Exchange Mill in 1825, and the contents, when advertised for sale in 1827, included twenty-four trimming looms, one broadloom, three Dutch looms and two braid looms.[26] In Congleton in 1822 three firms, Gent and Norbury, James Foden and Richard Edwards, were manufacturing ribbons in mills:[27] Gent and Norbury in Vale Mill and Richard Edwards in John Booth's mill at Ball's Croft.[28]

An alternative to housing looms within the multi-storeyed mill was to house them in adjacent loomshops. Slate's Dane Mill, Congleton, built by William Slate in around 1775,[29] was an integrated site by 1811, containing silk-throwing machinery in the main mill and looms in 'a good piece of building adjoining, which has been used for two weaving rooms'.[30] Stanley Street Mill, Macclesfield, was used in 1813 as a loomshop for adjacent silk-throwing mills which were in common ownership[31] (Figure 24).

The housing of looms in the silk industry before the mid 1820s entailed accommodating hand-operated broad and ribbon looms of various types. The organisation of the hand-weaving industry resulted in the building of garrets and loomshops, but the accommodation of looms within the multi-storeyed mill did not affect the design of mill building during this period. Similarly, the spinning of silk does not appear to have affected mill design at this time and although there are a small number of references to silk spinning, no mills have been identified in east Cheshire as being constructed specifically to house this process before 1826 (see p 74).

Figure 24
*Stanley Street Mill, Macclesfield, was used, in 1813, as a loomshop.*

The form of the mill building and the organisation of the factory system had already been established by the powered silk-throwing industry in the early 18th century, before the introduction of powered cotton spinning. It is necessary, therefore, to consider to what extent the manufacture of cotton yarn by the new technology, as well as the change from horse and water power to steam power, affected mill design. Whilst it is possible to put forward a number of hypotheses relating to the effect of technological change on the dimensions of mill buildings, it is worth noting a statement given by John Brocklehurst, a Macclesfield silk manufacturer, to a Parliamentary Committee of Inquiry, that 'parties built mills to suit their own convenience; men with larger capital built a proportionate mill, and men of less means built a smaller mill'.[32]

## Processes in relation to the design of mill building

### Mechanisation of the cotton processes

After the successful introduction and development of mechanised silk-winding and throwing machinery in the early and mid 18th century, technology in the silk industry was at a virtual standstill until the 1820s. The cotton industry on the other hand, possibly stimulated by the success of English silk-throwing machinery, developed a whole series of machines from the mid 18th century until 1810, which converted cotton spinning from an essentially domestic, hand-powered industry to a factory-based industry whose processes were entirely mechanised.

Although experiments had been made with powered cotton-spinning machinery as early as 1733 by Paul and Wyatt,[33] and later by Highs and Kay,[34] the most successful of the new, powered, cotton-spinning machines were the water frame (Figure .25), patented by Richard Arkwright in 1769 (see p 11), and the mule, perfected by Samuel Crompton in 1779. The water frame drew out the cotton roving by means of a series of rollers turning at differing speeds. The roving was then twisted by being passed through a loop in a wire flyer which rotated around the receiving bobbin, a method already established by the Italian silk-throwing machines. The water frame vastly increased productivity and produced a strong yarn suitable for the warp threads of weaving. It was the direct precursor of the throstle spinning machine, an iron ver-

Figure 25
*Arkwright's water frame was patented in 1769. The cotton roving passed from the spindles at the top of the machine, through a series of rollers which drew it out, before passing through a wire loop which rotated around the receiving bobbin and twisted the cotton into thread (Cossons 1972).*

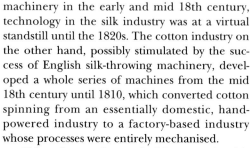

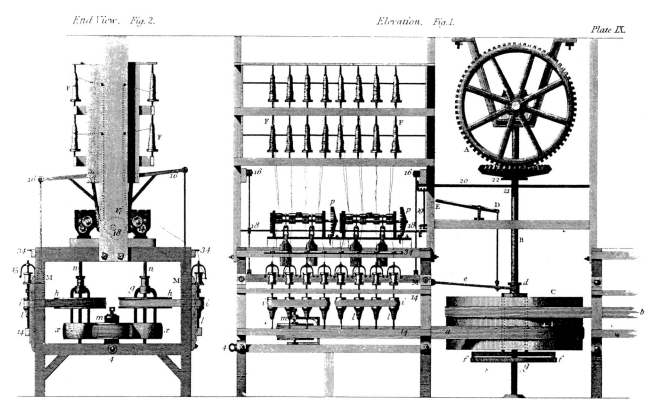

COTTON MANUFACTURE.

*WATER SPINNING FRAME.*

End View. Fig. 2.    Elevation. Fig.1.    Plate IX.

sion of the water frame, and ultimately of the modern ring-spinning frame. In east Cheshire, the water frame seems to have been phased out by the early 19th century, to be replaced by throstles and mules. Its use for spinning cotton at Quarry Bank Mill, Styal, near Wilmslow, until at least the 1830s,[35] and at Rainow Mill, Rainow, in 1821,[36] seems to have been unusual.

The mule (Figure 26) combined the method used by the spinning jenny, of drawing out the roving by stretching it whilst adding a strengthening twist, and the method of roller-drawing used by the water frame. In this way it could produce very fine cotton yarn. Initially, the mule was hand powered, but the power-driven mule, introduced in the 1790s, powered the draw, or first part of the spinning cycle, whereby a length of roving is drawn out and spun. This allowed the mule to increase in size to around 350 spindles, and enabled a spinner to work a pair of mules.

Figure 26
*The mule was perfected by Samuel Crompton in 1779. The cotton roving passed from bobbins at the back of the machine through sets of rollers which drew it out. The roving was then stretched further by the action of the carriage (figure 1) rolling away from the main frame (figure 2) whilst the receiving spindle turned and twisted the cotton (Cossons 1972).*

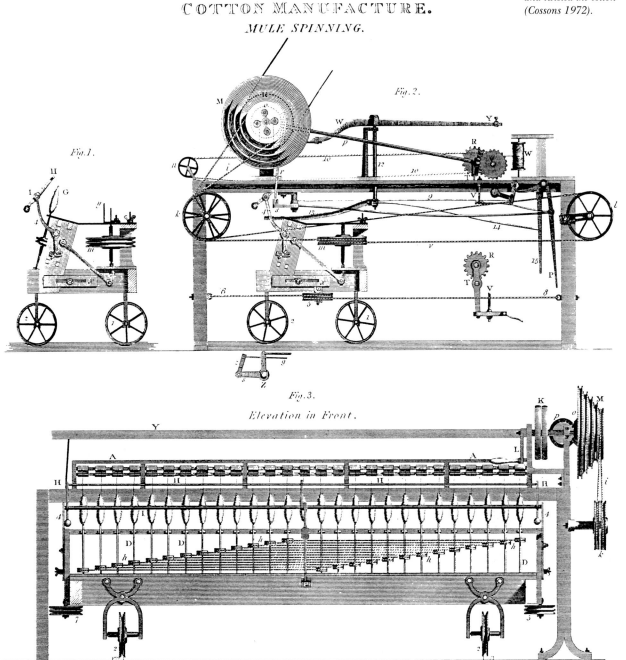

COTTON MANUFACTURE.

*MULE SPINNING.*

*Fig.1.*

*Fig.2.*

*Fig.3.*

*Elevation in Front.*

The success of powered spinning technology stimulated the need for efficient machinery in the preparatory processes. Until the 1770s carding was performed by hand cards: two flat-faced brushes with angled, wire teeth which, when drawn one across the other, combed the cotton fibres and untangled them. The first powered carding engine was patented by Daniel Bourn in 1748 and introduced the idea of cylinder cards. This involved mounting cards, for this purpose strips of leather pierced with metal teeth, on two or more cylinders. Bourn's machine seems to have been improved by Peel and Hargreaves around 1760, but these early cylinder cards had no mechanical method of removing the carded cotton, which had to be done by hand. However, in 1775 Arkwright patented a method which, by means of an oscillating metal comb known as a doffer, removed the carded cotton in a coherent sheet. This sheet could then be drawn together into a slubbing.[37] Although these advances mechanised the major elements of cotton processing, it was not until around 1810, when the cleaning processes known as devilling or willowing and scutching were also mechanised that the entire process of yarn production could be performed efficiently by machines.[38]

### Flexibility of mill use

The dominant characteristic of east Cheshire textile mills over the period, 1780 to 1826 was, with some notable exceptions, their use as multi-purpose industrial buildings. In the silk industry, manufacturing output and capital return were vulnerable to a capricious fashion market and were dependent upon protectionist legislation. By contrast, the cotton industry was under pressure to improve and refine its manufacturing processes in order to supply a steadily increasing demand for cheap and functional cloth. The silk industry therefore offered to the potential investor an established system of production, but with the risk of a sudden loss of market, whereas the cotton industry offered a more stable market with much higher demand, set against the need for substantial capital investment in experimental technology. For several entrepreneurs in east Cheshire, the solution lay in investment in both the silk and cotton industries, and the erection of textile mills which were suitable for either silk or cotton processes.

A survey of mills erected throughout England and Scotland between 1771 and 1795 shows that those buildings, described as Arkwright-type mills,[39] varied widely in their size. Planned on a simple rectangle, the widths ranged from 3·9 m to 16·5 m, the majority measuring 8·1 m to 8·4 m, whereas the lengths were variable, ranging from 8·1 m to 59·7 m, and the number of storeys ranged from two to seven. What emerges from these statistics is that, although all these mills housed Arkwright spinning machinery, they do not present a definitive design. There does not appear to have been a particular size of mill building specifically suited for Arkwright's machinery.

The important aspects of the new textile technology in relation to mill buildings are the dimensions of machinery and the organisation of processes. Arkwright's water frame, unlike the Italian silk-throwing machine, was rectangular in shape and adaptable in length, depending upon the number of spindles carried (Figure 27). By 1790 twelve drafting heads, driving forty-eight

Figure 27
*A plan showing water frames housed across the width of a mill (Birmingham Library Services, Boulton and Watt Collection, Miscellaneous Mills portfolio).*

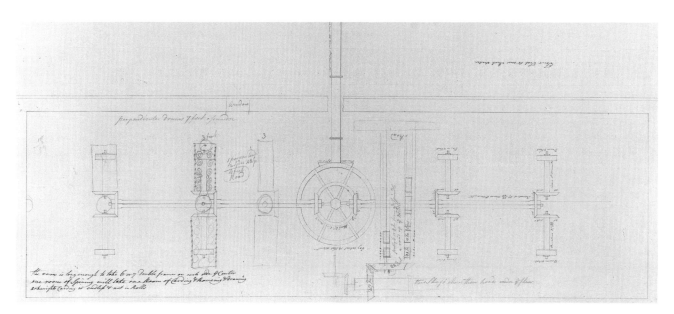

spindles, were arranged on either side of the headstock (driving mechanism), which resulted in a machine of *c*7 m in length.[40] It was apparently possible not only to house cotton-spinning machinery in mills built for silk throwing, or vice versa, but also to continue to build to the same specifications. It is noted in the deeds of Arkwright's Cromford Mill, Derbyshire, the first water-powered cotton-spinning mill, as it is too in those of the Old Mill, Congleton, one of the first British silk mills, that the mill was to be built 'for spinning, winding or throwing silk, worsted, linen, cotton or other materials'.[41]

This situation meant that there was little hindrance for those who wanted to move from silk throwing to cotton spinning, either in terms of familiarity with textile production and marketing or, more importantly, in terms of the mill building they required. In 1817 John Corry commented that 'Mr Roe and other silk throwsters allured by the prospect of gain engaged in cotton spinning.'[42] Roe was followed from silk into cotton by, amongst others, George and William Reade of Congleton in 1784,[43] and George Antrobus of Bollington in the 1790s.[44] In 1797 John Latham was involved in both silk and cotton,[45] as were Daintry and Ryle, who were processing both silk and cotton in the 1790s.[46] This ease of movement facilitated both the initial expansion of the cotton industry in east Cheshire and, when the economic situation demanded, the return to silk; for example, Daneinshaw Mill, Congleton, built by Richard Martin in 1784 for cotton spinning, was occupied by Hall and Johnson for silk throwing by 1822.[47]

The possibility of housing either silk or cotton processes in mills also encouraged speculative building, since a mill built for letting did not have to be designed for a particular industry, thereby increasing the variety of potential occupants. Advertisements in the *Macclesfield Courier and Herald* in the early years of the 19th century describe mill premises as being suitable for a variety of uses. For example, two rooms were advertised for letting in Common Gate Mill, Macclesfield, in 1811, 'each 25 yards by 8 yards wide, with a good regular turning for cotton or silk machinery'.[48]

Textile entrepreneurs who did not have the capital to build mills relied on leasing a whole or part of a mill, frequently only one floor. Demand for leasehold premises inevitably provoked building on a speculative basis, with the intention of letting the property to textile or other manufacturers. Building for this purpose enabled men from other fields to take advantage of the building boom in the thriving silk and cotton industries. Thomas Cockson, for example, builder of a cotton shop at Lower Heyes in Macclesfield in 1784, was a surgeon and apothecary,[49] whilst Charles Townley, builder of Park Mill, Congleton, in 1825, was a builder by trade.[50] Men from within the textile industry also built mills on a speculative basis. In 1812 Thomas Whitney, a cotton manufacturer who built Pickford Street 'A' Mill, Macclesfield, in 1811, let part of his factory to Edward and Robert Bailey for their silk-throwing business. The Baileys occupied the 'bottom floor' and half of the 'middle floor' and also had use of a small warehouse with half of the yard behind it.[51] It was also possible for new or small businesses to lease machinery as well as the floor space. In 1825 John Johnson of Congleton advertised rooms to let in his new mill: 'To silk throwsters. To let — and may be entered upon early in the ensuing spring — two or three rooms in a newly erected silk factory situate at Buglawton near Congleton. Each room will contain three hundred dozen spindles with requisite preparations and warehouse room.'[52]

Division of the mill floors in this way meant that some agreement was needed for the distribution of power. In Pickford Street 'A' Mill, Whitney retained ownership of the steam engine and divided its use between the tenants. The Baileys, for example, had the 'liberty of working and turning their silk machinery therein, by the steam engine of Thomas Whitney' but were limited to a maximum of 480 spindles. In a similar arrangement in 1819 James Cooper, a silk throwster in Pickford Street 'A' Mill, was limited to a maximum of 100 spindles. For his part Whitney agreed to work the engine at a regular speed but was not to be held liable for any loss of production due to a failure of the engine.[53] Although this is the only known evidence for this arrangement in east Cheshire, there is no reason to suppose it was not a widespread practice.

## Costing

Insurance values, in that they must to some extent reflect replacement cost, may give an idea of the building cost of an early textile mill. In 1796 George Antrobus, a Bollington cotton spinner, insured Higher Mill for £1,000 with the Sun Fire Insurance Company. Whilst the mill was valued at £400, the 'gearing' at £100 and his stock at £50, the most expensive item was the machinery at £450. The mill cost can be contrasted with his Lower Mill which was valued at £850[54] and with Aaron Clulow's Bollington 'cotton millhouse and machinery' which was insured in 1788 for £950.[55] Clulow insured a second cotton-spinning mill at Tytherington near Macclesfield, for £1,950.[56] All these mills were

Figure 28
*Thorp Street Leather Mill, Macclesfield, erected c1820. The fixed-light, small-pane windows would have been common in mills of this period.*

water powered, and their building costs and machinery valuation at around the end of the 18th century fall between £1,000 and £2,000.

Comparison of these figures with insurance valuations of cotton mills elsewhere in the country in the late 18th century implies that the east Cheshire mills were generally built and equipped on a slightly smaller scale. In 1779 a mill at Belper was insured, including utensils and stock, for £3,000. Furthermore, a 1783 mill in Manchester was insured on a similar basis for £6,000.[57]

However, insurance valuations were not a reflection of market values which themselves fluctuated widely, depending on the state of the economy. John Brocklehurst, the Macclesfield silk manufacturer, gave evidence that a silk mill which had cost between £6,000 and £7,000 about 1825, in a boom period, sold, independent of machinery, for £1,270 in 1827, a time of depression.[58] Furthermore, the number of influential factors involved in valuations of mill buildings and their contents — mill size, value of stock and machinery, relative fire risk of building materials and stock, variations in property markets and the health of the textile industry — all contribute to complications of interpretation.

## Mill architecture

### Characteristic mill design

The characteristic east Cheshire textile mill of the period from the 1780s to 1826 was three to four storeys high, and rectangular or L-shaped in plan. Although the majority of mills were plain, unadorned and functional, a small number were distinguished by style, by size and, in the case of Lowerhouse Mill, Bollington, built as a cotton-spinning mill, by the use of a fireproof structure. Power houses, warehouses and offices, and occasionally toilet blocks, were contained either in adjacent buildings or as extensions to the mill. Small dyehouses, loomshops and garrets were also sometimes an integral part of the mill site. Essentially, however, the multi-storeyed mill continued to function during this period without significant development or site expansion.

Throughout east Cheshire many mills of this type survive,[59] the primary phases of them similar in size and construction, despite being built for both silk and cotton processes (Figures 28, 29). Their overall size is small by later standards and does not differ greatly from those silk mills built before 1780. Internal widths are generally 7·5 m to 8 m, although in a few cases slightly wider (see below). Lengths are variable but within a range of 22 m to 38 m, and floor to ceiling heights average 2·5 m (Figure 30). The 1823 mill at Victoria Mills, Macclesfield (Figures 65a, 82), although it conforms generally to the standard mill type of this period, is nevertheless distinguished by having a ground floor to ceiling height of 3·8 m. This may imply that it was one of the first mills in Macclesfield to house Jacquard looms (see p 79).

Building materials and methods were frequently laid down by indentures of lease, as in the building of Bollin Mill, Macclesfield, for example: 'The said Thomas Ainsworth ... shall on or before the 25th day of March, 1826 ... build or finish ... with brick or stone or slate, and the floor and roof of timber, to be of good sound oak or foreign deal timber, in a workmanlike manner, a good substantial building or factory.'[60] Those mills situated in the south of east Cheshire, including the towns of Macclesfield and Congleton, were built of handmade bricks, being close to large resources of clay. Public elevations were most often built using decorative, Flemish bond, with English Garden Wall bond on elevations of lesser importance. The use of stone in these brick mills was largely confined to foundation walls, roof covering, sills and sometimes lintels. Stone foundation walls, often only three or four courses high but sometimes reaching to sill level, were used as damp courses for those mills built close to water; Brookside Mill, Thorp Street Leather Mill and Catherine Street Mill, in Macclesfield, are examples. The first two of these three mills are

Figure 29
*Park Mill, Park Street, Congleton, was erected in 1825 by Charles Townley, a Congleton builder.*

Cottages

0    10 m

Figure 30
*47 Sunderland Street Mill, situated between Sunderland Street and Charlotte Street, Macclesfield, was built in 1783–4. By 1804 it was in use as a cotton shop. L-shaped in plan, it was built with three adjoining cottages and was originally three storeys high. The columns are secondary and were perhaps added in the early 19th century and positioned where loadbearing was necessary.*

situated on the banks of the River Bollin, whereas Catherine Street Mill (Figure 31) was erected close by the now infilled Pinfold Lake. Roofs were stone-flagged, since stone from the quarries to the north of the area was the most easily obtained roof covering material and was plentiful.

There were at least fifteen mills situated in the northern part of the county in the gritstone districts of the Pennine hills, in Rainow, Bollington and Kettleshulme, which can be seen as a coherent group (see p 63). Mills from this part of east Cheshire, close to the stone quarries of Bollington and Kerridge, are characteristically constructed of regular sandstone blocks, laid to diminishing courses, with stone-flagged roofs (Figure 32).

Figure 31
*Catherine Street Mill, Macclesfield, c1820, was built with a stone foundation wall. These were used to provide damp-proofing for mills close to water.*

Figure 32
*Gin Clough Mill, Rainow, was built in 1794, and was water powered. The first phase is hidden behind the buttress and was possibly a jenny shop. The second phase, in the foreground, was built by 1827. This mill is typical of those built in the Pennine area in the north of east Cheshire (see Figure 58).*

Other features are shared between stone and brick mills. Windows are domestic in scale, evenly spaced, around 1 m apart, with cambered or segmental brick arches or stone lintels, and stone sills. In Congleton, window openings were often flat-arched with splayed stone lintels. From surviving evidence, small panes were held in place by wooden glazing bars; rarely were window frames of cast iron. All these structural elements have their precedents in the silk mills of the mid 18th century, and the basic elements of design for both brick and stone mills remained the same; plain, unadorned and functional.

Internally, traditional methods of construction were usually employed. Roof trusses and flooring were of timber. In the 18th century hewn oak was still used for heavy king-post trusses, with trenched purlins (Figure 33a), but by the early 19th century the increased demand for timber and the scarcity of oak brought about the general use of imported pine. The widespread use of softwood and the introduction of steam-powered saw-mills facilitated a reduction in the scantling of roof timbers and the construction of lighter queen-post trusses (Figures 33b, c), although hewn timber beams were often reused. The top floors of many mills of the period are open to the rafters. Roof trusses were often inscribed with Roman numerals, by which they were correctly assembled, and some beams were inscribed with marks that may have identified the timber for import and export purposes.

Internal supports were not necessary for the narrow spans, floors being carried by single-span wooden beams. With the single exception of the

Figure 33
*Roof trusses:*
*a) late 18th-century king-post roof at Park Green Mill, Macclesfield;*
*b) early 19th-century queen-post roof at Lumbhole Mill, Kettleshulme;*
*c) early 19th-century queen-post roof at Oxford Road Mill, Macclesfield.*

Figure 34 *(Above)*
*Early 19th-century stair tower with taking-in doors at Lumbhole Mill, Kettleshulme.*

Figure 35 *(Above right)*
*This privy tower at Lowe Street Mill, Macclesfield, would have housed dry shute privies in which the soil fell down a pipe into a box at the foot of the tower. The box could be removed for emptying.*

Figure 36 *(Right)*
*Some of the early mills were heated by open fires. This fireplace, in the basement of Park Green Mill, Macclesfield, is the only example in east Cheshire that has survived relatively unaltered.*

fireproof Lowerhouse Mill (see p 51), cast-iron columns were not used as a primary form of construction in mills in east Cheshire until the mid 1820s. As a secondary means of support, cast-iron columns could be positioned in an *ad hoc* manner where spot loadbearing was considered necessary, and removed when alternative use of floor space or of loading was required. This practice is still carried out today.

Access to upper floors was by open wooden stairs but by the end of this period stone staircases were more commonly constructed, housed either internally or in external towers (Figure 34). Toilet blocks were generally of the dry shute type with a collection point at the base of the shute; examples can be seen at Lowe Street Mill, Macclesfield (Figure 35), and in the primary phase of Brook Mills, Congleton. At Quarry Bank Mill, Styal, the soil was carried away by the mill leat.

Mills were heated by means of open fires or stoves which delivered warm air through vents to each floor, or by piped steam. The structural remains of these systems can now be seen in the mainly obsolete heating chimneys which remain attached to several mills. Although the workings have often been lost by the removal of stoves and cast-iron piping, occasionally evidence survives, as at Park Green Mill, Macclesfield, where a fireplace remains in the basement (Figure 36).

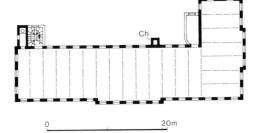

Newspaper advertisements confirm the early use of steam heating, although references of this kind are rare: 'All the silk machinery in the middle room of Messrs Johnson and Co's factory in Pickford Street ... turned by a powerful engine and the room heated by steam.'[61]

Artificial lighting, to supplement daylight and for night working, was initially provided by candlelight, but since this was insufficient, experiments were carried out during the early 1800s with gas lighting in mills.[62] In 1817 it was 'proposed, with the sanction of the corporation to establish a company in Macclesfield, to be called the Macclesfield Gas Light Company ... for the purpose of lighting the streets, shops and factories'.[63] A gas company was not established in Congleton until 1833.[64]

Warehousing at this time was usually provided within the mill building, on either one or more floors, in the attic, or in a wing. At Park Green Mill the gabled front projection was probably added for this purpose. At Alma Mill, Pickford Street (Figure 37), Lowe Street Mill and Brookside Mill, Macclesfield, warehouse extensions seem to have been added shortly after the erection of the main mill, since all these wings are constructed of the same type of brick and in the same architectural style as the primary wing. At Catherine Street Mill, Macclesfield, and Wheelock Mill, Wheelock, wings accommodating warehouse space are contemporary with the mill.

**Pedimented mills**

Chester Road Mill (Figure 38) is the most complete standing example of seven mills erected in Macclesfield between 1811 and 1831, which differ from the large number of unadorned mills of the period by virtue of their conspicuous

Figure 37 *(Above left) Warehouses were added to some mills. This warehouse at Alma Mill, Pickford Street, Macclesfield, was added shortly after the mill was erected c1820 and possibly contained offices heated by open fires.*

Figure 38 *(Above) Chester Road Mill, Macclesfield, built c1823, is the only complete surviving example of the seven pedimented mills erected between 1811 and 1831 in the town.*

Figure 39 *(Left) Union Mill, Statham Street, Macclesfield, was a pedimented mill erected c1820. It has now been demolished (Photo: J Massey 1959).*

pediments. Five of these mills, Wardle Street Mill, Park Lane Mill, Union Mill (Figure 39), Bridge Street Mill and Arbourhay Street Mill,

49

Figure 40
*Thorp Street Gas Mill, Macclesfield, was built in 1827 but not occupied until 1832 by Samuel Thorp for silk throwing. It is pictured here ablaze in 1977 and was subsequently reduced to three storeys.*

are now demolished, whilst Thorp Street Gas Mill stands only three storeys high having lost two storeys after a fire in 1970 (Figure 40).[65] In their classical pretensions these mills, built for silk production, reflect a period in the early 19th century described by John Brocklehurst, a Macclesfield silk manufacturer, as the industry's 'highest point of perfection',[66] and presumably, therefore, a time of great capital investment and confidence in trade.

Evidence indicates that Chester Road Mill was built during the 1820s as a steam-powered mill and that from an early stage in its history all the processes of silk throwing and manufacture, including dyeing, were integrated on the site.[67] In 1826, during a period of severe depression, the mill was advertised to let.[68] This could not have been long after the mill was built, as in 1826 it was still described as 'wholly new' and the steam engine as 'nearly new'.

*Lot I ... compact silk factories with the engine house and buildings belonging thereto and situate in Chester Road, Macclesfield, and late in the occupation of Messrs Hapgood and Parker, together with the steam engine and fixed and main gearing therein. Also 10 cottages, stables and join-ers' shops. The steam engine, which is of twelve horses power is nearly new and in good repair. The buildings are wholly new and very substantial*

*and from their excellent situation, compactness and superior convenience they are fully justified the most complete and desirable works in the town of Macclesfield.*[69]

The original L-shaped plan of the mill (Figure 38) was formed by the main block, 37·5 m by 8 m internally, with a shorter return wing probably used for warehousing. All other mills in this group varied from 29 m to 40 m in length, with a constant external width of 9 m, similar to the majority of mills built during this period. Overall heights were either four or five storeys; floor to ceiling heights at Chester Road are 3 m, and to judge from the photographic evidence of the now demolished mills, this would appear to have been a common dimension.

External decoration on these pedimented mills was restrained, their distinctive appearance arising from the pediment which crowned the central, projecting bays and created a harmonious balance between the horizontal and vertical elements of the building. The vertical emphasis was enhanced by the placing of a bell tower or cupola centrally on the roof ridge. The brickwork on Chester Road Mill follows the standard pattern of Flemish bond on the front elevation and English Garden Wall bond on other elevations, surmounted by a moulded, wooden, eaves cornice, and the pediment contains a working 19th-century clock. It is not clear whether all the pedimented mills had clocks. Window spacing and size on all these mills are regular, all windows having flat, gauged-brick arches (except Park Lane Mill which had splayed stone lintels) and stone sills. The main entrances of Chester Road Mill and Wardle Street Mill were built in the classical style with moulded stone pediments and pilasters.

These pedimented mills were built at a time of general expansion in the silk industry. An increase in productive capacity was made possible by the use of steam power to drive relatively large numbers of machines on sites where water power was not available. On-site weaving was also being introduced to complement throwing, and there is evidence to suggest that these mills were built or occupied by manufacturers. This usage is not reflected in these mills by an increase in size and scale — they are generally similar in this respect to contemporary mills of simple design — but rather by their assuming an elevated architectural style. Such classicism in mill architecture, designed to impress, is indicative of the increasing confidence at this time on the part of entrepreneurs and millowners.

### Fireproofing

Silk is not a highly combustible material and as a consequence owners of silk mills suffered no particular risk of fire and made no obvious efforts to protect their mills. The processes of cotton spinning, on the other hand, especially the preparatory processes, were particularly hazardous in terms of fire risk. Of the fifteen cotton mills built in Bollington, Rainow and Kettleshulme in the early 19th century, five were destroyed by fire whilst being used for cotton production: Ingersley Vale Mill in

1819, Lumbhole Mill in 1822, Sowcar Mill in 1831 and again in 1841, and Rainow Mill in 1856. In order to reduce the risk of fire in mills, particularly in cotton mills, attempts were made nationally, beginning in the 1790s, to build fireproof structures using a brick-arch and cast-iron beam construction to reduce the amount of combustible building material.[70]

Lowerhouse Mill, Bollington, was built as a fireproof, water-powered, cotton-spinning mill by Philip Antrobus in 1818 (Figure 41).[71] It was constructed of stone and was four storeys high with an attic. In plan it was 74 m long, including the wheelhouse, and 13 m wide. Its floors

Figure 41
*Lowerhouse Mill, Bollington, was built by Philip Antrobus in 1818 as a fireproof water-powered cotton-spinning mill. The engine and boiler houses were probably added by Samuel Greg in 1832.*

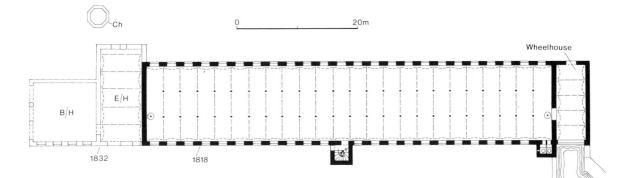

Figure 42

*Lowerhouse Mill, Bollington, has two rows of cast-iron columns supporting iron beams and segmental brick vaults. A bolting face on the underside of each beam, as well as a bolthole at the top of each column, allowed the attachment of the brackets which supported line shafting.*

Figure 43

*The roof trusses at Lowerhouse Mill, Bollington, were shrouded in iron sheeting to protect them from fire.*

were composed of brick arches of 2·7 m span and a 200 mm rise. The arches are levelled with sand and covered with brick tiles. Cast-iron, T-sectioned beams, together with two rows of cylindrical, cast-iron columns support the floors at the springing of each arch (Figure 42).[72]

Iron is also a feature of the roof trusses, which are timber with iron queen-posts, and have iron shoes at the junctions of the principals and the collar beams. To add to the building's fireproof qualities, the trusses were shrouded in iron sheeting (Figure 43).[73] This shrouding is also a feature of the trusses at Quarry Bank Mill, Styal, where in addition the rafters are boxed in with iron sheets.

Although a number of fireproof mills are known in the Manchester area, the design of Lowerhouse Mill is unique for its time in east Cheshire, where it was not until the middle of the 19th century that fireproofing became a more prominent feature in cotton mills and their ancillary buildings (see p 119).

**Mills of greater capacity**

As has been discussed above, mills built during this period are generally of a similar size and volume, but five stand out as markedly larger than their contemporaries. Lowerhouse Mill, Bollington, at 12 m wide internally and Lumbhole Mill, Kettleshulme, at 10·5 m wide internally, are notable for their greater than average width. Three other mills exceed the average in both width and height. These are Depot Mill, Pickford Street 'A' Mill and Crompton Road Mill, Macclesfield, the latter the only one of these three still standing (Figure 44).

Depot Mill, so-called because the mill served as an assessment office in 1824 for the return of

Figure 44
*Crompton Road Mill, Macclesfield, was erected in 1823 by Watters and Lund to house powered cotton looms.*

duties paid on raw silk, was built in 1810,[74] Pickford Street 'A' Mill was built a year later,[75] and Crompton Road Mill in 1823.[76] These three mills have a number of features in common: all were built to be powered by steam; all were tall, Depot Mill with six storeys, and Pickford Street 'A' Mill and Crompton Road Mill with five storeys; and all were wide in relation to the majority of contemporary mills, Depot Mill at 10·5 m,[77] Pickford Street 'A' Mill at 11·5 m and Crompton Road Mill at 11 m.

The spans of all five mills required intermediate support, and the use of cast-iron columns, recorded at the Depot Mill and Pickford Street 'A' Mill[78] can be seen as a primary and integral part of the structure of Crompton Road Mill (Figure 45) and Lowerhouse Mill.

The significance of these dimensions is difficult to interpret. Although there is documentary evidence for the processing of cotton on all five sites, there is no clear correlation between process and mill dimensions. Lowerhouse Mill (see p 51) was built by Philip Antrobus for cotton spinning and Lumbhole Mill (see p 63) probably for cotton spinning. Depot Mill and the adjoining Button Mill (see p 31) were owned in the early 19th century by William Ayton and described as 'extensive silk and cotton factories'.[79] The contents of one of these mills, probably Depot Mill, were auctioned in 1821 and are those of the cotton-spinning industry, comprising 9,894 spindles (7,278 mule and 2,616 throstle):

*At the factory late in the occupation of William Ayton, 21 carding engines, 18 mules 216 spindles each, 6 mules 204 spindles each, 2 throstles 120 spindles each, 19 throstles 96 spindles each, 5 throstles 72 spindles each, 4 throstles 48 spindles each, 4 drawing frames 4 boxes each, 4 drawing frames 8 boxes each, 1 roving frame 120 spindles, 2 blowing machines, 4 warping mills and winding frames.*[80]

Pickford Street 'A' Mill was built by Thomas Whitney for cotton spinning (see above) and Crompton Road Mill was occupied by Waters and Lund for powered cotton weaving.[81] The building dates of Depot Mill and Pickford Street 'A' Mill may be related to the full mechanisation of preparatory cotton processes, and the date of Crompton Road to the early stages of powered cotton weaving.

Figure 45
*Crompton Road Mill, Macclesfield, is likely to have had cast-iron columns as a primary feature to help the structure cope with the vibration of powerlooms.*

Figure 46
*A silk weaver in his garret.
The woman on the left is
filling quills with silk which
were then inserted into the
shuttle to form the weft.*

Figure 47
*In 1804 the garrets
situated on Little Street,
Macclesfield, were in common ownership with the
adjacent Little Street Mill
(see Figure 51).*

## Garret houses

In the textile industry generally, the factory
housing of powerloom weaving had superseded
the domestic system by the mid 19th century. In
contrast, handloom weaving in the silk industry
was only gradually absorbed into the factory system and the production of fine-quality and
fancy woven silks by handloom survived as a
domestic industry until the 1930s.

The housing and organisation of this branch
of the industry was varied. During the early 19th
century, when periods of growth and prosperity
stimulated the output of handloom weaving,
looms were accommodated in any suitable
premises, including cellars and small workshops
with suitable fenestration. However, specific types
of housing can be identified, together with the
associated organisation of manufacture: garret,
or upper storey, workshops housing independent
weavers or weavers employed as outworkers;
loomshops housing numbers of weavers, either
associated with a mill or independent manufacturing concerns; and housing within a mill.

According to evidence given to a
Parliamentary Committee of Enquiry, there
were 1,240 silk handlooms in Macclesfield by
1818; 234 of them were housed in the mills and
the rest, 1,006, in the workshops of outworkers.
Henry Critchley, a Macclesfield silk manufacturer, employed between 140 and 160 silk
weavers at this time, but only fifty of them were
employed at his Bridge Street factory, the rest
being outworkers weaving in their garrets.[82]
Garret weavers were supplied by the factory
owners with warp and weft which they then prepared and wove in their garrets before returning the finished product to the mill (Figure 46).
In some cases middle men or 'undertakers'
received warp and weft from millowners or silk
manufacturers and supplied it to garret weavers.
The whole family, it seems, had an active part to
play in the work, from filling the quills for the
shuttles, to weaving. Some weavers employed
boys as apprentices for seven years, although in
times of hardship the contracts were sometimes
ignored and the apprentices turned out.

Garret houses were built in many parts of
east Cheshire. Some still stand in Congleton,
Wilmslow, Bollington, Bosley and other villages,
but the vast majority were built for silk weaving
in Macclesfield, where in all there were about
600, about half of which have now been demolished. Although garret houses were built in the
18th century and throughout the 19th century,
most were constructed in a brief period in the
first two decades of the 19th century, at a time
when, according to Corry writing in 1817,
'weavers carried everything with a high hand: if
a new house was built, the upper storey was generally prepared with large windows fit for a
weavers workshop'.[83]

A small amount of evidence indicates that
some garrets were built or owned by manufacturers and millowners, implying that where mill
and garret are in the same ownership, the garret
acted as a loomshop for the mill. For example,
the 1804 Enclosure Award Map of Macclesfield
shows the garret houses which stand on Little

Street and share a yard with Little Street Mill (Figure 47). The schedule for the map shows the mill and garrets to have been in the common ownership of Edward Richardson.[84] In 1820 John Booth, owner of a cotton mill situated between Booth Street and Elizabeth Street, and another at Ball's Croft, Congleton, was listed in the particulars of his estates as owning 'six dwelling houses situate in Silk Street, over the whole of which is a large room or manufactory, and now or late in the several occupations of Joseph Buckley, Charles Staton and others'.[85]

An east Cheshire garret house is a three-storeyed building of handmade brick (only two or three are of stone) with a slate or stone-flag roof, and typically is 8 m long by approximately 4·5 m wide.[86] The brickwork on the front elevation is most commonly laid in Flemish bond, whilst the remaining elevations are of the plainer English Garden Wall bond. Commonly the doors and any ginnel entrance have arched heads, and the windows have segmental heads. However, the long garret windows generally have a single row of headers over them. The lower two floors form a domestic dwelling consisting of a small living room, kitchen and two bedrooms, whilst the top floor forms a workshop. This is usually lit by a wide, small-paned window on the front or rear elevation and by a small window on the other. Angus Bethune Reach, reporting for the *Morning Chronicle* in 1849, visited Macclesfield in order to write about its textile workers, and he described a garret loomshop:

> *ascending a ladder and making your way through a trap door, you reach the loom shop, which is always located in the garret, which is exclusively devoted to the operation of weaving ... One of the bedrooms was furnished, the other was littered with portions of the apparatus of looms. The garret was a lofty and airy room, the roof rising in a sort of peak — it was a corner house — to the height of about ten feet. The window extended longitudinally almost the whole length of the room. In the apartment there stood, I think, five treddle-looms and a Jacquard, and a young man and two girls were at work.*[87]

Although some garret houses were built individually, they were most commonly erected in groups of three or four dwellings, or as terraces forming entire streets (Figures 48, 49). Access to the garret was most often by a trap-door in the workshop floor, reached by a flight of wooden steps, and each was separated from its neighbour by a partition wall, into which the chimney flues were built. Occasionally, a terrace of garret houses was constructed with no partition walls in the garrets so that they

Figure 48
*The dwellings on Paradise Street, Macclesfield, are fine examples of garret houses built in long terraces.*

Figure 49
*A row of four garret houses, built on Rood Hill, Congleton.*

Figure 50
*These garret houses on Townley Street, Macclesfield, are under one continuous workshop. The stacks are at each end so as not to interrupt the workspace, and an extra doorway (with a cross in the fanlight) provided direct access to the garret.*

formed one continuous workshop (Figure 50). In this case the garret was reached either by an extra door at ground-floor level and an internal staircase, or by a doorway at garret level reached by an exterior staircase. The chimney breasts were built into the front or rear walls to ensure a clear work space in which the looms could be housed.

55

## Power systems in relation to the design of mill building

The demand for power created by the unprecedented rise in manufacturing output at the turn of the century was satisfied by a variety of power systems. The arrangement of these systems in relation to location and capacity was experimental, and was as variable as the consumers' needs. From the 1780s until the mid 19th century, horse power, water power and steam power were used, either independently or in combination. Clear patterns of use do emerge from an examination of sites but just as there is no strict correlation in the late 18th or early 19th century between processes and

Figure 51
*Little Street Mill, Macclesfield, built in the late 18th century, is the only surviving east Cheshire mill known to have been built to be powered by horses (see Figure 47).*

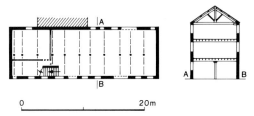

building specifications, so there is no such relationship between building specifications and power source. To judge from the evidence of sites in east Cheshire, small mills were not always driven by water power, and large mills were not always driven by steam power. As the processes did not make greater demands upon the buildings or upon the power capacities of either steam or water than could be accommodated, the layout and construction already established for the silk industry and for water-powered sites continued until the 1820s with little, if any, alteration.

### Horse power

The Macclesfield historian John Wootton wrote in 1866 that 'within living memory of a large proportion of the inhabitants now living ... the machinery of our silk mills was turned by means of a horse gate'.[88] Despite the importance of horse power to early industrialisation, no structural evidence of horse wheels or of their housing has been identified in east Cheshire. However, some dimensions were recorded in 1821 at textile 'premises recently occupied by Christopher Adkinson, Calenderer, near the Unicorn in Lower Hillgate, Stockport': 'The complete gearing for a horse walk ... with the horse walk adjoining, which is 2 stories high and 23ft long by 22ft 6 inches wide. Also a water wheel of 20ft diameter with a supply of water thereto.'[89] This particular combination of power sources has not been identified in east Cheshire, although advertisements attest the use of horse-power in mills:

> All that edifice or building, used as a silk mill with stable, horse gate and appurtenances thereto belonging, situate in Silk Street, Congleton aforesaid ... together with a horse wheel with cast-iron gearing belonging to the said mill ... together with two useful ponies which have been accustomed to work the said mill. The mill is four storeys high and built in a strong and substantial manner.[90]

Evidence also indicates that Little Street Mill, Macclesfield, was powered by horses. This is an example of an 18th-century urban silk mill typical of contemporary mills in most aspects of its construction but unique as the only surviving mill known to have been built to be powered in this way. It formed part of a site on which all the processes of silk production, including throwing, dyeing and weaving, were integrated as early as 1814 (Figure 51). The site was described in 1804 as, 'houses, silk shop, garden', occupied by Edward Richardson,[91] and on 20 April 1811 the mill was advertised for sale:

*The factory is three storeys high, thirty yards long and nine yards wide, or thereabouts, and full of silk machinery, the most part whereof is new and which the tenant may be accommodated with ... The machinery has hitherto been turned by horses, but a steam engine may be erected at a trifling expense ... For particulars apply to Mr J Pickering, Grocer, Macclesfield.[92]*

The present dimensions of Little Street Mill, 24 m by 7·2 m, differ little from those recorded in documentary evidence.[93] The mill's overall dimensions are directly comparable to those of mills built exclusively for silk processes, to be powered by water, and comparable also to the mills built during the early 19th century for the processes of both silk and cotton and powered by either water or steam.

An advertisement of 1814 records that the mill had the facilities for washing and dyeing silks.[94] A small, early 19th-century building of handmade brick with a stone-flag roof stands to the rear. This had a louvred ventilator on the roof, a typical feature of dyehouses, for the purpose of allowing steam to escape. An advertisement of 1826 indicates that the processing of raw silk through to the preparation of the warp was carried on in the mill:

*To be sold at auction by Mr Wayte, At the silk factory, Little Street, Macclesfield, by the assignees of Mr Henry Barlow ... 4 throwing mills containing 11 dozen spindles each, 2 single rowed, 3 heighted spinning mills, 22 dozen each, 10 hard silk engines, containing 718 swifts, 2 doubling frames, 72 bobbins each, 2 soft silk engine, containing 100 rices, warping mill with creel and box complete, doubling wheels and jacks, staff pegs and post, press, tram and organ boxes, wet silk press, sundry silk tubs and boxes and extensive assortment of engine tram, warp, and shute bobbins, quantity of engine weights, stove box and pipes, a boiler, iron and copper stove piping and all the wrought and cast iron shafting in the different rooms.[95]*

All this evidence describes a small site in which all the processes of silk manufacture were integrated from an early phase in its history and possibly at a time when the mill was powered by horses.

Although it is not possible to quantify the use of horse power, it is probable that the importance of this system has been underestimated because of the lack of surviving structural evidence. A number of mills built in Macclesfield and Congleton in the late 18th and early 19th centuries were positioned away from known water sources and have no

recorded primary power system. Although steam powered by the 1870s[96] they could originally have been horse powered. Examples in Congleton are Swan Bank Mill, Square Mill, Wagg Street Mill and Moody Street Mill. As far as is known, all these mills, now demolished, were built for silk throwing, requiring a relatively low power capacity. Of the equivalent group of mills in Macclesfield which included Newgate Mill, King Edward Street Mill, Samuel Street Mill and Charles Street Mill, only two, Pickford Street Mill (Figure 52) and 47 Sunderland Street Mill remain standing (see Figure 30).[97]

The dimensions of the demolished sites are recorded on the 1871 Ordnance Survey map and range in length from 31·5 m to 21 m with a constant width of 7 m to 8 m. Both the standing mills, Pickford Street Mill, built between 1789 and 1804,[98] and 47 Sunderland Street Mill, built in 1783 to 1784,[99] are L-shaped in plan with main ranges measuring 7·5 m in width by 21 m and 27·5 m respectively. The known dimensions of these mills correspond to those of contemporary powered mills, and it is likely therefore that they were also powered and may well have been driven by horse power.

It is not known for which processes 47 Sunderland Street Mill and Pickford Street Mill were built, but the Enclosure Award Schedule of 1804 lists 47 Sunderland Street as a 'cotton shop' owned by Hannah Orme.[100] This is the only recorded mention of cotton in the mill, which was thereafter used for silk throwing and manufacturing. Pickford Street Mill was recorded in 1804 as a 'silk shop', owned by Nathaniel Higginbotham, and remained in use as a silk-processing factory. The similarity in the dimensions of these two mills, and comparison

Figure 52
*Pickford Street Mill, Macclesfield, was built between 1789 and 1804. By 1804 it was being used as a silk mill. Sited away from watercourses, it is possible that it was originally powered by horses.*

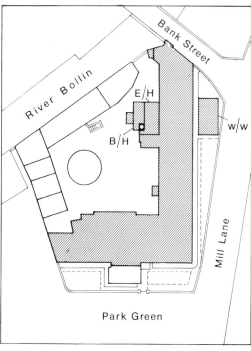

Figure 53
*Park Green Mill,
Macclesfield, was built by
Daintry and Ryle in the
late 18th century as a
water-powered mill. The
wheel was situated
against the main, Mill
Lane, range. Steam power
was added to the site from
the mid 1790s and an
engine house was erected
opposite the waterwheel in
1811. Rain-water heads
which were positioned on
the Park Green elevation
were dated 1785 and may
have related to the addi-
tion of the Park Green
wing or the projecting
gable, both of which are
secondary. The original
mill, the Mill Lane range,
was destroyed by fire in the
1970s and rebuilt with a
two-storeyed façade (plan
taken from 1871
Ordnance Survey map,
1:500).*

with water-powered mills, indicates that neither the process nor the power was the principal factor in determining size.

### Water power

Developments in waterwheel technology stemmed largely from the research of John Smeaton in the later 18th century. He established that the most efficient type of wheel was the overshot, turned by the weight of water falling into buckets at the top of the wheel, rather than the undershot, which was turned by the impetus of water striking paddles as it flows under the wheel. However, the overshot wheel requires a considerable head of water which was not available on most rivers. The compromise was the breastshot wheel, which was turned by water delivered at around axle level, utilising the weight of the water but not requiring such a large head as the overshot wheel.

Early wheels were made entirely of wood, but greater demands for power placed an increasingly heavy burden on them so cast-iron axles were introduced, initially by Smeaton but not successfully until the early 19th century.[101] Gradually the wooden parts of the wheel were replaced by iron, although wheels were often constructed using a combination of both. Even the cast-iron axles could not cope with the amount of torque that high-horsepower wheels placed upon them. Further developments by Thomas Hewes and William Strutt around the beginning of the 19th century resulted in the suspension wheel, which took the drive from the rim of the wheel and reduced the stress on the

axle. The axle could now be lighter in construction and the spokes in effect became tension rods.[102] For undershot wheels which remained in use where only a small head of water was available, the improvements made by J V Poncelet increased efficiency by directing the flow of water into curved paddles. Poncelet's developments in the early 19th century were later taken further, mainly by Lesley Pelton who encased the wheel, and they led to the development of the water turbine.

In east Cheshire, cast iron was used in the construction of waterwheels from the early 19th century. A wood and iron suspension wheel was installed by the millwright Thomas Hewes at Quarry Bank Mill in 1807, and between 1817 and 1820 the 'great' iron wheel was installed. In the same year, an advertisement described a wheel at Waterside, Disley, probably at Waterside Mill, as being 'nearly new and iron shrouded'.[103] As a final example, when Samuel Greg took over Lowerhouse Mill, Bollington, in 1832 he set about repairing the cast-iron waterwheel which had probably been installed when the mill was built in 1818.

Clear patterns emerge from an examination of water-powered sites in east Cheshire. In Macclesfield, because of the scarcity of sites with available water power, the number of mills built to be powered by water was small in relation to the number of mills powered by either horse or steam. Between 1785 and 1826 only six sites out of the sixty-eight mills erected in the town are known to have made use of water power, and the structural evidence is correspondingly scarce. Of these six, Lower Heyes Mill, Sunnyside Mill, Lower Beech Mill and Johnson's Mill were used for cotton spinning, and Pickford Street 'B' Mill and Park Green Mill were used for silk and cotton.[104] This bias towards cotton is due to the fact that building during the 1780s was prompted by the take-off in the cotton industry. The majority of the mills built in Macclesfield town during the period under review in this chapter were erected during the early 19th-century boom in the silk industry, by which time adequate steam power was widely available.

Park Green Mill (Figure 53), built by Michael Daintry and John Ryle, is the only one of these water-powered mills to survive in Macclesfield. It was, however, partly dependent upon steam power from the mid 1790s,[105] when a steam engine was installed to supplement the water power. The building is of more than one phase, although all the main phases are of 18th-century date.[106] Differences in floor heights and the brickwork at the junction of the two wings[107] indicate that the Mill Lane wing predates the Park Green wing. Furthermore, straight joints indicate that the front gabled projection is a later addition.[108] A rain-water head which was positioned on the Park Green elevation bore the date 1785,[109] and this has been previously accepted as the building date of the mill, but may relate either to the Park Green wing only or to a later phase of construction.

The mill is four-storeyed with a basement and attic. Internal construction utilises traditional building methods, with an oak king-post truss roof, and wooden floors with unsupported spans of 6·5 m in the Mill Lane wing and of 5·5 m in the Park Green wing. The gabled front projection was probably used as a warehouse.

The waterwheel was positioned against the Mill Lane wing. The length of the leat, 400 m, and the lie of the land indicate that the wheel was undershot. The wing measures 43·5 m, but the maximum distance in this wing from the wheelhouse is 30 m, which is consistent with the dimensions of 18th-century water-powered mills in east Cheshire.

In Congleton, water-powered mills were built over a longer period than in Macclesfield, reflecting the advantage in this respect of the powerful River Dane and its tributaries. Fourteen of the thirty or so mills built in Congleton during this period were water powered, although a number had the additional support of a steam engine: Slate's Dane Mill and Daneside Mill, for example. Of these, eight were originally used for silk processing, five for cotton, and one is uncertain. Four of the mills had wheels positioned internally: Dane Mill (Figure 54), Daneinshaw

Mill, Stonehouse Green Mill and Brook Mills, and in the first three of these mills, the wheels were in the centre of the basement/ground floor. At Daneinshaw Mill, for example, a substantial wheel pit measuring 6·9 m by 2·5 m accommodated a breastshot wheel. The pit has the fine ashlar masonry commonly found in association with the housing of waterwheels. Other mills housed their wheels either in wheelhouses, or externally, as at Vale Mill, Congleton, and Flint Mill, Buglawton (see p 99).

Stonehouse Green Mill and Brook Mills, urban mills which became equally reliant on both steam and water power, are typical of the mills of east Cheshire in that both silk and cotton were processed on the site. Stonehouse Green Mill was built as a water-powered mill in 1785 by George and William Reade, silk throwsters, for cotton spinning.[110] Although the original machinery housed in the mill is not known, the date would indicate that the mill was built in response to the annulment of Arkwright's patent, to house water frames. By 1830 the Reade family had returned to silk throwing and had acquired the Brook Mills site, immediately adjacent to Stonehouse Green Mill, whilst retaining Stonehouse Green Mill for cotton spinning[111] (see also pp 71, 87). Stonehouse

Figure 54
*Dane Mill, Congleton, is situated within a meander of the River Dane which almost forms an island site, and retains evidence of its water-power system in the overspill leat and a large weir. A leat carried water from the river to the wheel positioned centrally within the mill.*

Green Mill (Figure 55) and Brook Mills (Figure 56) show many similarities in construction and development. An unusually fulsome advertisement of 21 April 1821 describes one of the mills on the Brook Mills site, and gives valuable evidence about the mill building, its power systems and production:

*silk mill or factory, situate at Stonehouse Green, with the engine house and an excellent steam engine of six horse power, recently erected ... and the brook or stream of water there, for the use of the said factory ... The factory is a substantial and handsome brick building, four storeys high and furnished with every necessary convenience. The machinery is worked during the day by the steam engine and the stream of water together (the latter of which is constant and sufficient to turn a water wheel of two horse power) and the same is worked during the night by the stream of water alone. The factory is in the immediate neighbourhood of col–lieries, and coals are laid down at it at about six pence per cwt ... The factory is completely fitted up with new machinery of the best and most modern construction, containing upwards of 200 dozen spindles for throwing and spinning, with a pro-portionate quantity of winding engines, doubling machines etc.[112]*

Maps of the Stonehouse Green and Brook Mills sites[113] show watercourses and culverts which indicate that the wheels were housed internally; in the centre basement of the 1785 Stonehouse Green Mill (Figure 55), and within

a wheelhouse at the south-west end of the early Brook Mills (Figure 56). As with Park Green Mill, the gentle lie of the land, which could not have provided much fall of water, indicates that the wheels were probably undershot. By 1821 both water power and steam power were in use on the sites as complementary systems, as was common in the early 19th century.

In the rural districts of Macclesfield borough, all of the mills of this period were, without exception, water powered; such power is recorded in use on several sites well into the mid 19th century. However, the water supply was not always reliable and consequently approximately 40 per cent of the thirty mills are known to have installed supplementary steam power during this period. Cotton spinning pre-dominated in these districts, although silk throwing was introduced during the boom years of the early 19th century, often replacing cotton spinning on the same site.

Quarry Bank Mill, Styal (Figure 57), is an outstanding example of an early, rural, cotton-spinning mill, reliant on water power. The fine range of late 18th and early to mid 19th-century buildings has survived largely unaltered. The first mill was built by Samuel Greg and John Massey in 1784, and measured 8·5 m by 27·5 m; a gabled wing housed the staircase and a small room used for storage or, as it was heated, per-haps as a counting house. The mill was almost certainly intended to house water frames and was driven by a wooden waterwheel positioned at the north end of the mill. In 1796 the early

**Figure 55**
*The earliest phase of Stonehouse Green Mill, Congleton, to the left, was built by George and William Reade for cotton spinning in 1785. It was originally water powered but steam power had been added by 1821. The waterwheel was positioned within the mill, approxi-mately behind the position of the later chimney. In the 1830s the large mill was added (right) for silk spinning.*

mill was extended southwards by 27 m and a fifth floor was added. To power this increased capacity, Greg's new partner, Peter Ewart, reorganised the existing water-power system by rebuilding and extending the weirs, leats and dams to power a new waterwheel which was installed in 1801 at the opposite end of the mill. By means of these alterations the mill capacity was increased from 2,425 to 3,452 spindles by 1805, and two years later one of the waterwheels was replaced by a wood and cast-iron wheel. By 1796 a Boulton and Watt steam engine had been installed to complement the water-power system. This engine was replaced in 1806, and again in 1810 by a 10 horsepower engine. A capacity of 10 horsepower is not large in comparison to other engines installed at this time in cotton mills in the locality and underlines the continuing reliance on water power for production at Quarry Bank Mill.

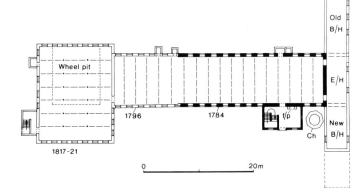

Figure 57
*Quarry Bank Mill, Styal, built by Samuel Greg and John Massey in 1784 for cotton spinning, was water powered. The original mill was extended in 1796 and again between 1817 and 1821.*

Figure 56
*The earliest phases of Brook Mills, Congleton, were water powered and are late 18th or early 19th century in style. By 1821 they were occupied by George and William Reade for silk throwing.*

Figure 58
*This wheel pit, along with fragments of the water-wheel, survives at Gin Clough Mill, Rainow. The wheel seems originally to have been overshot. Axle mounts can be seen in the wall to the right. Latterly the water was supplied to the wheel via the cast-iron pipe visible at the top of the photograph (see Figure 32).*

Further improvements were made between 1817 and 1820 for the replacement of the earlier wheels by a cast-iron suspension wheel designed and constructed by Thomas Hewes, the Manchester engineer and partner of William Fairbairn. This wheel, 9·6 m in diameter and 6·3 m wide, weighed 44 tons, could generate 100 horsepower and together with the new tunnelling cost £7,736. It was housed in the basement of the second mansard-roofed extension, architecturally unique for its period within east Cheshire, which was constructed as part of a wider programme of expansion taking place within the Greg concern.[114]

Gin Clough Mill, Rainow, is, like Quarry Bank Mill, a *c*18th-century rural cotton-spinning mill but conceived on a much smaller scale (Figure 32). It was built by John Lowe in 1794[115] and measured around 9 m by 7·5 m.[116] By 1827 the mill had been extended to its present length, 18·5 m, was still reliant upon water power and was described as a silk mill.[117] For most of its life as a textile mill, until about 1860 when a steam engine was installed, Gin Clough Mill was powered by water. In the basement of the mill remains the wheel pit which housed an overshot wheel (Figure 58). The position of the pit relates to the primary phase of the mill, at which time the wheel would have been internally housed at its north end. Wheel fragments show that the final wheel in use measured 5 m in diameter, with a concentric 3·5 m iron gear ring, and was constructed of wood, the rim sections held in place by a wrought-iron strap.[118]

**Complementary power systems**

On sites where water supply was unreliable, the most efficient way to take advantage of the available power sources was to combine water power with steam power. Both structural and historical evidence of this complementary system has survived in east Cheshire mills.

In 1806 a case was brought before the Chancery Court by the Adlington Hall estate,[119] which claimed that the estate corn mill had an insufficient supply of water to employ its waterwheel regularly, and that this insufficiency was due to the number of cotton mills built on the River Bollin and its tributaries, upstream of the estate. The Court received a deposition from a Rainow millwright, William Richardson, who described the positions and power sources of the offending Rainow and Bollington cotton mills. Of the fourteen mills built in Bollington and Rainow by 1806, all were water powered and five also used steam engines as a supplementary power source: Brookhouse Mill, Millbrook Mill, Lowerhouse Mill (Rainow), Ingersley Vale Mill and Sowcar Mill. Millbrook Mill in Rainow had two waterwheels of 6 m diameter placed one above the other, but according to Richardson it did not have sufficient water 'in dry seasons to turn the whole of [the] works without the assistance of a steam engine'. Similarly, Edward

Collier at Ingersley Vale Mill had 'a steam engine of eighteen horsepower attached to this factory which he occasionally uses when the water is scarce and whilst the reservoir replenishes'.

At Lumbhole Mill, Kettleshulme (Figure 59), outside the area covered by Richardson's evidence, an example survives of the combined use of water and steam power. The mill was built between the years 1797 and 1798, was heightened from two to four storeys in 1815, burnt down in 1822 and was rebuilt some time between 1823 and 1835. It is thought that the present power system of suspension waterwheel and beam engine were installed during the rebuilding phase.[120] The dimensions of the mill were recorded in 1816 as '30 yards long and 11 yards wide' (27·7 m by 10·6 m).[121] This advertisement, however, did not identify the process

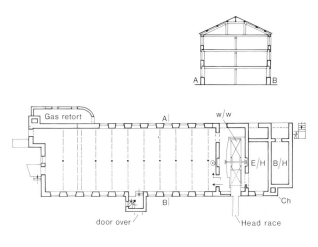

Figure 59
*Lumbhole Mill,
Kettleshulme, was originally built between 1797
and 1798, but a fire in
1822 led to its rebuilding
between 1823 and 1835.*

for which the mill was used. In 1816 the mill was owned by a silk manufacturer, George Brocklehurst, and in a later advertisement[122] is described as a 'cotton factory'.

Although the existing waterwheel and beam engine at Lumbhole Mill (Figure 60) are thought to have been installed by about 1835 to operate as complementary systems, the use of water power, with steam power as an alternative, was recorded on this site as early as 1816, when the engine was described as having 10 horse-power.[123] The existing suspension waterwheel measures 7·6 m in diameter and 1·7 m wide and the cast-iron gearing from the rim of the wheel is twinned with the gearing from the beam engine.[124] The wheel is housed in a wheelhouse

which adjoins the mill, and the engine is housed in a lean-to extension, adjacent to the wheel-house (Figures 61a, b). This complementary power system was designed to drive a mill in which all the processes of cotton spinning, including the preparatory processes of scutch-ing and carding, were carried out.

Richardson's evidence to the Chancery Court does not make it clear whether the steam engines discussed were driving machinery directly or were pumping water on to the water-wheels, but it is likely that in 1806 steam engines would have been turning machinery directly, especially one as powerful as that of 18 horse-power at Ingersley Vale Mill. Nevertheless, the introduction and early use of steam power was

Figure 60
*Lumbhole Mill, Kettleshulme, houses a steam engine and water-wheel which were installed c1835 to work as a complementary system.*

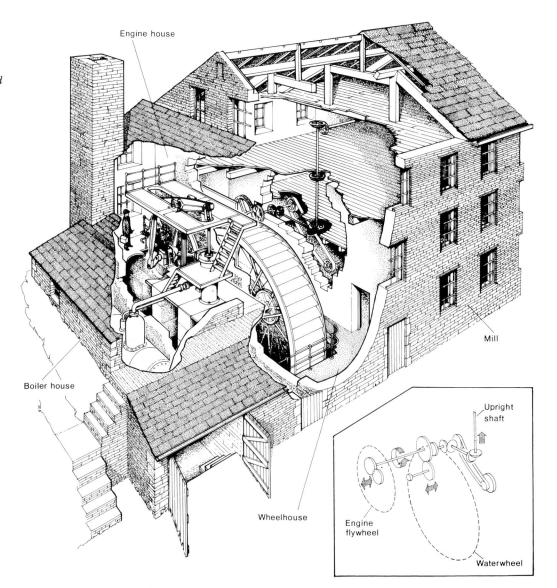

Engine house

Boiler house

Mill

Wheelhouse

Upright shaft

Engine flywheel

Waterwheel

primarily as a substitute or supplement for less reliable sources of power, rather than as a means of extending capacity, and, in consequence, the size of mill buildings.

### Steam power

The evolution of steam-power technology for use in the textile industry was the result of a number of refinements to the steam water-pumping engines which were used in the mining industry during the 18th century. Undisputed credit for the most successful of these refinements goes to the partnership of James Watt, an instrument maker, and Matthew Boulton, entrepreneur and industrialist. Their development of the separate condenser increased the efficient use of steam power for pumping engines. The patent for this improvement lasted from 1769 to 1800. Further improvements patented by Watt — the use of expansive steam force, parallel motion of the piston rod, and, above all, the centrifugal governor — resulted in greater efficiency, regularity and economy, and enabled engines to provide the primary power for driving machinery.

There is evidence for the installation of six Boulton and Watt engines in east Cheshire mills between 1801 and 1809.[125] Thomas Slate erected a rotative beam crank engine at his Congleton Dane Mill in 1801, and in 1811 the *Macclesfield Courier and Herald* advertised that 'There is a large steam engine adjoining this work which has lately been erected on Messrs Boulton and Watt's Patent, and capable of turning machinery on an enlarged scale for another factory which was intended to have been built and for which there is a foundation 15 yards long already laid.'[126] In March 1801, Daintry, Ryle and Co ordered a 32 horsepower rotative sun and planet engine for a cotton mill in Macclesfield, and in July 1802 a 40 horsepower rotative beam crank engine was installed, also for Daintry and Ryle, in a Macclesfield cotton mill.[127] In 1805 a 20 horsepower engine was installed for the firm of Daintry, Wood and Daintry, at a site owned by them in Sutton.[128] In October 1804, a 20 horsepower rotative beam crank engine was installed for J and G Pearson in their silk mill in Macclesfield. This is likely to have been Sunderland Street Mill, since the Pearsons owned this mill in 1804 (see Figure 64). The last of these engines was a rotative side-lever independent, installed by Jesse Drakeford at Daneside Mill in Congleton, before 1809.[129]

Boulton and Watt attempted to control the market until 1800 by demanding premiums for work done by their engines and payments for production of their separate condenser under licence. This situation engendered the pirating

*a*

*b*

Figure 61
*Lumbhole Mill, Kettleshulme:*
*a) cast-iron suspension wheel, installed c1835 and recently restored;*
*b) steam engine installed c1835.*

Figure 62
*Sutton Mill, Macclesfield, is typical of east Cheshire mills erected c 1820 to be powered by steam.*

of their technology by rival engineering firms. The services of these firms were used by textile manufacturers who were reluctant to pay Boulton and Watt's charges for what was not always an efficient and satisfactory service.[130] Furthermore, local engineering firms were able to supply the engines more cheaply and were more accessible for maintenance work. There is evidence that several firms supplied engines in the Manchester and east Cheshire areas: Francis Thompson of Chesterfield, Bateman and Sherratt of Salford, and Galloway and Bowman, Ormerod, and Joshua Wrigley, of Manchester. In 1793 Francis Thompson supplied a double-cylinder atmospheric engine to Michael Daintry for a cotton mill in Macclesfield, thought to have been Park Green Mill.[131] Contemporary newspaper advertisements record engines which were installed by Thompson and others: 'To be sold by auction at the factory and premises of Messrs Thomas Buxton and Co, situate at Bank Top, Macclesfield. All that valuable silk machinery ... together with a capital steam engine of 2 horse power, nearly new, with three horse boiler, made by Thompson of Chesterfield.'[132]

Newspaper advertisements also carry valuable information relating the mill size to the engine capacity. It is clear that the larger engine capacities relate to cotton spinning and, taking into account the figures given on the Boulton and Watt engines, range in size between 14 and 40 horsepower during this period. These figures are much higher than those recorded for the power requirements of the majority of steam-powered silk mills, which operated at between 2 and 12 horsepower, although the 20 horse-power engine supplied to J and G Pearson by Boulton and Watt was for a silk mill.[133]

All of these engine capacities were within the power range of contemporary waterwheels. Steam-engine capacities, therefore, would not at this stage have determined the dimensions of mill building. However, there is an obvious correlation between steam engines of greater power and the increased width of cotton mills from $c\,7 \cdot 2$ m to $c\,9 \cdot 9$ m. This increase would have related to a combination of the demands of machinery and the intended level of production rather than to the capacity of the steam engine. For the same reason, the dimensions of silk factories powered by steam do not differ from those powered by water or horse.

The availability of steam-power technology thus does not appear to have altered the basic design of mill building. Although a substantial proportion of these early 19th-century mills have been demolished, their dimensions are recorded on historical maps and in advertisements, and have an unerring consistency.[134] Of the standing mills, Alma Mill, Pickford Street, Brookside Mill, Catherine Street Mill, Commercial Road/Queen Street Mill, Lowe Street Mill, Sutton Mill (Figure 62) and Thorp Street Leather Mill in Macclesfield, and Royle Street Mill and Park Mill in Congleton, can all be regarded as conforming to a standard format of construction which is generally viewed as typical of early textile-mill architecture.[135]

Wheelock Mill, Wheelock (Figure 63), stands as a typical example of a mill built during this period, around 1809, to be powered by steam. Three-storeyed and L-shaped in plan, its main

Figure 63
*Wheelock Mill, Wheelock, was erected c1809 as a steam-powered silk-throwing mill. It survives largely intact although the plan restores the engine and boiler houses and the chimney to their original form.*

range measures 28·5 m long by 7·5 m wide internally. The adjoining wing appears to be have been built for warehousing since there is no evidence of power transmission and the window arrangement was not designed for maximum lighting. To the north-west, adjacent to the mill, are the much altered engine and boiler houses which originally formed an L-shaped building. The engine house, just 3 m wide, is tall and narrow. An entablature beam lying in the mill yard, and one in the engine house but probably not in its original position, indicate that it once housed a beam engine. The original chimney which stood against the mill, to the south of the boiler house, was square in plan and as such was typical of early mill chimneys. Wheelock Mill, although representing a large number of steam-powered mills, was as simple in plan and construction as, and identical in scale to, mills built to be powered by either horse or water.

The housing of steam engines often added an extra dimension to mill building. If a mill was already water powered, the engine had to be placed where it could connect with the existing gearing. This could be adjacent to the wheel as at Lumbhole Mill in Kettleshulme (see p 63), at the opposite side of the mill as at Park Green Mill and Sunderland Street Mill, or at the opposite end of the mill as at Lowerhouse Mill, Bollington. Engine houses were built as extensions to all of these mills, except at Sunderland Street Mill where the engine house and adjacent boiler house were positioned fronting Sunderland Street (Figure 64), some 3·6 m away from the mill. This siting may be explained by the fact that the 20 horsepower rotative beam crank

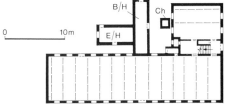

engine was amongst the first of its kind to be used in Macclesfield, and it may be that the mill-owners, J and G Pearson, were concerned about the risk of fire, explosion, or the possible damaging effects of vibration on the mill itself. The boiler house has been demolished, but the engine house, which is clearly visible on an 1810 sketch of Waters Green (Figure 4), still stands today. It is three storeys high, three bays in

Figure 64
*The engine house at Sunderland Street Mill, Macclesfield, was probably erected in 1804 to house a Boulton and Watt steam engine. It can be seen in an 1810 sketch of Waters Green (see Figure 4).*

*a*

Figure 65
*Engine houses.*
*a) The 1823 mill at*
*Victoria Mills,*
*Macclesfield, has an*
*engine house (left) which*
*abuts the main mill. The*
*boiler house was under-*
*ground.*

*b) The engine house at*
*Wheelock Mill, Wheelock,*
*erected c 1809, is an*
*example of an engine*
*house built separately*
*from the main mill.*

*b*

Figure 66
*The engine house at
Thorp Street Leather Mill,
Macclesfield, here shown
partially demolished, was
of lean-to type. The chimney was incorporated into
a privy tower.*

length and two bays wide. Although without decoration, the building has a refined architectural
style, with Flemish bonded brickwork to the
Sunderland Street elevation, a hipped stone-
flagged roof with modillioned eaves, and tall
window openings with cambered brick arches,
stone sills and hung sash window frames. The
treatment given to this engine house signifies
the importance attributed to this building and
its contents.

There is evidence from other mills of this
period for the construction of engine houses,
but none possesses the architectural style of
Sunderland Street Mill engine house. Of the
remaining structures, three different types can
be identified: lean-to buildings attached to a
mill as at the Leather Mill, Macclesfield; more
substantial additions in the form of single or
multi-storeyed projections as at Victoria Mills
(Figure 65a) and Alma Mill, Pickford Street,
Macclesfield; and small separate buildings as at
Wheelock Mill, Wheelock (Figure 65b), and
Higher Mill, Bollington.[136] At Alma Mill,
Pickford Street, the engine house is distin-
guished by semicircular arched windows which

became a typical feature of engine house architecture.

Contemporary with the engine house at
Thorp Street Leather Mill, Macclesfield, are the
chimney and adjacent toilet block (Figure 66).
The chimney is typical of the early 19th century
in that it is, like that at Commercial
Road/Queen Street Mill and Victoria Mill,
Macclesfield, and Millbrook Mill, Rainow,
square in plan, tapered and relatively short.
These early chimneys seem often to have been
incorporated into the structure of the engine
and boiler house (see Figure 65a). Boilers of the
period would generally have been of the simple,
single-flue type, of which none remains *in situ*.

The significance of steam power was two-
fold: first, its use enabled mill builders and textile entrepreneurs to choose sites for expansive
concerns which were not restricted by the need
to be adjacent to a source of water power, or the
small power capacity of a horse gin. Second, the
harnessing of steam power created the potential
for increased capacity which, because of the lim-
its of early steam technology, was not applied
until the mid and late 19th century.

# 4  Housing the silk industry 1826–1990

By the mid 1830s the silk industry in its various branches had become predominant in the towns of Macclesfield and Congleton, whilst the cotton industry was more specifically based in the northern districts of east Cheshire (see Chapters One and Five). In Macclesfield, silk throwing continued as the predominant industry for the greater part of the 19th century, with waste-silk spinning carried out by the major firm of J and T Brocklehurst and by a limited number of smaller concerns. Powered silk weaving gradually increased in production to the extent that towards the end of the 19th century Macclesfield's silk industry ultimately came to depend for its survival upon this branch. Silk dyeing and finishing were also important in the town. Although the depression of the early 1860s damaged the entire silk industry, in Macclesfield its greater resources and diversification enabled it to recover and survive until the mid 20th century.[1] Mill building thus continued throughout the period under review for all branches of the silk industry, but the design of new mill building after the late 1820s was generally for the purpose of housing those processes which regenerated the industry in the 1830s and 1840s.

In Congleton during the 1830s and 1840s, silk spinning and ribbon manufacturing became of major importance. The depression of the early 1860s, however, caused such serious harm to the silk industry in Congleton that the process of fustian cutting was introduced to take up available labour and mill space left idle by the contraction of silk. Subsequent mills were therefore built almost exclusively for fustian production (see p 104).

Evidence exists for the construction of twenty-four mills in Macclesfield during the periods of prosperity which took place between the major slumps of 1826 and 1860. This figure, only about one-third of the number built in the previous forty years, reflects the consolidation of manufacturing interests and represents a period in which investment in expansion often took the form of building extensions on existing sites or of re-using underused or empty mills, rather than the erection of new mills on new sites. In Congleton borough during the same period of time, at least fifteen new mills were built, including one at Wheelock. This number compares with the figure of about twenty-four mills built during the preceding forty years and indicates a steadier rate of economic progress than in Macclesfield.

## The development of the silk industry in east Cheshire

Investment in silk weaving (known also as silk manufacturing) in the mid to late 19th century seems to have been a significant factor in the survival and development of the east Cheshire silk industry. The number of firms either specialising in weaving or producing both thrown and woven silk formed an increasingly large proportion of the total. It was noted in 1866 that:

*A French manufacturer applies himself to one class of goods — he throws into it all his resources and ingenuity in order that he may excel in that particular species. Another firm would apply themselves to a different species ... In England, however, and in Macclesfield especially, the silk manufacturer is so circumstanced that he is obliged to combine half a dozen branches under one management, and if he does not excel in any one depart-*

*ment, the superior machinery at his command for economising labour, and the skill and perseverance of his workmen enable him to produce goods that stand in fair competition with his foreign rivals, whilst his mixed trade stands him in need should one particular branch fail.*[2]

Examples of the 'mixed trade' referred to above are to be found in the organisation of processes by three firms awarded medals at the Great Exhibition in 1851, for 'craftsmanship, design and cheap at the prices quoted',[3] namely, J and T Brocklehurst, Critchley, Brinsley & Co, and H & T Wardle. Critchley and Brinsley, and H & T Wardle were weaving companies, whilst the Brocklehurst family firm had been involved in all stages of silk trade and production at varying times of their existence, from silk-button manufacture, to throwing and weaving, and, by the mid 19th century, to silk spinning. Of these three firms, Critchley and Brinsley and J and T Brocklehurst had London addresses.[4] Since the organisation of processes and company assets by these firms enabled them not only to survive the trade cycles of booms and slumps, but to reach standards of excellence, a brief outline of their individual histories will illustrate the successful developments in the silk industry during the mid 19th century and to provide comparison with smaller firms which also continued in production.

From their beginnings, Brocklehursts had occupied a site at Hurdsfield on the eastern edge of Macclesfield. The company expanded and diversified its production on this site so that by the early 19th century the processing of silk through all its stages, from throwing to weaving and finishing, was carried out at the Hurdsfield mills (see p 17). Other premises were acquired in Macclesfield during the immediate post-1826 depression, at a time when, on John Brocklehurst's own admission,[5] premises were worth only a fraction of their original cost. These were Pickford Street Mill in 1827, Lower Exchange Mills 'F' and 'B' by 1830, and Pleasant Street Mill at an unknown date in the mid 19th century. In this way Brocklehursts were poised to take advantage of the healthier silk trade in the 1830s. After 1832 the company diversified into silk spinning and powered weaving, and to house this expansion new mills were built at the Hurdsfield site: 'B' Mill in the 1830s and Albert Mill in the 1840s. It is also worth noting that Brocklehursts owned the most successful of Macclesfield's private banks. So successful was the Brocklehurst silk-manufacturing firm that it survived until the 1990s, having entered into a partnership with the silk printing and dyeing firm of Whiston in 1926.[6]

Critchley and Brinsley, although not so long lived, were also large employers and bankers in Macclesfield. Henry Critchley, in addition to his interests in the firm, was a partner in the Critchley and Turner bank from 1802 until 1816, when the bank failed and was taken over by the Brocklehursts. In the earliest record of the firm in 1805, Critchley and Brinsley were described as manufacturers,[7] and from the early period of their history they occupied Bridge Street Mills, a site on which they remained until 1886. Henry Critchley described himself in 1818 as a manufacturer of bandanna handkerchiefs, employing between 140 and 160 (varying with trade) of the estimated 1,500 looms in Macclesfield, fifty or so of which were housed in his factory.[8] Although Critchley and Brinsley remained in occupation of Bridge Street Mills, they did so together with a number of other companies, including silk throwsters, but it is impossible to know what level of interdependency, if any, existed between the companies, or whether the site operated as an integrated site.

Maps show the development of the Bridge Street Mills site from one to three adjoining mills by 1838.[9] Although the firm operated as manufacturers (weavers) during the first half of the 19th century, when they were listed amongst the top ten manufacturers in Macclesfield,[10] there is no structural evidence to show that the looms were initially housed in any building type other than the multi-storeyed mill on the Bridge Street site since weaving sheds were not added until after 1871. In 1872[11] and 1878[12] Critchley, Brinsley & Co were listed in trade directories as silk manufacturers and as silk throwsters. This diversification, from manufacturing to throwing and manufacturing, at a late stage in the firm's history, was the reverse of a general trend which had taken place between ten and twenty years earlier whereby throwsters had expanded their investments into weaving. However, the history of this firm's organisation is not unusual in that, without the type of massive expansion undertaken by the Brocklehursts, they were still sufficiently stable to survive the serious slumps of both 1826 and 1860. The later diversification may have been an attempt to recoup the firm's prosperity after 1860, which, if so, was not a long-term success, since there is no evidence for the firm's existence after 1886.

In Congleton, Reade & Co can be taken as an example of a company which survived by changing its activities from silk throwing to cotton spinning in 1785, returning to silk throwing and weaving by 1830, changing from throwing to spinning by 1834, whilst retaining their interests in weaving. These changes of branch and process involved the Reade family in a number of different family consortiums. The Reade family firms occupied and extended the adjoining sites of Stonehouse Green and Brook Mills (Figures 55, 56), which were ultimately amalgamated to form an extensive silk-spinning site. Although the Reade family sold out in 1852 to the Solly family, the company name was retained and the firm of Reade & Co remained in production in these mills until 1929.

The variety of organisation by firms both large and small makes it difficult to draw conclusions about the reasons for their survival. However it seems that, for many firms, investment in silk weaving was a contributory factor, and that the number of firms either specialising in weaving, or producing both thrown and woven silk, formed an increasingly large part of the industry.

In addition to the continued existence of large firms such as those described above, there persisted numbers of small firms, which flourished in an industry where hand processes, particularly weaving, were not easily or quickly replaced by large-scale mechanisation. Furthermore the required capital outlay was not necessarily prohibitive to anyone willing and able to speculate. As was the case in the early 19th century, premises in mills were advertised to let floor by floor, for example, for throwing: 'To be let and may be entered upon the 25 March, the first and second storeys in the Oxford Road Silk Factory, in Macclesfield, now in the occupation of Mr Joseph Arnold containing 250 dozen of silk mill spindles, with the silk machinery and fixtures attached thereto',[13] and for weaving: 'To let, Two rooms in the silk factory situated in Catherine Street, Macclesfield, well adapted for silk manufacturing purposes, and now in the occupation of Mr Josiah Smale. The rooms are heated with steam. The rent is moderate. Particulars from Mr William Green, iron founder, Macclesfield.'[14] The premises were almost certainly used as part of diversified production of the firm of Josiah Smale and Son (see below). The last sentence of this advertisement further corroborates the still speculative nature of factory ownership and occupancy.

Small lots of machinery were also available:

*To be sold by private contract, fine swivel looms, for weaving doubles, with shafting, strapping and gearing compleat. One soft silk engine, one doubling frame, a warping mill, a blocking machine, warehouse fixtures and other materials for the convenience of a small manufacturer. The above are contained in part of Jackson's factory in Duke Street Macclesfield, [in Sutton, see p 101] and will be sold on reasonable terms. To anyone wishing to*

*engage in the silk manufacture on a moderate scale, the present is a favourable opportunity, as the machinery is in most compleat working condition and may be forthwith used to advantage.*[15]

This advertisement refers to powered ribbon looms housed in a mill built probably about twenty years earlier for throwing purposes.

Where expansion needed to take place, the common arrangement, in urban areas where land availability was limited, was for firms to acquire other mills. In this way a small number of firms came to own several sites, with the result that organisation of their production became dispersed. This pattern of organisation was characteristic of the greater proportion of the silk industry from about 1860 until the almost total demise of the industry in the mid 20th century. The single-structure, multi-storeyed mill was an important element within this system in which small firms could establish themselves, and which large firms could acquire for the expansion of processes and production.

Josiah Smale and Son in Macclesfield and Berisfords in Congleton are firms whose histories demonstrate this pattern of development but are unusual in that both companies survived until the 1990s.[16] Josiah Smale and Son has its origins in the 18th-century silk-throwing industry.[17] By the 1850s the company's stock books show them to have invested in weaving — manufacturing ties, handkerchiefs, silk twill and crêpe de Chine, both on powerlooms within their factories, and on handlooms by outworkers, and increasing their turnover from £9,000 to £19,000 during the 1850s.[18] By 1864,[19] Josiah Smale and Son, describing themselves as silk manufacturers and throwsters, had come to occupy Bollin Mill. They had also acquired the adjacent Alma Mill, Townley Street Mill and Brookside Mill, and between 1872 and 1885 built the George Street Mill and George Street New Mill (see p 88), the whole site known collectively as the Bollin Mills. During the course of their expansion the family firms of Josiah Smale and Co and Smale Bros became the largest owners of mill property in Macclesfield, owning the Bollin Mills, Royal George Mills and Park Lane Mills (a total of ten mills grouped within these complexes), together with King Street Mill, Waterloo Street Mill, Langley Weaving Shed and Bond Street Mill. All the varying stages of production in silk throwing and weaving were carried out in these mills.

In Congleton, the firm of Berisfords, established in 1858, occupied Foundry Mill, known later as Victoria Mill, for powered ribbon weaving. Expanding their production to include varieties of tapes and bindings, the company acquired

Lower Park Mill and Spratt Street Mill in Congleton, Thorp Street Gas Mill and the King Edward Street/Waterloo Street Mills in Macclesfield, and Edward Street Mill, Buglawton, by the mid 20th century.

## Processes in relation to the design of mill building

A number of notable technological advances in silk spinning and weaving, introduced during the 1820s and 1830s, were fundamental to the recovery of the silk industry in the mid 1830s. The introduction of powerloom weaving was perhaps the most important, but the application of the Jacquard mechanism to looms and the successful mechanisation of waste-silk spinning were also influential. These processes, however, could not be housed adequately in the mills of traditional construction and scale. Although the system continued whereby a number of different firms often carried out different processes

within a single mill building, increasingly mills designed to accommodate a particular process became more characteristic of building for the silk industry after the hiatus of the late 1820s and early 1830s.

### Silk throwing

Throwing technology had made only little advance by the late 1820s. The wooden parts of the early throwing frames were replaced by metal, which speeded up but did not alter the process. In 1829 it was recorded that: 'having previously operated on machinery of the old construction ... the machinery of Macclesfield and Congleton had been improved upon a principle that increased the revolutions of the spindles as far as was necessary and the cast-iron gearing and tin cylinder had been employed'.[20] It is likely that the new form of machinery came into widespread use during the recovery period of the 1830s. Although recognisably similar to the throstle machine used for cotton spinning,[21] rectangular rather than circular in form, silk-throwing machinery (Figure 67) retained only

Figure 67
*Rectangular throwing frames came into widespread use during the 1830s and were constructed of metal rather than wood (Ure 1861, 50).*

relatively low spindleage and so imposed no further demand upon mill architecture. It was therefore possible to continue to house throwing machinery in existing mill buildings, and several of the new multi-storeyed mills built during the mid to late 19th century retained the proportions and construction of the earlier mills for this purpose.

## Silk spinning

Silk spinning is the process by which silk yarn is produced from waste silk which is composed of short fibres. In the processes of producing thrown silk from the continuous filament emitted by the silk worm — reeling, winding, cleaning and throwing — a great quantity of waste silk is generated, estimated in 1765 to be at least half of all raw and thrown silk.[22] Damaged cocoons, from which it was not possible to reel a continuous filament, were also a major source of waste silk. Silk was such an expensive commodity that methods were devised to produce the equivalent of woollen shoddy by shredding used woven silk and reducing it to a fibrous state. As the gross product of thrown and woven silk was increased by mechanised systems of processing, so the volume of waste silk was increased. It was imperative therefore to find mechanised systems of dealing with waste silk, the hand spinning of which has a history as old as the manufacture of silk.

The development of powered cotton-spinning machinery enabled similar mechanical principles to be applied to silk spinning, but the application was not without difficulty since cotton-spinning machines were designed to deal with standard short fibre lengths rather than the unequal fibre lengths of waste silk. The cutting of silk into short staples of between 25 mm and 50 mm, which could be spun on machinery designed for cotton, damaged the quality and lustre of the silk, and it was therefore necessary to concentrate on the methods used for spinning the longer staples of worsted or flax. In 1836 Gibson and Campbell of Glasgow patented a machine which successfully adapted the principle of the throstle spinning machine for the spinning of long silk, with a staple of up to 250 mm.

Mechanised silk spinning was still impeded by the problems of mechanising the preparatory processes of combing and carding waste silk, known jointly as dressing. Although machines for combing and carding had been in use since the early 19th century, most notably that invented in 1821 by the Frenchmen, Didelot and Bauwens, much of the dressing was done by hand on factory premises.[23] This last hindrance to the progress of silk spinning was removed by Lister's invention of the self-acting dressing machine in 1877.[24] The yarn ultimately produced by these

refinements of machinery held qualities of softness and adaptability to blending with other fibres which thrown silk did not possess.[25]

By the early 19th century a silk-spinning industry was established in Yorkshire and Lancashire, and in Cheshire at Macclesfield and Congleton, although it never challenged the pre-eminent process of silk throwing in Macclesfield. Two of the firms amongst those responsible for pioneering the industry in Cheshire were the Brocklehursts in Macclesfield and the Reades in Congleton. J & T Brocklehurst (see p 70) formed a business alliance with Gibson and Campbell, the patentees of the long-silk spinning process. When Gibson and Campbell were faced with the traditional reaction to major textile inventions, that of challenge to the validity and rights of their patent, Brocklehursts offered their support, both moral and financial, in legal defence. In return Brocklehursts 'were given the right to use the [long-spinning] process, free of further cost, and to participate in any extension or renewal of the amended patent rights'.[26] Brocklehursts continued as the major producers of spun silk in Macclesfield until the 1950s.

Although silk spinning became an important industry in Congleton, production in the mid 19th century was based at only three sites, at Stonehouse Green and Brook Mills, occupied by Reades (see p 71), at the Forge Mill, occupied by the firm of Peter Wild and Co, and at Bath Vale Mill, occupied by Conder and Co.[27]

Silk spinning during the early and mid 19th century, prior to the full mechanisation of the preparatory processes, was housed in mills of traditional design and construction. In 1848 Waters Green Mill in Macclesfield was advertised for sale, together with its spinning machinery:

*all the valuable and modern made machinery for preparing and spinning silk and crape [including] silk spinning mills, from 200 to 264 spindles, principally in iron frames, made by Ritson and Waters and Langford ... sixty eight power-looms by Sharp, Roberts and Co ... condensing steam engine, cylinder 26 inches diameter, 5 feet stroke, 30 horses' power, fly wheel 21 feet diameter, mortice wheel 6 feet 2 inches diameter, and Ashlar stone foundation, by Bowman & Galloway.[28]*

This list describes the machinery of a mill in which the processes of powered silk spinning and weaving were integrated, and the engineering detail indicates that the machinery was of up-to-date technology. However, the dimensions of the mill as taken from historical maps are recorded as 10 m wide by 32 m long.[29] The lack of additional building on the site indicates that this machinery was housed within the single mill

SILK SPINNING. 4. Dressed Silk Spreading - Silk waste.

building, the dimensions of which are an increase of only about 1 m on the width of late 18th and early 19th-century mills. Although improved technology in the processes of both silk spinning and powered weaving placed increased stress upon buildings in terms of load-bearing, where spindleage remained low, as at Waters Green Mill, existing mill structures were still used for the accommodation of the newly mechanised processes. This solution was short term, however, since larger and heavier machinery, brought about by the increase of spindleage, the mechanisation of preparatory silk-spinning processes and greater numbers of powerlooms, could not be housed in traditional multi-storeyed mills.

As more of the preparatory processes of silk spinning became mechanised, the organisation and accommodation of processes on site became increasingly structured. All the major sites in east Cheshire used for the production of spun silk have been demolished, with the exception of Brook Mills, Congleton. Stonehouse

Green Mill, Congleton, was recorded prior to its demolition in 1988. Plans of Stonehouse Green and Brook Mills, dated 1853 (in the possession of the owner), and of Forge Mill, dated 1865,[30] record the contemporary layout of processes. These plans are a rare and invaluable record of the organisation of processes in the silk-spinning industry, which were more akin to the organisation of similar short-fibre processes in the cotton and worsted/woollen industries than to other processes in the silk industry.

Since the spinning of short-staple fibre requires many stages of preparation, scutching, combing, carding and roving (or lapping for silk), and the machinery for these processes was cumbersome and heavy (Figure 68), the weight of this machinery necessitated its housing at ground or possibly first-floor level, and so site layout, incorporating the sequential arrangement of the processes, was of paramount importance in the silk-spinning industry.

The layout of Forge Mill, Congleton, shown in plan on the 1845 Tithe Map of Congleton,

Figure 68
*The firm of Brocklehursts began spinning silk in their Macclesfield mills in the middle of the 19th century. This photograph, taken in the early 20th century, shows the spreading of dressed silk, part of the process of preparing the combed silk fibres for spinning and illustrates the weight and bulk of silk-dressing machinery (Warner 1921, 409).*

75

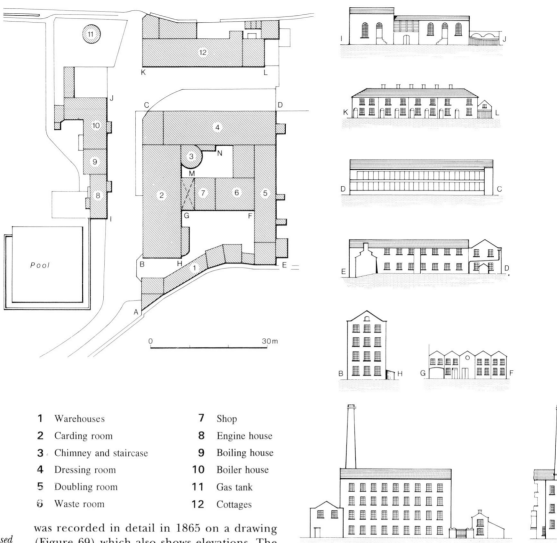

Figure 69
*Plan and elevations based on an 1865 drawing of Forge Mill, Congleton, which details the layout of a silk-spinning site.*

| | | | |
|---|---|---|---|
| 1 | Warehouses | 7 | Shop |
| 2 | Carding room | 8 | Engine house |
| 3 | Chimney and staircase | 9 | Boiling house |
| 4 | Dressing room | 10 | Boiler house |
| 5 | Doubling room | 11 | Gas tank |
| 6 | Waste room | 12 | Cottages |

was recorded in detail in 1865 on a drawing (Figure 69) which also shows elevations. The buildings appear to have been specifically and efficiently designed for the needs of the silk-spinning industry, since Peter Wild & Co continued to use the site for silk spinning, with the same basic layout, until 1952. The plan of 1865 shows that the waste silk, on arrival, was stored in the waste room (G–F on plan), adjacent to a building called a shop whose purpose is unknown. The elevation shows a row of two-storeyed, attached, gabled buildings with a loading-bay door into the waste room. From there the waste silk was taken to the boiling and wash houses (I–J on plan), shown as a range of single-storeyed buildings with round-headed windows. The washed and dried silk was then taken to the dressing room (C–D on plan) where the heavy machinery for combing (dressing) was housed; from there the dressed silk was taken for carding on the ground floor of the four-storeyed mill building (C–B on plan), which is comparable in scale to silk mills of the mid

19th century, measuring 8·5 m wide by 24 m long, with floor to ceiling heights of 3·6 m. Since there is no mention on the key to the plan of the processes of drawing (the equivalent of cotton roving) and spinning, it is reasonable to assume that these were carried out on upper floors.

The site layout for silk spinning at Stonehouse Green and Brook Mills, Congleton, comes from a plan drawn in 1853 in response to a change of site ownership in 1852 (Figure 70). Although the mills had previously been used for cotton spinning, short-silk spinning (Stonehouse Green Mill), silk throwing and silk weaving (Brook Mills), the site was converted

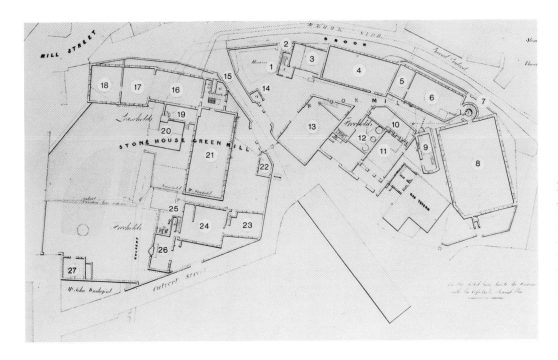

Figure 70
*Although Stonehouse Green Mill, Congleton, had been used for cotton spinning and short-silk spinning, and Brook Mills, Congleton, for silk throwing and weaving, when this plan was drawn in 1853 the whole site was being used for long-silk spinning.*

into a production line for long-silk spinning. The plan shows the early mills (outlined as 4, 5, 6, 16, 17, 18), which were built between 1785 and an unknown date in the late 18th or early 19th century (see Figures 55, 56). The later mill at Brook Mills (outlined 8) was built in 1835 (date on rain-water head) (Figure 71), and its partner at Stonehouse Green Mill (outlined 21) was almost certainly of similar date. Ancillary buildings, including engine and boiler house extensions, would also have been built as part of the site expansion at this time, and are all in evidence on the 1845 Congleton Tithe Map.[31] The building date of the two larger mills relates their construction to the introduction of short-silk spinning at Stonehouse Green Mill, and to silk weaving, almost certainly powered at this date, at Brook Mills (see p 87). The site plan of 1853 shows dressing and carding at first-floor (meaning here ground-floor) level, whilst spinning was carried out on the second (first), third (second) and fourth (third) floors.

Thus all the processes involved in silk spinning were most efficiently carried out on one site, many at ground-floor level, which necessitated extensive site development. However, although the arrangement of processes and their adequate housing was essential to industrial efficiency, the architectural response was never exclusive to a single process or branch of the industry.

## Jacquard weaving

The finest silk cloth was the product of hand weaving, and although by the end of the 19th century powered weaving had replaced hand weaving in terms of quantity, hand weaving was not finally abandoned in east Cheshire until 1981, with the closure of Cartwright and Sheldon at Paradise Mill, Macclesfield. The most intricate designs of colour and pattern were produced on the Jacquard loom by means of the alternate raising and lowering of numbers

Figure 71
*The 1835 mill at Brook Mills, Congleton, was built to house powered silk weaving (see Figure 83).*

Figure 72
*The hand Jacquard loom was introduced into England in about 1821, possibly by the entrepreneur Stephen Wilson. The looms pictured still survive at Paradise Mill, Macclesfield, now a museum.*

of warp threads through which different shuttles, fed with a variety of colours, were passed. Before the invention of the Jacquard loom, this form of weaving had been made possible by the use of a draw loom operated by a weaver and by a boy who was responsible for altering the arrangement of the warp threads by pulling a harness card to raise the necessary heddles (cards with eyelets carrying the warp threads). The method was tedious and time consuming.

Many attempts were made, especially in France, to improve efficiency, but it was not until 1801 that Joseph-Marie Jacquard patented a method by which all the mechanisms were operated directly by the weaver. Power was not applied to Jacquard weaving until late in the 19th century. In essence the Jacquard loom, whether hand or power-operated, remains the same today. The Jacquard mechanism uses hole-punched cards which regulate the raising and lowering of the warp threads and is still housed in a frame positioned directly above the loom, thus creating a machine which required about 3·6 m head height (Figure 72).

The Jacquard loom was first introduced into England in about 1821, possibly by the entrepreneur Stephen Wilson, of the firm Lea, Wilson and Bousfield (also known as Lea, Wilson & Co), probably at his factory in Streatham, London.[32] An exact date cannot be found for the first use of this machinery in east Cheshire, although in 1821 it was reported that:

> The quality of our silk manufacture is in many respects equal to that of the French; equal in the articles of piece goods, inferior in ribbons, very superior in gloves and hosiery, as well as in poplin and other mixtures of wool and silk, but in price we are 20–26% dearer; a portion of which difference is perhaps to be accounted for by a piece of machinery which has been for some years in use at Lyons, and which is described to be an inestimable advantage in weaving the finer and varied patterns of silk. This machinery is now well known, and has been brought to perfection by a gentleman in this country who has very considerable skill by making himself master of it, but it has not yet been brought into use.[33]

Oblique references to the use of the loom in Manchester and Macclesfield were made in evidence to a Parliamentary Committee in 1823.[34] Evidence has also come to light from the deeds to Victoria Mills, Macclesfield, which associate the ownership and possible building of the early phase of the mill in 1823 with Stephen Wilson, Charles Pritchard Bousfield, Samuel Wilson (brother of Stephen) and Matthew Jackson, apparently an associated company of the London firm of Lea, Wilson and Bousfield (see Figure 82).

There is also an early reference to the loom in Macclesfield in 1828:

> To the manufacturers of Macclesfield, J Hall, sole agent to J Jacqier (from Lyons), manufacturer of machines a la Jacquard, respectfully informs the manufacturers of Macclesfield and its vicinity, and the fancy weaving trade in particular, that these machines are at length from intense perseverance, brought to the highest perfection. Neither expense nor exertion having been spared on the completion of this object. M. Jacqier's machines are now generally used throughout the three kingdoms, for every figured article woven in looms — viz, silks, ribbons, china, crapes, damasks, muslins, carpets, hollis lace etc. They will be found particularly advantageous, as the pattern can be changed in five minutes at the option of the weaver, and the work is more correct than by any English

> machine. J Hall guarantees the purchasers of these machines against any claim the patentees may presume to have, and it may be added that they have been manufactured and sold about six years.[35]

A small number of advertisements record the use of Jacquard looms in mills, where greater control could be exercised over a costly process, but the bulk of work was still put out to weavers working in garrets. The organisation of production, with the weaver tied to the master manufacturer for the lease of his loom but otherwise paying for his own expenses from the price he was paid for his finished cloth, is indicated by the following testimony:

> I am at work at present on fancy silk with a Jacquard loom … The piece I've got to weave will be about fifty four yards long when wove and I get £2. 5sh. for it. I expect to finish it in a month. Out of that I shall have to pay one shilling a week for winding, three pence a week for the hire of the loom and if I didnt work at home I should have to pay one shilling a week for loom hire. The oil to burn at night will be 6d. a week at least, for I know I will have to work fifteen hours a day to get it done in one month. The piece that I am at work on is what some people call 'shotted' silk, it is a green cane and pink shute; they pay extra for that in London but do not give us nothing extra here for it. Well, out of my £2. 5sh. I shall have to take off 4sh. for winding, 1sh. for loom hire and 2sh. at least for oil — that makes 7sh.; 7sh. from 45sh. leaves 38sh., thats 9sh. 6d. a week.[36]

The introduction of the Jacquard loom does not appear to have altered the existing organisation of the manufacturing industry, except in so far as the capital investment needed for the new machinery would, in most cases, have been beyond the reach of a domestic weaver. Weavers were therefore generally reliant upon the master manufacturer for the provision of the loom. This situation, already well established, is likely therefore to have become more widespread with the introduction of the Jacquard loom.

A by-product of the Jacquard weaving industry was the accumulation of huge amounts of hole-punched cards which were held for future repeats of pattern, so that whole floors of mills became occupied by card storage. The bulk of the problem and the economic consequences of the duty imposed on paper and card production were reported in 1850:

> Paper cards are used. To these cards have to be transferred the patterns and beautiful designs which have to be interwoven upon the silken fabrics by the jacquard weaver. The quantity of cards

*used in the trade is enormous. In some of the fabric for waist-coating now produced in Manchester, there are as many as 90 picks (one thread of the weft) of silk in every inch of cloth and some patterns will require the weaver to be furnished with 900 or 1,200 cards. One really elaborate pattern required 1,088 cards. The weight of the cards is 4¹/₂lbs per 100, so that the total weight of 1,088 would be about 49lbs. The duty paid to Government on 49lbs of cardboard at 1¹¹/₂d per 1lb gives a total of 6sh. 1¹/₂d. This set of cards will only serve one weaver. If the design is one that takes, and he (the manufacturer) has to put 1,000 weavers at it, a thousand times 6sh. 1¹/₂d has to be paid in duty. Each weaver will be three weeks in producing his 20–30 yards of waist-coating. The number of cards used is in proportion to the number of colours introduced into a pattern, or the extent of it. In bed furniture and figured window curtains, a large pattern took 7,000 to 8,000, and in the other 12,000 to 14,000 cards, produced by a large manufacturer in Manchester. Now in France and Germany, there is no duty on paper, and in some of the figured velvets and more elaborate designs for silk goods, the manufacturer in this country cannot compete because of the greater number of cards required.*

Interestingly, the writer of this article reckoned that 'English artisans and capitalists began to throw their attention to the Jacquard loom ... but 12–15 years ago', which gives a date of about the late 1830s, which could actually relate to the use of this type of loom becoming widespread in this country. However Lardner, writing in 1831, claims widespread adoption of the loom by that date.[38]

### Powered weaving

The application of power to weaving was a long and laborious process which began in response to the increased volume of yarn produced by mechanised spinning processes during the 18th century. Powerloom weaving in the silk industry was initially suitable only for coarse, plain weaves, since fine silk yarn was too delicate a material for the relatively insensitive technology of powered weaving. Brocades and other cloth of quality continued to be produced by hand weaving.

In 1836 it was estimated that there were 414 powerlooms in operation in the Cheshire silk industry,[39] whilst in 1840, in Macclesfield alone, 'The number of hand looms is stated in all at about 4000 hand looms. Very few hand loom cotton weavers. No linen weaving.'[40] As late as 1849 it was noted:

*Very little silk, and that only of the coarsest kind, is woven by power. A small quantity of bandannas*

*[a richly coloured yellow or white spotted handkerchief] are thus turned out in Macclesfield; but in the production of the higher class of silk fancy goods, the delicacy and intelligence of human labour is requisite, and the Jacquard is never beholden for its motion to the steam engine.*[41]

In conclusion, the accommodation of silk spinning, Jacquard weaving and powered silk weaving placed stresses and made demands upon mill building which were untenable in the old mills. Silk spinning was comparable in its range of preparatory processes to cotton spinning, and the use of heavy machinery for these processes necessitated a greater area of well-supported floor space than was available in mills of a pre-1826 date. Neither could the weight and vibration of powerlooms be supported above ground-floor level without additional flooring support, and even with additional support the placing of this machinery above first-floor level could be detrimental to the fabric of the building. The height of a Jacquard frame, at around 3·6 m, could not be fitted within the average floor to ceiling heights of pre-1826 mills, which were between 2·3 m and 2·5 m, although height could be found by the use of loft or roof space. In the late 1830s, therefore, with the widespread uptake of new technology, alternative means of housing these processes had to be found.

## Mill architecture

### Multi-storeyed mills

'Very good attics' and 'rooms exceedingly light and lofty and suitable for any kind of looms' are noticeable phrases in mid 19th-century advertisements of mills. They indicate that a structural change in the building of multi-storeyed mills was taking place in response to the housing of a wider range of processes, including Jacquard weaving which required greater head height for the mechanism attached to the loom. Indeed looms continued to be housed in mill attics until the closure in 1981 of Paradise Mill, the last handloom establishment in Macclesfield.[42]

At least seven of the fourteen extant mills built in Macclesfield during the periods of prosperity after the depression of the late 1820s and before the depression in the 1860s have floor to ceiling heights of 3·7 m to 4 m on at least one floor, as for example Charlotte Street Mill, built in about 1840. The 1823 mill at Victoria Mills, Macclesfield (Figures 65a, 82), has a ground-floor ceiling height of 3·8 m and may be an early example of a mill accommodating

Jacquard looms (see p 79). Some mills have a high, spacious and well-lit top storey, as at Royal George Mills, built about the late 1840s (Figure 73). In Congleton, a number of mills of this period also conform to the same pattern, including Albany Mill and its neighbour, Sunnyside Mill, both of them built in about 1845, and Victoria Mill, built in two phases, the first mill in 1859 with an extension in almost identical style of construction during the 1870s.[43]

In plan, east Cheshire silk mills of the mid 19th century had comparable floor lengths to earlier mills, ranging from 20 m to 38 m. Floor widths had increased by about 1 m, averaging between 8·5 and 9·5 m. Cast-iron columns for intermediate support became a feature of mills built during this period. Although introduced as an integral part of the primary structure, for example in the 1837 mill at Victoria Mills, Macclesfield (see p 85), the characteristic use of columns in silk mills, unlike those in cotton mills, was as individual supports, unconnected to the columns directly above or below. The flexibility of this method of construction enabled the columns to be used as primary or secondary support, responsive to the rearrangement of machinery or to the demands of

increased loadbearing. Consequently, the alignment of columns in mills sometimes became irregular, with great reliance still placed upon the loadbearing properties of the cross-beams. This practice continues today.

Floors and roof trusses were of timber, although imported softwoods were used instead of native oak. Queen-post truss roofs with lighter, softwood members, suitable for wider spans, were more commonly constructed, as at Charlotte Street Mill and Royal George Mills (see Figure 73), although king-post truss roofs, with lighter, smaller-section timbers, continued to be used as a form of roofing support, as at Victoria Mill, Congleton. No fireproof construction has been identified in any silk mill, in contrast to cotton mills of the period.

Typically, silk mills of the mid to late 19th century range in height from three to six storeys, with the average mill being four storeys and fifteen bays long, figures little different from mills of 18th and early 19th-century date. Externally the later mills, with rare exceptions, have the traditional, plain façades common to their earlier counterparts, using the same form of brickwork, including Flemish bond to denote public elevations and the simple use of brick

**Figure 73**
*The hand Jacquard looms required about 3·6 m head height and were therefore often accommodated in mill attics. The high, top storey of the late 1840s mill at Royal George Mills, King Edward Street, Macclesfield, could have housed hand Jacquard looms.*

and stone for window heads and sills. Whilst in Macclesfield brick remained the common material for window arches, in Congleton splayed stone lintels became the preferred style of window head, as at Albany Mill (Figure 74), Sunnyside Mill and Flint Mill. Windows of mid 19th-century date were generally taller, for example at Royal George Mills, Henderson Street Mill and Charlotte Street Mill, Macclesfield, and at Victoria Mill, Congleton, a consequence of the need to light the increased room heights and deeper floor widths.

No change from the arrangements of the earlier period has been noted in the systems of warehousing, hoisting facilities, heating or lighting. Warehouses and offices, if not incorporated within the mill, could be attached as a secondary wing, as at Brown Street Mill, Macclesfield

(Figure 75). Goods were hoisted either by means of an external winch through loading-bay doors, or internally by manually operated hoists as at Royal George Mills and London Road Mill, Macclesfield. Heating was supplied by steam pipes, using surplus steam from the mill boiler. There is no evidence of open fires from this period. The general method of lighting industrial buildings in the 19th century was by gas. A most graphic description of gas lighting in Pitt Street Mill, Macclesfield, built in 1840, was recounted by a mill worker who remembered that as late as the earlier part of this century the gas mantles were attached to handloom frames, causing the light to flicker erratically.

Improvements were made in the provision of access between mill floors and in toilet facilities for the mill workers. Stone generally replaced wood for stairs both in new mills and as additions or replacements to existing mills, reducing the risk of fire spreading and improving the means of escape. Stone stairs were positioned either internally as at Royal George Mills, or in stair towers, which were either circular in plan, as at Charlotte Street Mill, Bollinside Mill and Paradise Upper Mill (Figure 76), Macclesfield, or square, as in the 1837 mill at Victoria Mills, Macclesfield (see Figure 82). In one instance, at Stonehouse Green Mill in Congleton, toilets were positioned within the core of the stairwell (Figure 77). Stair towers and toilet blocks of the dry shute type are features normally to be found on the rear elevation of mills of this period.

*Figure 74 (Right) Albany Mill, Canal Street, Congleton, erected c1845, has splayed stone lintels.*

*Figure 75 (Below) Warehouse and office wing extension of Brown Street Mill, Macclesfield, erected c1840.*

*Figure 76 (Below right) Stone stairs, replacing or supplementing wooden stairs, were positioned either internally or in external towers, as here at Paradise Upper Mill, Old Park Lane, Macclesfield.*

Exceptionally, the finest example of a dry shute toilet block in the county can be seen on the gable elevation of the 1835 Brook Mill at Congleton (Figure 78a). At the base of this semicircular-ended brick tower is a substantial stone collection point for the soil (Figure 78b). The scale of this structure is hardly apologetic.

*a*

Figure 77
*In the c 1830 mill at Stonehouse Green Mill, Congleton, the privies were situated within the core of the stairwell.*

Figure 78
*Brook Mills, Congleton.
a) The dry shute toilet block, of brick with a rounded end, is contemporary with the 1835 mill.
b) The unusually large soil collection point at the base, which is of ashlar masonry.*

*b*

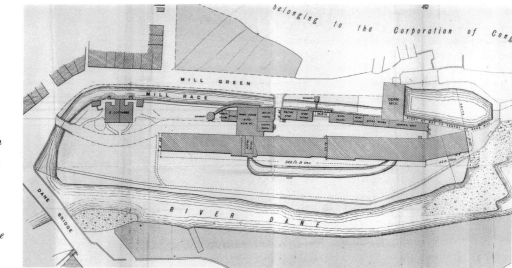

Figure 79
*Drawn in 1887, this plan of the Old Mill, Congleton, shows how the original mill, erected in 1753, had been extended eastwards in the 1830s. The small range of out-buildings had existed since at least 1845 (deeds in possession of the owner).*

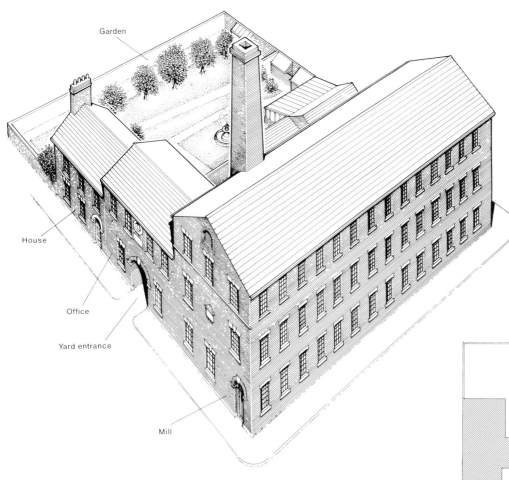

Figure 80
*Meadow Mill, Congleton, was built in 1860, probably for silk throwing. However, the collapse of the silk industry shortly afterwards meant that the mill was being used for fustian cutting by 1867. Meadow Mill is a good illustration of how the multi-storeyed mills of the silk industry continued to be built to a relatively small scale. The perspective drawing attempts to reconstruct the mill, mill house, offices and garden as they would have looked in the 1870s.*

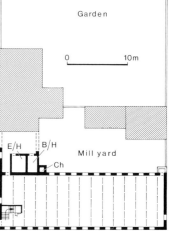

The approach of mill builders to construction during this period was that which had resulted in the standard early textile mill, that is, a careful weave of pragmatism and expediency. Buildings were constructed using traditional methods and materials, taking advantage as necessary of the loadbearing capacity of cast-iron columns.

This simple type of multi-storeyed mill was nevertheless suitable for the accommodation of a variety of processes in the production of textiles. For example, when Samuel Pearson bought the Old Mill, Congleton, in 1830, his plans for expansion into silk weaving involved the enlargement of the existing five-storeyed mill by the addition in line of a five-storeyed extension (see Figure 15), built in identical style, and with methods of construction similar to the earlier phase of building constructed in 1753 for silk throwing. A plan of the site dated 1887 (Figure 79) outlines a small range of buildings which had been in existence since at least 1845,[44] and which, apart from the washrooms, were not peculiar to the silk industry. They included stables, coach house and joiners' shop. When Pearson needed more factory space in 1836, he acquired Dane Mill, Congleton, so that, in a manner typical of all branches of the silk industry except spinning, processing for one firm would have been carried out on more than one site, all of them simple multi-storeyed mills. This system, which evolved because of the relatively light machinery used in the silk industry, particularly in the preparatory processes of silk throwing, and possibly because of the lack of space to expand within an urban environment, remained

characteristic of the silk industry until its closure.

With the exception of mills in which silk spinning was carried out, for example at Hurdsfield Road Mills, Macclesfield, and Forge Mill, Congleton (see p 74), site expansion through additional building was limited. The majority of these mills stood as individual buildings, the most common extension taking the form of an attached warehouse/office wing with one or two-bay single-storeyed weaving sheds generally situated at the rear of the mill. The continuity of style and construction of the relatively small-scale multi-storeyed mill is best exemplified by the erection in 1860 of Meadow Mill, probably for silk throwing (Figure 80). This pleasing range of mill, office and millowner's (or manager's) house retains the essential simplicity of design of mills built a century earlier for silk throwing. It has also the dubious distinction of having been built in the year in which the silk industry suffered a catastrophic collapse, particularly in Congleton.

The greatest challenge to construction methods for mills in the silk industry was the accommodation of powered weaving which required buildings of a strength adequate to withstand the constant heavy vibration of the powerlooms. An early solution to this problem was the construction of multi-storeyed mills with strengthened flooring, supported by cast-iron columns which were an integral part of the structure and permitted wider floor spans. In Macclesfield, the 1837 mill at Victoria Mills and London Road Mill are both examples of this kind of construction. The former mill (Figure 81) was almost certainly built by the firm of Winkworth and

Figure 81
*The largest mill at Victoria Mills, Macclesfield, was built in 1837, probably by the silk manufacturing firm of Winkworth and Proctor.*

Figure 82
*Plan of Victoria Mills, Macclesfield, showing the three phases of development. The first phase is the central block built in 1823, possibly for hand Jacquard weaving. The looms may have been accommodated in the tall ground floor. The next*

*block was built in 1837. The increased width and the loadbearing capacities of the cast-iron columns were designed to accommodate powered looms. The final phase was two storeyed and built c1870. It is not clear for what purpose it was originally used.*

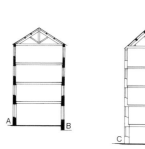

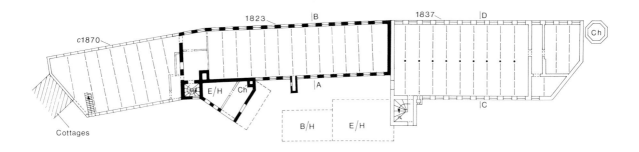

Figure 83
*The 1835 mill at Brook Mills, Congleton, was probably built to house powered silk weaving. The use of cast-iron columns and box-beam construction increased the strength and loadbearing capacities of the structure (see Figure 71).*

Proctor, silk manufacturers.[45] A name and date-stone was positioned above the mill yard entrance on Mill Lane. The mill is 11 m wide, and the beams are supported by a single row of cast-iron columns. The columns are an integral and regularly disposed part of the structure (Figure 82). They decrease in diameter from 150 mm at basement/ground-floor level to 100 mm at top-floor level.[46] The roof members are composed of timber cross-beams, rafters and purlins, with wrought-iron queen-rods and struts. As a building material, iron has been used in this mill not only for strengthening but, in the roof trusses, for lightness of construction at the upper level.

Externally this mill is traditional in appearance, functional and plain. Windows have cambered brick arches and stone sills. The loadbearing walls are constructed of handmade brick, laid unusually to English Garden Wall Bond on all elevations. The mill owes its unusually acute-angled shape at the south-west corner to a situation not uncommon in the siting of urban mills, that of fitting the maximum area of mill building into available land space, in this case, between the river and Windmill Brow.

In Congleton, the five-storeyed mills on the Stonehouse Green and Brook Mills sites have the same form of construction as the two Macclesfield mills just noted. The date of Stonehouse Green Mill, built during the 1830s, relates its construction to the introduction of silk spinning at the site, and Brook Mill (Figure 83), built in 1835, to silk weaving, possibly powered at this date. Both mills were built by methods of construction designed to increase the strength and loadbearing capacities of their floors in order to accommodate the extra load of silk spinning or weaving machinery even when the heaviest machinery was housed at ground and first-floor levels only. Both mills relied upon primary cast-iron columns for internal support and upon the use of box-beam construction for strength. The 1830s Stonehouse Green Mill was built 2 m wider than the adjacent 1785 mill, and with primary cast-iron columns. The 1837 Brook Mill is 7 m wider than the earlier mills on the site.

London Road Mill, Albion Mill and Brown Street Mill in Macclesfield, all built during the 1840s by silk manufacturers, demonstrate a restrained but increased awareness of architectural style, each mill having clasping corner pilasters. Whilst Brown Street Mill and Albion Mill (Figure 84) have the simplicity of the earlier style of mill building, London Road Mill has elements of mid 19th-century Italianate architecture. Although in plan and scale it is the twin of Albion Mill, London Road Mill is unique in

Figure 84
*Albion Mill, London Road, Macclesfield, was built in 1843.*

Figure 85
*George Street Mill,*
*Macclesfield: a)built*
*c1875, its tall windows,*
*continuous stone sills and*
*moulded stone gutter*
*brackets are indicative of a*
*late 19th-century silk mill.*

style in Macclesfield. Its brick walls are mounted on stone foundation walls which extend to first-floor height. The tall, segmental-arched windows have a decorative effect achieved by a dentilled arrangement of brickwork, and the reveals have curved, moulded brickwork. The projecting eaves cornice is supported on carved timber brackets. London Road and Albion Mills dominate the main London approach road into Macclesfield in a powerful display of mid 19th-century mill architecture.

No further structural developments occurred in multi-storeyed mill architecture until the construction in 1885 of George Street New Mill in Macclesfield, which marked the change from traditional methods of building for the silk industry to those employed in the early years of the 20th century. As one of the final

expressions of traditional silk mill architecture, its neighbour and predecessor, George Street Mill (Figure 85), was built about 1875 in the traditional form. This mill is three-storeyed and constructed of handmade brick on stone foundations. Architectural details which indicate its late 19th-century date are the prominent, moulded, dentilled stone gutter support, the continuous stone sills which form string-courses, and the size of the tall windows. Internally the mill is constructed with timber floors and king-post roof trusses and relies partially for its load-bearing capacity upon substantial cast-iron columns. Its narrow internal width of 8 m, which is directly comparable to 18th and early 19th-century mills, does not require this level of intermediate support. Its construction therefore suggests that the building housed powered

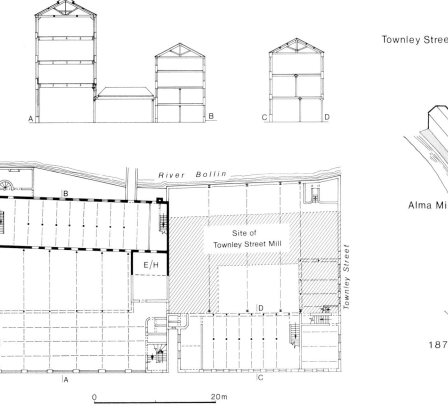

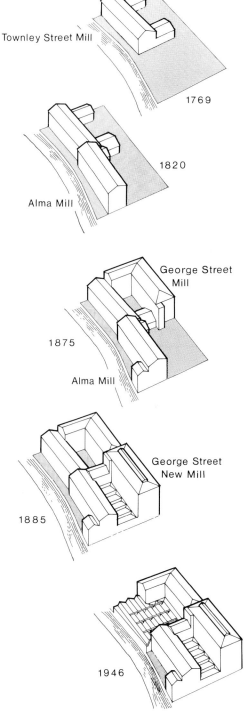

*b) The above plan shows the site as it was at the time of survey. To the left, on the river bank, is Alma Mill, Pickford Street, built c1820. To the right, fronting George Street, is George Street Mill, erected 1872–85. George Street New Mill of 1885 adjoins, with a weaving shed to the rear. Behind George Street Mill is a north-light weaving shed which was erected in 1946 on the site of Townley Street Mill.*

looms at least at ground-floor level. The mill stands as a testimony to the slow evolution of mill construction for the silk industry in east Cheshire, over a period of some 130 years.

In 1885 George Street Mill was extended by the construction of George Street New Mill

(Figure 86), a four-storeyed mill with an attached, single-storeyed, four-bay-deep weaving shed with north-light roof trusses. The new mill was built to accommodate powered Jacquard weaving and was used for this purpose until 1988 when the looms were removed, retaining only those in the adjacent 1946 weaving sheds.

The multi-storeyed mill was built of stock brick with a slate roof. Above ground-floor level, the style and construction of the mill is similar to its predecessor, George Street Mill, having tall, regularly spaced windows with stone sills and splayed stone lintels. However, in contrast to George Street Mill, the design of George Street

New Mill marked a departure from traditional methods of construction in that reliance was placed upon a cast-iron and steel framework as a primary loadbearing element of construction (Figure 87).

The purpose of this design was to provide the maximum amount of light possible over a wide floor area, sufficient to illuminate tall machinery. This was achieved by the construction of large, almost square windows, measuring 3·8 m by 4·6 m on the George Street elevation. Despite the size of the openings, the loadbearing capacity of the brick wall was maintained by building thick piers of 600 mm between the windows and

Figure 87
*The design of George Street New Mill marked a departure from traditional methods of construction in east Cheshire having a cast-iron and rolled steel loadbearing framework.*

Figure 89 *(Opposite top)*
*Peel Street Mill,*
*Macclesfield, is a two-*
*storeyed mill built c1870*
*for powered weaving. It is*
*unusual in having semi-*
*circular-headed windows*
*at ground-floor level.*

Figure 88
*Park Mill, Hobson Street,*
*Macclesfield, was erected*
*in 1852, probably by John*
*Barnett Wadsworth, for*
*powered silk weaving. L-*
*shaped in plan and two*
*storeys high, it is one of*
*several two-storeyed mills*
*designed to accommodate*
*powered looms.*

by the use of cast-iron window lintels in the form of inverted T-section joists which carry the bricks at the window heads. The east wall of the mill, adjoining the contemporary weaving sheds, is carried at first-floor level by iron columns of 200 mm diameter as a substitute for walling between the main body of the mill and the contemporary north-light truss weaving sheds built on the opposite side.

The mill thus stands as an important and innovative building in east Cheshire in its early

use of rolled steel for supporting beams, and as an early form of loadbearing metal framework. The confident style of this building reflects the pre-eminent position of the firm of Josiah Smale and Sons in Macclesfield. It can also be seen as a continuation of the tradition in which mills particularly associated with the weaving industry, for example a number of the pedimented mills, manifest, in their architectural distinction, the importance of that branch of a luxury industry. However, since the silk industry never reached the capital expenditure level of other textile industries, the architecture of these weaving mills remains relatively modest.

**Two-storeyed weaving mills** In east Cheshire, two-storeyed weaving mills or sheds have been identified as an alternative early means of housing powered looms.[47] In Macclesfield these are Park Mill, Peel Street Mill and the weaving shed adjacent to Albion Mill. Other examples of this building type, built for cotton weaving, are at Waterside Mill, Disley, and Clarence Mill, Bollington (until its demolition in the late 1980s). Park Mill (Figure 88) on Hobson Street bears its name and the date 1852 in a small pediment above the main door. The mill was possibly built and certainly occupied in its early

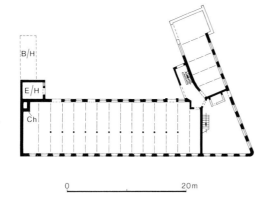

phase by John Barnett Wadsworth, manufacturer.[48] A building date for Peel Street Mill (Figure 89) has not been established, but from 1872 it was occupied by silk manufacturers. Both Park Mill and Peel Street Mill were steam powered and, although with spans of only 8·5 m, were built with cast-iron columns for increased stability. The columns at Peel Street Mill have been replaced with steel stanchions. The layout of these mills is simple, with a main range for weaving and an adjoining smaller wing for warehouse and office accommodation. Park Mill retains its harmony of scale, with small panes held in the tall window frames (recently replaced), surmounted by gauged brick lintels. Peel Street Mill, unusually, has stock brick, semicircular-headed windows at ground-floor level. The weaving shed next to Albion Mill is, unusually, seven bays wide, and together with Albion Mill and London Road Mill forms an imposing display of mid 19th-century mill architecture.

The erection of two-storeyed sheds for the accommodation of powered weaving continued until the most recent phase of building for the silk industry. Wood Street Mill, Macclesfield (Figure 90), built about 1900 and situated immediately adjacent to the site of the Button Mill, the first powered throwing mill in the town, is a fine example. In the construction of its two phases the mill also demonstrates the transition from a traditional structure to the free-standing, metal-frame form and has elements in common with the George Street mills. The mill was built of stock brick, with a pitched

Figure 90
*Wood Street Mill, Macclesfield, is a two-storeyed weaving mill which was built c 1900. It was enlarged in 1909 by a flat-roofed extension designed by Stott and Sons.*

Figure 91
*Green Street Mill, Macclesfield, was built in 1928 for powered Jacquard silk weaving. At the time of survey it still contained its original looms.*

slate roof, and regularly spaced tall windows on the Pickford Street elevation where walls are loadbearing. On the Wood Street elevation the windows are large and square, of similar design to those at George Street New Mill. For this reason the loadbearing capacity of the wall is diminished and compensated for by the support of the internal cast-iron columns.

The later phase, built in 1909 for J Barlow, manufacturers, was designed by the Manchester firm of architects, Stott and Sons. The extension was constructed of 'brick with stone dressings; bottom floor wood blocks on concrete; first floor wood; joists supported on steel girders and columns and boarded on top; and the roof supported on steel girders and iron columns, constructed with wood joists boarded on top and covered with patent vulcanite roofing.'[49] The use of both rolled steel and cast iron in this building echoes the design of George Street New Mill. The scale and design of the windows on the Wood Street elevation is repeated on the extension, for the same reason, which was to light the extended floor area and the Jacquard looms. Walls are of stock brick, laid to English

Garden Wall bond on all elevations, thus abandoning the tradition of using Flemish bond on public elevations. The roof is flat and in its construction was not designed to provide a source of light. Generally, the top storey of two-storeyed weaving sheds was utilised for ancillary processes, for example card storage and bobbin winding, which did not need to be well lit.

Green Street Mill (Figure 91) was also built for powered Jacquard weaving and in the late 1980s it housed the oldest powerlooms in Macclesfield, made by William Smith & Bros of Heywood and installed in the mill in the year of its construction, 1928.[50] The mill was constructed of stock brick, with steel stanchions enclosed within the brickwork supporting rolled-steel joists (Figure 92).[51] The ground floor and foundations are of concrete; the first floor is of timber, and the roofing is asphalt. Across a width of 9 m there is no intermediate support; the metal framework stands incorporated into the walling. Windows and wall are in about equal proportions, obviating the need for other loadbearing elements. Although essentially modern in construction, Green Street Mill and the second phase of Wood Street Mill echo the small scale and simple, functional style of the early Macclesfield textile mills.

**Single-storeyed sheds** The solution most widely adopted as suitable for housing not only powered looms but the various processes involving the use of heavy machinery such as in the preparatory stages of silk spinning was that of the single-storey north-light roof-truss shed (see also p 127). The design of this type of building arose out of the need to sit heavy machinery at ground-floor level and provide the maximum steady, clear light over a wide floor area. These single-storeyed sheds were constructed with cast-iron columns supporting the timber-framed roof trusses of saw-tooth-profile, multiple-span roofs. Light was diffused through glazing on the north faces of the roof pitches, whilst the south faces were covered in flags or slates. In Macclesfield, however, in spite of the advantages of this form of construction, there is evidence for the building of only four single-storeyed sheds of mid 19th-century date.[52] All were

Figure 92
*Green Street Mill, Macclesfield, was designed in 1928 and built as a two-storeyed mill with a structure of brick, steel stanchions and rolled-steel joists. It was designed to accommodate ten women workers in the winding room and twelve men in the weaving shed.*

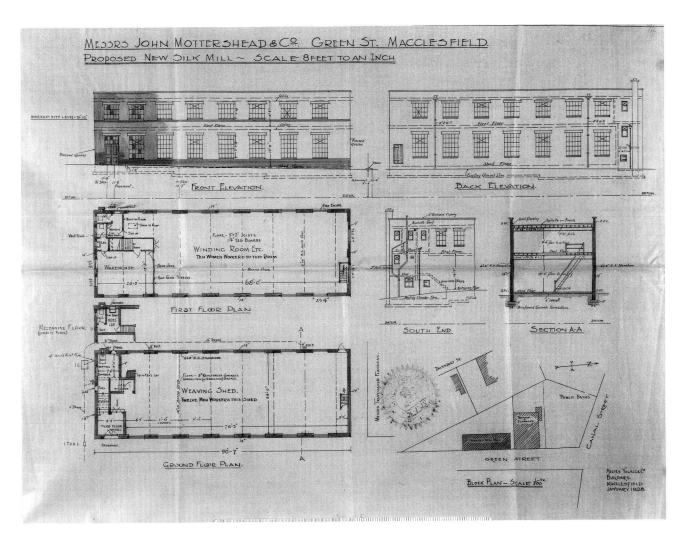

positioned at the rear of pre-existing sites: at Chester Road Mill (Figure 93), Oxford Road Mill, Royal George Mills, built for silk weaving, and Lower Heyes Mill, built for cotton weaving. In Congleton, sheds were at the rear of Dane Mill by this date, and at the Forge Mill site, although these sheds were used for silk-spinning processes.

Single-storeyed sheds were often situated in the angle formed by the L-shaped plan of a mill, standing sometimes on the infill of a redundant reservoir. This latter development occurred during the last period of building, during the 20th century, when steam power had been replaced by electricity. North-light sheds were also built, but more rarely, as structures independent of existing mill building, as at Buckley Street Mill and Ryle Street Mill, Macclesfield, and Victoria Mill, Congleton. Interestingly, Buckley Street Mill, an extensive shed, sixteen by eighteen bays, was built to house powered embroidery machinery by the firm of A W Hewetson's Ltd in 1932. Although sheds of this style were generally built for powered weaving, several were in fact

built by the silk industry for a number of processes, including the preparatory processes of silk spinning.

**Warehouses**

An increase in the building of warehouses in the late 19th and early 20th centuries occurred as a response to the expansion in the powered-weaving industry. Most of these were unremarkable additions to existing mill sites but two warehouses deserve mention because of their particular architectural and historical distinction. Hope Mill 'A' in Macclesfield, demolished in 1985, was built in 1876 for J O Nicholson, silk manufacturer and throwster, by the architect William Sugden.[53] As befitting a man whose father established the Nicholson Institute for the improvement of design in the silk industry, and who collaborated with William Morris in the production of the latter's damask silks, Hope Mill 'A' had more conscious elements of design than most other buildings of the silk industry in Macclesfield. The main Elizabeth Street elevation had attractive groupings of

Figure 93
*Mid 19th-century single-storeyed weaving sheds at the rear of Chester Road Mill, Macclesfield, with Oxford Road Mill in the background.*

triple-light windows with stone surrounds and mullions, arranged within two pedimented bays.

The Royal Silk Warehouse (Figure 94), standing in a commanding position on the west side of Waters Green, was built in 1903 by the firm of Robinson Brown, silk merchants.[54] A datestone above the main door is inscribed: 1903 R B. The building is probably unique in that it was the only retail warehouse known to have been built specifically for the sale of manufactured silk goods which could also be made up into garments on the premises, although wholesale and retail warehouses were built in Manchester during the same period for the sale of a wide variety of cloth. The prestigious function of this building, certainly in east Cheshire, is reflected in its commanding style and location.

The warehouse is four-storeyed, with a flat asphalt roof, and built of Accrington brick laid unusually to English bond on sandstone foundation walls on the main and return elevations. These three elevations are each subdivided by brick pilasters and framed by clasping corner pilasters, all of which are terminated by spherical stone finials which project above the parapet. The vertical lines are crossed by stone string-courses forming the continuous sills and lintels of each window. The rear elevation is of rough stock brick and does not have the same decorative treatment. The central main bay is surmounted by a single room which was originally roofed with a sail-vaulted dome, constructed of wood and covered with scalloped zinc.[55] The Italianate style of the external design is reflected

Figure 94
*The Royal Silk Warehouse, Waters Green, Macclesfield, was built in 1903 by the firm of Robinson Brown, silk merchants. It is the only warehouse in east Cheshire known to have been built specifically for the sale of manufactured silk goods.*

Figure 95
*Mid 19th-century wheel-house at Washford Mill, Buglawton, near Congleton.*

internally by the design of Corinthian capitals on the cast-iron columns. The entrance hall is embellished in an art nouveau style, with decorative door furniture on the panelled mahogany double doors and patterned tiles. Almost identical in style, and built in the same year, 1903, is Bond Street Mill, Macclesfield, but the treatment of this mill was more restrained in both construction and decoration.

The Royal Silk Warehouse is a fine example of the use of decorative brickwork and stonework, characteristic of even modest building for the silk industry during the late 19th and early 20th centuries. Varieties of glazed yellow and red brick were introduced from about the 1870s, incorporated into lintels and string-courses, as at Waters Green Mill, Macclesfield. Accrington brick was later used, generally with restraint, for the same effects, for example at Green Street Mill, Macclesfield, built in 1928, where it was used for walling up to the level of the ground-floor sills, and for the quoins, window sills and string-course between storeys.

Engineering blue brick was occasionally used for foundation walling, for example at Bond Street Mill, and for decorative effects. Moulded brickwork was also a particular characteristic of the façades of north-light truss weaving sheds, where the main elevations were often constructed with a blind arcading treatment, as at Buckley Street Mill, Oxford Road Mill, Bond Street Mill and Hurdsfield Road Mills, all situated in Macclesfield. Moulded stone architraves surrounding main entrances, and bearing date and name stones, are also typical features of the period. Stonework generally was used for decorative rather than structural reasons, in contrast to early 19th-century mills.

The buildings constructed during the final years of prosperity for the silk industry display the highest level of architectural embellishment for silk-mill architecture in east Cheshire. This characteristic is a development of the tradition where the finest quality of building seems almost always to have been associated with the process of silk weaving.

## Power systems in relation to the design of mill building

Clear distribution patterns emerge in the use of power systems in east Cheshire during the mid 19th century. Water power continued to make a significant contribution as a power system for textile mills both in the rural districts and in Congleton. Although it is not known when waterwheels in Congleton's silk mills became redundant, at least two mills, Flint Mill and Washford Mill (Figure 95), are known to have retained and used their waterwheels until the mid 20th century. Flint Mill (Figure 96), on the bank of the River Dane, has a history of multiple use, flint grinding, corn milling and silk throwing, with evidence for at least three different wheel positions. The primary wheel was housed in a basement wheelhouse, whereas the secondary wheels were on the outside of this wheelhouse. The latest wheel, which is still in place, remained operational until 1973. It is of the Poncelet type and was probably added in the mid 19th century. At Havannah Mills, Eaton, and Dane Mills, Bosley, both of which relied upon several wheels, and at Flint Mill, Buglawton, water-powered systems are known to have been renewed and replaced throughout this period. At Riverside Mill, Sutton, water power was installed as late as the 1870s, probably for driving calendering (pressing and finishing) machinery.

Despite the continued use of water power, none of the new mills built after 1826 in Macclesfield and Congleton, with the exception of Primrose Vale Mill, Congleton, of about 1828, appears to have been built as a water-powered mill. Steam power was preferred for a variety of reasons. It was more reliable and it enabled mills to be built on land away from the already congested water sources. However, the capacity of steam engines recorded in association with mills built after 1826 does not differ substantially from the horsepower recorded on mill sites in the late 18th and early 19th centuries. Advertisements for Macclesfield mills record several engines by

Figure 96
*The Flint Mill, Buglawton, near Congleton, has evidence for at least three different wheel positions. The latest wheel is cast iron and of the Poncelet type. It remained operational until 1973.*

various manufacturers: an engine of 12 horse-power by Thompson of Chesterfield, with 21 horsepower boilers, in a mill at Commongate;[56] one of 16 horsepower with metallic piston by Thompson in Oxford Road Mill;[57] one of 12 horsepower, also by Thompson, with a 17 horse-power boiler in Silk Street Mill[58] and an 8 horse-power engine with metallic piston by Galloway and Bowman (so far unlocated), in a mill in the Watercotes.[59] The relatively small capacities of these engines were considerably less than those of contemporary cotton mills, which ranged from about 30 to 100 horsepower. For east Cheshire silk mills the power ranged between about 6 and 30 horsepower, which evidently met the requirements of powered throwing machinery and looms housed in these mills, but was not in itself a catalyst for change in the specifications of mill building.

Contemporary comment on steam power testifies to its widespread use by 1828, and inter-estingly indicates early concern about the effects of industrial pollution:

> *The extra-ordinary circumstances [of the weather], the clouded atmosphere, the long rains, the fre-quency of lightening, have made some people think that the steam engines, which are working in great numbers in various parts of the world, do gener-ally cause a change for worse in the atmosphere ... The number in Great Britain alone is supposed to be ten thousand, which send up sulphurous and bitumous gasses.[60]*

Engine houses built to accommodate steam engines of relatively low capacity were corre-spondingly small in scale. Although many have been demolished, a number of engine houses do remain, particularly where the engine has been housed in the basement or lower storey of a mill wing as at Albion Mill (as a secondary phase), and the 1820s Victoria Mills, both in Macclesfield. However, all trace of the engines have disappeared, except occasionally for the cir-cumscribed arc of the flywheel against the wall, as at the old Victoria Mills and at Pitt Street Mill, Macclesfield, or the stone engine-mounting block at Albion Mill.

In Congleton two engine houses of particu-lar significance and of greatly contrasting struc-ture remain. At the Old Mill, the engine house which was almost certainly added by the new owner, Samuel Pearson, in the 1830s, to house a single-beam engine, is architecturally the most decorative engine house in east Cheshire (Figure 97). The semicircular-arched window on the end elevation has an imposing moulded sandstone surround; on the same elevation the parapet is surmounted by elaborate moulded stonework in the form of a scalloped shell

**Figure 97**
*This architecturally distin-guished engine house at the Old Mill, Congleton, was almost certainly added by Samuel Pearson in the 1830s. It housed a small beam engine of which only the beam floor survives.*

**Figure 98**
*The engine house at Higher Washford Mill, Buglawton, near Congleton, is a simple brick structure contained within the ground floor of the mill. It may have been similar to other small engine houses, the removal of which would have left little or no trace of the source of power in the mill.*

flanked by two scrolls with stone urns at either end, only one of which now remains. Internally the building retains the beam floor.

In contrast, at Higher Washford Mill an engine house of no structural distinction but possibly of greater significance survives as a free-standing square brick-built enclosure at ground-floor/basement level in the mill (Figure 98) and probably housed a low-capacity vertical cylinder engine. The complete removal of this structure would leave little or no trace of its existence, which may indicate why little evidence remains of the housing of primary drive systems in a number of small mills.

In Macclesfield two extant engine houses may be typical of others now demolished. At Sutton Mill, the engine house and neighbouring boiler house remain enclosed in the mill yard (Figure 99). At London Road Mill, the engine house is attached to the rear of the mill (Figure 100). Both engine houses have the semicircular-arched opening which identifies engine house architecture of the mid 19th century. Within the London Road engine house are the mounting block, cast-iron frame and flywheel (Figure 101) of the mid 19th-century vertical single-cylinder steam engine recorded in later documents as of 12 horsepower.[61] These also give details of the gearing, shafting, gas and steam pipes running throughout the mill. It is probable that this type of engine was common in mills of this period which required relatively low horsepower. Chimneys of the mid 19th century were typically hexagonal or octagonal in plan, as at Victoria Mills, Macclesfield, Victoria Mill, Congleton, and Dane Mill, Congleton.

Figure 99 *(Below left)*
*The engine house at Sutton Mill, Macclesfield, is tall with a semicircular-headed window typical of engine houses of the mid 19th century.*

Figure 100 *(Left)*
*The engine house at London Road Mill, Macclesfield, is a small extension at the rear of the mill.*

Figure 101 *(Below)*
*The engine house at London Road Mill, Macclesfield, contains the flywheel and frame of a small single-cylinder vertical steam engine.*

During the late 19th century the development of power systems for the silk industry was unremarkable. In Congleton the deteriorating silk industry was replaced as a major concern in the town by fustian cutting (see p 104). Since fustian cutting was, until the early 20th century, a hand process, new mills built for this industry were built without power systems. In Macclesfield changes or extensions to power systems in the form of new building are hardly marked in the registration of building plans, which date from 1852, even where site extension might indicate that modifications were needed. The nature of building for the silk industry during this period, in comparison with the cotton industry, was generally small scale and *ad hoc*. In consequence, the power requirements for silk-mill sites generally remained within the upper limit of about 40 horsepower, recorded at Park Green Mill, Macclesfield, in 1906. As a result it would appear that small, vertical or horizontal single-cylinder steam engines, and even beam engines, as at Bridge Street Mills,[62] continued to supply these needs until and even after the introduction of gas and electric power.

There is very little evidence for the use of gas as the source of power for primary drive systems, although it had been used to provide heating and lighting in mills since the early 19th century. In 1894, the Minutes of the Macclesfield Silk Manufacturing Society, occupants of London Road Mill, recorded that 'Mr Johnson procure a gas engine at the best possible price and that he fix the same on the ground floor and correct the shafting'. The engine seems to have been a substitute for the 12 horsepower steam engine. Powerlooms were gradually installed by the Society at the London Road Mill from 1901. In May 1904, about two months after the gas engine had been fitted, the Minutes recorded 'that the saving of the gas engine amounted to about £2 a week'.[63] A Crossley gas engine[64] was installed for James Arnold & Co at Wood Street Mill, Macclesfield, which was built about 1900 for the accommodation of powered Jacquard looms. In 1920, a plan was registered for the building of a new engine house,[65] which shows the removal of a boiler. This would indicate the replacement of a steam engine by the gas engine. The original wing of the mill, on Wood Street, measured 10 m by 40 m, but these measurements can only be related to the earlier phase of primary drive. As far as is known, no mill or shed was built to be powered by a gas engine.

In 1916 it was reported that the Macclesfield Electricity Company Ltd, which had been established in April 1914, was supplying over 1,300 horsepower and lighting 7,000 lamps daily in Macclesfield.[66] Wm Frost and Sons Ltd, throwsters, installed electricity as early as 1914 in Park Green Mill, Macclesfield, but initially for lighting only. The date for the first use of electricity for machinery drive is not known. In 1928, Green Street Mill, Macclesfield, was built to be powered by an electric generator housed in a small shed attached to the rear of the mill. The drive to the looms was and still is supplied by horizontal line shafting. Since only two new sites were developed after this date, at Goodall Street Mill and Buckley Street Mill, and since both these buildings were for the housing of embroidery and making-up processes, the application of electricity to drive machinery cannot be considered as having affected the design of mill building. The extent and capacity of weaving sheds added on existing sites may have been influenced by the use of electricity, but they do not, in their variation of size, show any significant change from sheds constructed during the phase of steam power.

## Patterns of late 19th and early 20th-century mill building

In Macclesfield after the depression of the 1860s almost all new textile-associated building was for silk weaving or warehousing. New building in the outlying districts was for cotton processing (see Chapter Five), except at Langley, where silk finishing and weaving predominated. Of ten new mills erected in Congleton during this period, six were built for fustian cutting (see p 104), and three were built for silk processing: Albert Mill in 1871, replaced by Edward Mill in 1924, Dane Bridge Mill about 1875, and Roldane Mill in 1934, for making up garments from fabric knitted at the adjacent Old Mill site.

For Macclesfield borough, a wider perspective on the overall picture of building is possible because of the survival of building plan registrations from 1852. These show a flourishing building trade involved with the erection of weaving-shed extensions, warehouses, toilet and office blocks, boiler houses and chimneys, in addition to ten new mills on new sites. From 1852 to 1890, after which the regulations changed, plans were registered for the building of five new mills, ten weaving sheds, four buildings categorised as 'house and weaving shed', five warehouses, three dyehouses, two boiler/engine houses and one mill chimney. The registration of plans in this period was not compulsory; alternative evidence indicates that ten new mills were built during this period rather than five, so that the registrations account for only one half of that number. All the plans for new mills – Knight Street Mill in 1853, St George's Street Mill in 1853, Waters Green New Mill in 1875, Elizabeth Street Mill in 1878 and George Street New Mill by 1885 – were registered by firms already established in the silk industry. The first three of these mills were probably built for silk throwing, Elizabeth Street Mill for powered weaving and George Street New Mill for powered Jacquard weaving. Other registrations reflect the trend towards building for powered weaving, in which the greatest activity took place during the post-depression years of 1875 to 1890. Only a fraction of the building for the dyeing industry is recorded.

Changes or extensions to power systems are hardly marked. Between 1890 and 1947 almost all new building was for powered weaving. The registrations show plans for five of the eleven new mills built during this period: Bond Street Mill in 1903, Bank Street Mill in 1923, Buckley Street Mill in 1932 and Goodall Street Mill in 1933. About sixty-five site extensions, ten WC blocks and ten warehouses were registered, all in association with existing mills. Site extensions, easily the most common form of building development for the industry at this time, included at least seventeen weaving sheds; other buildings were for warping, finishing, calendering, offices and unspecified uses. The last application for a weaving shed, built at the rear of George Street, was registered in 1949, but by 1947 applications for change of use began to appear, the most frequent being the application for conversion of mill premises to light engineering use.

Figure 102
*The area around Worrall Street, Congleton, became a centre for fustian mills. This aerial view shows Shepherds Mill (1870s) in the foreground, Fair Mill (1870s), centre, and Riverside Mill (1878–87), centre right, all built for fustian cutting, whilst to the left of this group is Meadow Mill which was built in 1860, probably for silk throwing, but was subsequently used for fustian cutting. Stonehouse Green Mill and Brook Mills can be seen in the distance.*

Figure 103 *(Above)*
*Riverside Mill, Congleton,*
*was built by the firm of*
*Collinge & Co, fustian*
*cutters, between 1878 and*
*1887.*

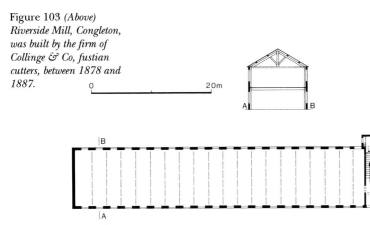

Figure 104 *(Right)*
*Fair Mill, Congleton, was*
*built in the 1870s and is*
*typical of the long and*
*narrow fustian mills.*

The pattern is one of building for the powered weaving industry and the building types are a continuation of those established during the mid to late years of the 19th century, that is, the two-storey weaving shed and the north-light truss, single-storey weaving shed. This pattern of building extensions is reflected to a certain extent in Congleton, for the silk-spinning and ribbon-weaving industries. Many of the mills have extensions and minor alterations, but these additional constructions are often of Second World War date, when the mills were commandeered as billets for American troops, or were added more recently for the industrial reuse of the mills. In Congleton, however, a distinct and characteristic building type can be identified, erected after 1867, when the fustian-cutting industry was introduced to the town.

## Fustian mills

The decline in the numbers employed in the Congleton silk industry in the mid 19th century created a need for alternative industry. In 1867 Thomas and John Shepherd of Royton in

Lancashire brought their fustian-cutting business to Congleton and set up in a mill at Eaton Bank, probably the Meadow Mill, formerly a silk-throwing mill[67] (see below). By 1874 there were six fustian-cutting firms established in the town.[68] One of the largest firms was that of Collinge and Co who built the Riverside Mill between 1878 and 1887. This mill stands out in design amongst what are very simple buildings (Figure 102). Other notable firms were owned by the Jackson family, fustian and velvet cutters. In 1924, Fred Jackson occupied Moor Street, Wallworth Bank, Park Street, Spindle Street and Silk Street Mills for velvet cutting, whilst Annie Jackson and Son occupied Victoria Street Mill and William Jackson and Sons occupied Lawton Street Mill.

Fustian, supposedly named after Fostat, a suburb of Cairo from where it is said to have originated, is a thick twilled union cloth, formerly cotton and linen but which could include silk, which is woven in such a fashion that a part of its weft is close to the surface and can be cut to form a nap. The cutting is now performed by a machine successfully introduced in the mid 20th century, but was previously performed by hand. The cloth was laid on long tables and the fustian cutter slit the weft with a long slender knife. The knife needed to pass along the whole length of the cloth many times before the weft across its entire width was cut and consequently the cutter walked up and down the room many times in one day. The process was described as it was carried out by the Shepherd family in Meadow Mill in 1887:

> *The rolls of material, either cotton or silk, usually measuring 100 yards, are manufactured in the Lancashire districts. These are tightly stretched on narrow frames of different lengths. The cutters knife consists of a piece of delicate flexible steel, slotted into the guide which holds the point in its proper groove. This is taken by the cutter down the whole length of the frame running along the material, over which it produces a soft, rich pile. After cutting the material is taken to another department where the interesting process of stiffening and drying is proceeded with, and the pieces made up ready for the dyer.*[69]

The skill of the work lay in being able to keep the knife in the line of the wefts being cut. It therefore placed a great strain upon the eyes of the cutter, especially at times when artificial light was needed. This took the form of flickering gas light and a candle at each end of the table. To supplement this the cutter also wore a candle on his hat, and those who still remember the fustian mills in Congleton today

describe how the cutters' candles could be seen passing from window to window along the length of the mill.

Fustian mills are simple in design. The foremost requisite was for a long, uninterrupted floor space on which the cutting tables could be erected. Shepherd Mills and Fair Mill, two mills erected for fustian cutting on Worrall Street, Congleton, in the 1870s, are 55·8 m and 49 m in length respectively and the two ranges of Riverside Mill are 50 m and 51 m long (Figure 103). In relation to their length these mills are narrow, Riverside Mill being the widest at 11·8 m and Fair Mill the narrowest at 8 m. Built of brick, fustian mills are either two or three storeys high and have regular fenestration (Figure 104). Characteristic features of the later fustian mills are the wide, segmental-arched windows, highlighted in red Accrington brick or, in the case of Riverside Mill, blue brick (see Figure 103). Roof trusses are generally of king-post type (Figure 105), although Riverside Mill has a queen-post truss to enable the roof space to be used for warehousing. The floors are of timber and, because of the amount of walking the cutter needed to do, are extremely thick. The floorboards at Fair Mill are 100 mm thick. As with mills used for early silk processing, these mills stand as simple rectangular or L-shaped structures with little or no ancillary building.

Fustian cutting continued in Congleton into the early part of the 20th century, carried out in many of the old silk mills as well as in purpose-built mills. Today these mills are used for a variety of other small industries.

Figure 105
*A view of the top floor of Shepherds Mill, Congleton, built in the 1870s, emphasises the length of floor space needed to house fustian-cutting tables. Only the lower section of the trusses are shown here but like most fustian mills they are of king-post type.*

# 5   HOUSING THE COTTON INDUSTRY 1826–1950

William Fairbairn wrote in 1863 that, 'Irrespective of the external appearance, the results of the improvements in mill architecture were manifest in ... the improvements that were introduced in the general arrangements of the buildings, their adaptation for the reception of the different kinds of machinery; security from fire and other requisites for carrying on a large and successful manufacture.'[1] His comments related to mill building nationwide, but were as true for the cotton mills of east Cheshire as they were for the rest of the country. The continued exploration of the use of cast-iron for structural members and for fireproofing, as well as the upgrading and adaptation of power systems to drive greater and more varied machinery, formed the basis for further developments in east Cheshire cotton-mill building. These developments, most of them pioneered in Lancashire, by then the major centre of Britain's cotton industry, altered the design and scale of cotton mills so that they less and less resembled those of the silk industry, and by the end of the 19th century the two were generally architecturally distinct.

## The development of the cotton industry in east Cheshire

The cotton industry in east Cheshire was seriously affected by both the post-war slump in the years following the Napoleonic Wars and the depression of the late 1820s (see p 12). In Macclesfield and Congleton, where cotton production was comparatively small scale, firms were forced out of business and the industry never recovered. At the beginning of the 19th century,

thirteen cotton firms had been established in Macclesfield, but by 1834 there were only three.[2] In Congleton there were six in 1800 but only one by 1834.[3] The national economic recovery in the mid 1830s was accompanied by the strengthening of the cotton industry in outlying districts to the north of Macclesfield and Congleton rather than in the towns themselves. Thus the east Cheshire cotton industry came to be centred in Styal, Disley, Rainow, Kettleshulme and, mainly, Bollington (see Figure 1). In these centres spinning cotton was the principal activity, although powered weaving was introduced to several large spinning sites during the 1830s. Additionally there were the more specialised products of fine cotton yarn for lace, produced in Bollington, most notably at Waterhouse Mill by the firm of Thomas Oliver, and candlewick, produced in Disley and by the Sheldon family at Lumbhole Mill, Kettleshulme.

Raw cotton was shipped, mainly from the United States, to the port of Liverpool from where it was distributed and sold by hundreds of brokers and merchants from all the major centres in Britain and abroad.[4] One shipping company used by the Swindells family was that of Andrew Low & Co, who, for example, in April 1834 shipped eighteen bags of Sea Island cotton, 'all under deck', from the port of Savannah, Georgia, to Liverpool. The total cost was £425 13s 9d, and it was the Swindells' responsibility to insure their cargo.[5] At the other end of the production process, finished goods were sent to Manchester for sale by partners, agents or warehousemen, depending on what particular arrangement any individual firm had. In the second half of the 19th century Manchester eclipsed London as the most important centre for the sale of cotton cloth and yarn.[6] Raw and finished goods were moved by horse and cart, and the opening of the Macclesfield Canal in 1831 meant that goods could be moved by barge. However, by the middle of the 19th century the canal was eclipsed by the railway. Macclesfield had rail communication from 1845 onwards when the Manchester and Birmingham Railway connected the town to Manchester, and in 1849 Macclesfield and Congleton were linked to the Potteries by the North Staffordshire Railway. There was no railway to Bollington until 1872 when a branch of the Sheffield and Lincolnshire Railway was laid from Marple to Macclesfield.

Although these cotton-producing areas were on the edge of the Lancashire cotton industry, which was increasing in strength, building bigger mills and developing large-scale production, perhaps the most important factor in the move of the cotton industry to outlying districts of east Cheshire was the influence of a few cotton-manufacturing families. These families, most notably the Gregs and the Swindells, but to a lesser extent the Olivers, Woods and Sheldons, controlled the industry in east Cheshire, ensuring the supremacy of cotton production in these districts.

The Greg family dominated the cotton industry in Wilmslow from Quarry Bank Mill at Styal, and also purchased Lowerhouse Mill, Bollington, in 1832. Outside east Cheshire they took over Low Mill at Caton near Lancaster from 1817, Lancaster Mill at Lancaster from 1822, a mill at Bury in 1827, and a mill in Ancoats, Manchester, in the mid 1820s. They purchased a Derbyshire thread mill at Calver around the middle of the century, selling it in 1864, and took over a mill at Reddish, near Stockport, originally built by the Gregs for letting, in 1847.[7] In 1844 the French commentator Faucher said that the Greg concern held 'first rank among the manufacturers. It consumes nearly four million pounds weight in cotton, possesses five factories, four thousand power looms and employs more than two thousand people.'[8] The Swindells family dominated the cotton industry in Bollington. They occupied or owned, with various partners, Ingersley Vale Mill and Rainow Mill from 1821 and 1822 respectively until 1841, Higher and Lower Mills from 1832 until 1859 and Waterhouse Mill, in partnership with Thomas Oliver, from around 1832 until 1841. They built Clarence Mill with their partners, the Brooke family, in 1834–8, extending it in 1841, 1854 and 1877 (Figure 106), and built the Adelphi Mill in 1856.

There were smaller firms who owned or leased smaller premises, often only part of a mill: for example, James Leigh, a cotton spinner

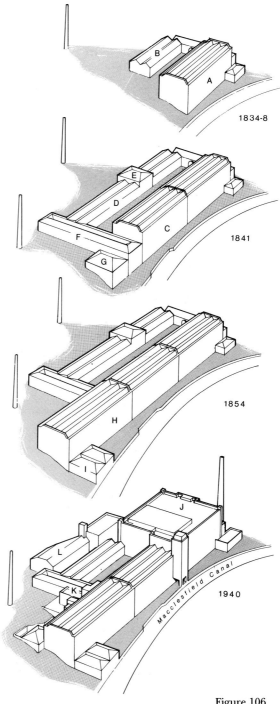

| | | | | |
|---|---|---|---|---|
| **A** | 1834-8 Spinning mill | | **G** | 1841 Gas retort |
| **B** | 1834-8 Weaving mill | | **H** | 1854 Spinning mill |
| **C** | 1841 Spinning mill | | **I** | 1854 Boat house |
| **D** | 1841 Weaving mill | | **J** | 1877 Spinning mill |
| **E** | 1841 Delivery room | | **K** | 1877 Engine house |
| **F** | 1841 Boiler house, engine house, mechanics shop, smithy and dressing room | | **L** | 1930s Canteen |

Figure 106
*Clarence Mill, Bollington, was built and developed by the Swindells family from 1834 onwards.*

who occupied Rainow Mill, Rainow, in the 1840s;[9] George Holden, a cotton spinner who was leasing part of the Oak Bank Mill, Bollington, when it was destroyed by fire in October 1882;[10] and Hooton and Hocknell, cotton manufacturers, who occupied part of Paradise Mill, Macclesfield, in 1867 and purchased it in 1870.[11]

The larger firms which came to dominate the east Cheshire cotton industry had several advantages over the smaller ones. Economies of scale meant that as production capacity was increased, production costs per unit remained the same or decreased. The larger companies were also more financially resilient in times of recession, and in times of expansion had a larger pool of capital to draw upon. Moreover, being financially more stable, the banks considered them to be more creditworthy.[12] There was also an advantage in dominating the local labour market and the dependency this engendered amongst the work-force.

These larger east Cheshire firms were careful not to lose those elements which were advantageous to the smaller concern, especially direct supervision of day-to-day business and the ability to keep down capital costs by purchasing sufficient quantities of secondhand machinery.[13] Size was not the sole criterion for success since foresight and initiative were crucial, particularly in the adoption of new technology. A note in the minutes of a meeting of the board of Swindells and Brooke, stating that they should 'embrace every opportunity of ascertaining the merits of using sized warps', serves to show how new developments were keenly pursued to assess their worth.[14]

### Specialisation and amalgamation

Throughout the second half of the 19th century the cotton industry nationally, dominated by Lancashire, turned away from the integration of spinning and weaving on one site, towards specialisation. The spinning industry was increasingly spinning yarn for the open market, rather than for weaving. Meanwhile, the weaving industry concentrated on the production of calico and coloured goods, looking to purchase yarn rather than spin it on site. The emphasis for the specialised firms came to be placed on producing large quantities of a limited range of goods for export, leaving the surviving integrated firms to produce a wide range of goods for the fluctuating home market.[15] This specialisation made it increasingly difficult for the relatively small investor to compete at the highest level. The large amounts of capital needed were beyond his individual means. However, by forming a joint-stock company with other investors, under

legislation of 1856 and 1862 which limited the amount of money they could lose, their capital could be relatively safely pooled.[16]

East Cheshire cotton-producing firms remained exclusively private, family concerns until 1862 when a joint-stock company was formed to build the Beehive Mill in Bollington. It was followed in 1865 by the Rainow Spinning Company Ltd and the Globe Cotton Spinning and Manufacturing Company Ltd. In 1866 Samuel Greg and Company Ltd was formed, followed in 1876 by Brooke Swindells and Company Ltd, which erected the 1877 extension to Clarence Mill. On the whole, these companies did not prove to be a success. Samuel Greg and Company Ltd, which became Lowerhouse Mills Company Ltd in 1910, survived until 1942, and the Globe Cotton Spinning and Manufacturing Company until 1933. However, the Rainow Spinning Company Ltd only survived until 1869. Brooke Swindells & Company was formed by Martin Swindells and Joseph Brooke, amongst others. They issued a prospectus aimed at encouraging the purchase of £10 shares in an effort to raise £120,000 to cover building costs. Their optimism proved to be unfounded and the company went into liquidation in January 1881, followed in around 1883 by the Bollington Cotton Spinning and Manufacturing Company.[17]

It has been argued that the limited success of joint-stock companies in the cotton industry was largely the result of the lack of the direct, self-interested management necessary to survive turbulent trading conditions in the late 19th century.[18] George Cawley Swindells blamed the failure of Brooke Swindells and Company Ltd on the replacement of owners by managers.[19] Their failure marked the end of cotton-mill building in east Cheshire and, although the Lancashire industry continued to build and remained relatively healthy into the 1920s, the east Cheshire cotton-spinning companies increasingly struggled to survive.

Reflecting the national trend, east Cheshire companies generally came to specialise in either yarn or cloth production. The major Bollington firms reverted to spinning, investing in new mules and ring-spinning frames. By the time of the Second World War 53,000 mule spindles and 27,000 ring-doubling spindles were employed at Clarence Mill, and 57,000 mule spindles and 20,000 ring-doubling spindles at Waterhouse Mill.[20] However, in order to survive, these spinning companies joined the Fine Cotton Spinners and Doublers Association Ltd (later the Fine Spinners and Doublers Ltd). This association, formed in 1898, was one of several national amalgamations of companies pioneered by Horrocks of Preston in 1887[21] and created in an attempt to reduce competition between British companies in order to increase their competitiveness abroad.

Under the Fine Cotton Spinners and Doublers Association Ltd, George Swindells & Co, owners of the Clarence and Adelphi Mills, Bollington, and Thomas Oliver & Sons, owners of Waterhouse Mill, came under national, combined control although they were still run at a local level by the owning companies. Although no significant new building was undertaken, the company invested heavily in new machinery, as well as in research and development, building a research establishment at Clarence Mill in the early 20th century. The company specialised, as traditionally Thomas Oliver & Sons had done, in the spinning of extremely fine yarns for lace and muslins, and by the 1940s had developed 'Sylex', a cotton yarn so fine that they could claim it was comparable to silk. Encouraged by the Cotton Spinning Industry Act of 1936 which, in an attempt to cope with the decline in the cotton-spinning industry, aimed to reduce the number of spindles in use nationally, the Fine Cotton Spinners and Doublers Association looked to diversify their production. In 1938 Clarence Mill was partly converted for the production of spun silk yarn and by 1949 Adelphi Mill housed entirely silk-spinning machinery, with a twisting capacity of 25,000 spindles. The company also spun man-made fibres in its east Cheshire mills, including nylon and its own rayon yarn known as Fiscobelle.

The Gregs at Quarry Bank Mill, Styal, were not part of this national association. After dabbling briefly with ring spinning in the late 1880s and early 1890s, they abandoned spinning altogether in 1894 and turned to weaving. They had installed 465 powerlooms by 1909 and by 1914 had added to them 109 automatic Northrop looms.[22] At Lower Heyes Mill in Macclesfield the Globe Cotton Spinning and Manufacturing Company also specialised in weaving, mainly of calico, operating 1,560 looms by 1916.[23] This company was a Manchester-based, joint-stock company formed in 1865 to purchase Lower Heyes Mill and in 1867 built a large weaving shed on an adjoining site (see below).[24] They also owned or leased part of Clarence Mill for a short time from around 1889 to 1894[25] but remained at Lower Heyes Mill until 1933 when the company seems to have gone out of business.

By the mid 1970s the cotton industry in east Cheshire had completely died save for a small amount of spinning and weaving which is carried out at Quarry Bank Mill, not now in order to compete in the world or even the domestic market, but as part of its function as an industrial museum. Most cotton firms established in east Cheshire at the end of the 18th century and the beginning of the 19th century were small concerns housed in one mill or one floor of a mill. They were likely to be owned by someone more experienced in the silk industry. As the 19th century progressed, however, the shadow of the Lancashire industry grew larger and the small and weak east Cheshire companies could not compete and died out. The smaller group of larger east Cheshire cotton companies which expanded in the middle of the 19th century were not, by and large, new companies, but established concerns that had survived the depressions of the early 19th century.

That east Cheshire companies could prosper serves to show that it was not essential to be based in the great Lancashire cotton spinning and weaving districts. By knowing their market, by being flexible and efficient in production, by knowing when to expand or reorganise, and by making the most of communications by road, rail and canal, it was possible for east Cheshire companies to compete successfully against Lancashire companies and survive. The Greg family based at Quarry Bank Mill and the Swindells family of Bollington were cotton manufacturers of national and, certainly in the case of the Greg family, international importance.

## Processes in relation to the design of mill building

High profits in the cotton industry were generally achieved through high productive capacity. This meant that manufacturers needed ever more efficient machinery in order to reduce production costs to a minimum. Millowners saw the development of both the powerloom and the automatic or self-acting mule as major steps in increasing productivity whilst reducing labour costs.

Two developments in mule-spinning technology brought about increased productivity. The mule had been partly powered since the 1790s (see p 41). However, the putting-up, or second part of the spinning cycle in which the spun cotton was wound on to the cop by means of the return of the carriage, remained a skilled, manually powered operation. This limited the number of spindles a spinner could control. Perhaps in the late 1820s, but certainly by 1832,[26] it had been realised that the spinner could be aided by partially powering the putting-up motion in such a way that although less manual power was needed the action remained under the spinner's control. This development allowed the mule to increase in size from approximately 350 to around 600 spindles.

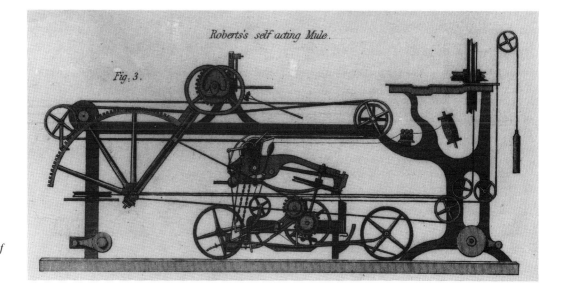

Figure 107
*The self-acting mule, developed between 1825 and 1830 by Richard Roberts, a Manchester engineer, automatically performed the full cycle of the cotton-spinning process.*

In 1825 Richard Roberts, a well-established Manchester engineer, was approached by a group of millowners and commissioned to invent a wholly self-acting mule which could run through the full cycle of the spinning process under power, and which could control automatically the rate at which the spun yarn was wound on to the cop and the amount of slack yarn left after the completion of the draw. In 1830 Roberts obtained a second patent for a self-acting mule which was powerful enough to accelerate the spindles and cops up to 5,000 revolutions per minute whilst at the same time being sensitive enough to wind the spun yarn correctly on to the cop at slow speeds. Mules could then be built with around 1,000 spindles. Initially the self-acting mule was most successfully used in the spinning of coarse yarn and it was some time, it is not clear how long, before it was able to spin the finest yarns. In consequence the part-acting mule was only gradually superseded (Figure 107).[27]

The throstle continued to be used in conjunction with the mule. Whereas the mule could easily provide fine cotton yarns, for some cloths a coarse yarn was needed, at least for the warp. For this the throstle was better suited than the mule, and it was used in east Cheshire mills until the widespread introduction of the ring-spinning frame in the last decade of the 19th century. In general, throstle spindles in east Cheshire were outnumbered by mule spindles. The first mill at Clarence Mill, Bollington, completed in 1838, was planned to house 6,400 throstle spindles and 8,640 mule spindles.[28] Lower Heyes Mill, Macclesfield, contained 536 throstle spindles in 1857 and 4,400 mule spin-

dles,[29] and, as a final example, the 1877 mill at Clarence Mill contained 20,724 throstle spindles and 36,992 mule spindles when it was advertised for sale in 1882.[30]

The mule remained the preferred spinning machine of the British cotton industry until the first decades of the 20th century. By this time, however, the industry worldwide had adopted the ring-spinning frame. This machine was developed in the United States of America by John Thorpe in 1828, but did not generally find favour until the bearings and spindles were improved in the later 19th century. The ring spinning of cotton yarn used a technique evolved from the throstle. A wire hook, or traveller, through which the thread passed, rotated within a metal ring positioned around the base of the receiving spindle. As the traveller turned, the yarn ballooned out and the resulting air drag slowed down the traveller causing a difference in the turning speed of the traveller and the spindle. Thus a twist was imparted to the thread.[31] This technique was particularly successful in spinning strong yarns and its slow adoption in Britain resulted in the industry losing ground to foreign competition.

The desire of cotton manufacturers to increase spinning productivity in the early to mid 19th century was partly prompted by a growing foreign market and partly by the need to supply the weaving industry which expanded following the introduction of powerlooms. The first patents for a powered broadloom for weaving cotton were taken out by Edmund Cartwright in the 1780s, but problems were encountered in sizing the warp as well as in making the powered movements precise, especially in driving the shuttle and beating up the weft. These problems were largely overcome by 1813, mainly owing to a series of inventions by Henry Marsland, William Horrocks and William Radcliffe, of Stockport. Nevertheless, it was not until the 1820s that powerlooms for the weaving of cotton cloth were made sufficiently reliable to come into widespread use.[32] The successful introduction of the powerloom marked the beginning of the decline of the domestic, hand-loom, cotton-weaving industry and a time of distress and hardship for handloom weavers. By 1840 there were very few handloom weavers in the area.[33]

By 1834 several firms in east Cheshire had introduced powered weaving. Charles and William Vaudrey were listed in Pigot and Co's trade directory of that year as 'cotton spinners and manufacturers' in Buglawton (at Bath Vale Mill), and Moseley and Howard of Waterside Mill, Disley, are similarly listed. Whilst these entries may include hand weaving, several are more specific. The Wood brothers, Joseph Watters and Co, Swindells and Brooke, and Samuel Greg and Co were entered as being cotton spinners and 'manufacturers by power'.[34]

Watters and Lund who in 1823 erected Crompton Road Mill, Macclesfield, for power-loom weaving,[35] and housed 130 powerlooms there in 1826 (see p 53), were possibly the first firm to weave cotton by power in east Cheshire. The Swindells had introduced powered weaving to complement their cotton-spinning business by 1826. In that year the *Macclesfield Courier and Herald* reported that troops were called to Ingersley Vale Mill, Rainow, then occupied by Fernley and Swindells. Mr Fernley, in the light of the deliberate smashing of some looms in Macclesfield by those opposed to the introduction of powered weaving, was 'under the greatest apprehension, from information he had received, that an attack would that night be made on their premises which contained 330 power looms'. In the event the attack did not occur.[36] Samuel Greg Junior was the first of the Greg family to install powerlooms: he began weaving cotton at Lowerhouse Mill, Bollington, in 1832, four years before Robert Hyde Greg introduced them at Quarry Bank Mill, Styal.

In general, during the middle part of the 19th century, many east Cheshire cotton firms added powered weaving to complement their spinning, carrying out both operations on the one site. The Swindells found that the integration of spinning and weaving on one site, as opposed to having them in different factories, improved efficiency 'for various reasons but chiefly the advantage we shall have over and above anything we can have as the works now

are'.[37] Improvements in the efficiency of machinery were also helping to reduce production costs. In an attempt to see how efficiency had improved, the Swindells compared the cost and output of machinery at Clarence Mill in 1842 with that at their Ingersley Vale Mill in 1821. It was calculated that whereas it had taken £2,100 worth of machinery to produce 1,000lbs of yarn at Ingersley Vale Mill, it took £1,552 16s worth of machinery to produce 1,600lbs of yarn at Clarence Mill, and that to have produced the latter amount of yarn at Ingersley Vale Mill would have required machinery worth £3,360. In other words, the efficiency of the machinery and production had more than doubled in twenty-one years. Furthermore they estimated that the machinery ordered for the new end of Clarence Mill in 1841, 'will be at least 20% better both as to principle and durability, and capable of producing yarn of superior quality'. It was also noted that 'The present machinery will have an advantage as to the cost of labour in proportion to the amount it produces; that is to say, that labour goes hand in hand with machinery — cheap machinery is attended with cheap labour.'[38]

## Mill architecture

There are four significant aspects to east Cheshire's cotton-mill architecture from 1826 onwards: first, an increase in the size and scale of cotton mills; second, the further development of cast iron in the construction of fireproof industrial buildings; third, the gradual introduction of weaving sheds as additions to existing sites; and fourth, the improved systems by which these mills were powered. Together these changes brought about an evolution of the housing of cotton production from the small, traditionally constructed mills of the late 18th and early 19th centuries, used in common with silk manufactories, to the great mills built on the 'Oldham model'[39] and now seen as typical of British cotton mills.

### Multi-storeyed mills

In the early 19th century a few cotton mills in east Cheshire were built with a width slightly greater than that of earlier mills. As already noted (see p 53), Pickford Street 'A' Mill, Crompton Road Mill and Depot Mill in Macclesfield, all built before 1826, were 11 m wide, wider than most east Cheshire mills of the time. Lowerhouse Mill, Bollington, was built in 1818, 12 m wide internally, and Lumbhole Mill, Kettleshulme was built between 1823 and 1835 10·5 m wide internally (see p 53). These small increases in width did not represent a new pattern in mill design.

It was with the building of the extension to the Higher Mill at Bollington, 13·2 m wide internally and probably dating from the 1830s (Figure 108), and the first Clarence Mill, built over the period 1834 to 1838, and 16·5 m wide, that there

was a distinct increase in cotton-mill width to almost twice that of early cotton mills. They were followed by the 1841 and 1854 extensions to Clarence Mill, both 16·5 m wide (Figure 109).

These buildings, each five storeys high, were around 8 m to 8·5 m wider than mills of the late 18th and early 19th centuries and are generally

Figure 108
*Higher Mill, Bollington, erected c1835, is 13·2 m wide internally, almost twice the width of earlier cotton mills.*

Figure 109
*This plan of Clarence Mill, Bollington, was drawn by the firm of Stott and Son in 1877. It shows the 1834–8 mill (right front) and its 1841 extension (centre front). To the rear of these mills are the 1834–8 and 1841 weaving mills. It also shows the 1854 fireproof mill (left front).*

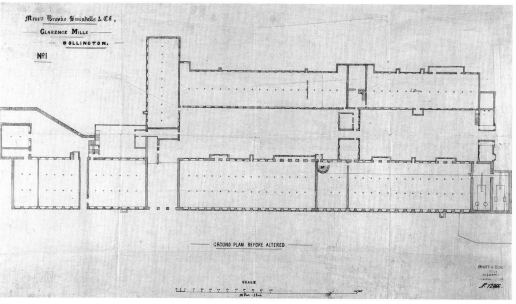

112

similar to each other in design. Cast iron was used to support the increase in span, either in the form of beams and columns in a fireproof design (see below) or in the form of columns supporting timber beams. The 1841 extension to Clarence Mill has two rows of columns down the length of each floor and in section these form a continuous vertical alignment of columns (Figure 110) and are an integral part of the structure, indispensable for the stability of the building. In this way they are similar to the columns incorporated into the silk mills of the same period, such as the 1837 mill at Victoria Mills in Macclesfield, and the 1835 mill at Brook Mills in Congleton (see p 87).

The floor to ceiling height of these cotton mills was between 3·1 m and 3·2 m, an increase over previous mills, in part to allow for taller windows and the better light they gave. The walls, lintels and sills were built of stone, using material from local quarries.[40] In terms of roof structure the increase in width was coped with in one of two ways. For those mills of a modest increase in width a single-span king or queen-post roof was still feasible. The Higher Mill, Bollington, for example, has a queen-post roof allowing the larger roof space to be used as an attic. For the much wider mills, such as Adelphi Mill or the 1841 and 1854 extensions to Clarence Mill, a multiple-span roof was needed consisting of a series of king-post trusses across the width of the mill.

These mills were probably built wider than their predecessors in order to house more or larger machines, or both. As far as the self-acting mule was concerned, it was possible for it to be housed in relatively narrow mills. In 1857 at the Lower Heyes Mill, thirteen self-acting mules totalling 5,400 spindles were housed in mills 8·1 m wide. Two of these mules contained only 336 spindles each.[41] It was, therefore, not the type but the size of the mule and its alignment within the mill that was of importance in relation to mill size. Evidence concerning the Clarence Mill buildings indicates that their width may have been determined by the way in which it was decided to position the mules. The Swindells intended to commence spinning at the first Clarence Mill, completed in 1838, with twelve mules, totalling 6,000 spindles, an average of 500 spindles each.[42] These were probably a mixture of mule types, as by early in 1842 Clarence Mill was housing both self-acting and 'other mules'.[43] Although the Swindells also intended to house twenty-two throstles in Clarence Mill, it would have been the housing of the much larger mule that was the more important consideration in relation to the mill's dimensions.

Figure 110
*The 1841 extension to Clarence Mill, Bollington, has two rows of columns down the length of each floor which are an integral part of the structure.*

Unfortunately it is not known how the mules were housed, but it seems probable that the increase in width was designed to allow the mules to be housed across the mill in pairs. In planning the machinery for the 1841 extension to Clarence Mill, it was intended to house the mules in this way with eight pairs on each of the third and fourth storeys. The development in mule design from the part-acting through to the self-acting mules enabled larger and larger numbers of spindles to be supervised by the same number of spinners. The housing of mules in pairs, with one pair per spinner, was part of this process.

The next significant development in east Cheshire cotton-mill construction came with the building of Adelphi Mill, Bollington, in 1856 (Figure 111). This is five storeys high, 58 m long and with an internal width of 26 m, 10 m wider than the extension to Clarence Mill built only two years before. Intermediate support is in the form of three rows of cast-iron columns, integral to the structure, which diminish in diameter from 300 mm at the fireproof, ground-floor level

to 150 mm at top-floor level. The mill is of stone, with stone sills and flat-arched lintels. The multiple-span roof is made up of rows of four king-post trusses each spanning 6·5 m. Unfortunately there is no evidence about the type of the original cotton-spinning machinery which was originally housed in the mill, but it would not be unreasonable to suppose that this expansion in mill size was intended to house self-acting mules of a much greater spindle capacity than those housed in Clarence Mill, but again across the width of the mill. This expansion in mill width was repeated in 1857 at Waterhouse Mill, 23 m wide, and in 1863 at Beehive Mill, 28 m wide.[44] These have been demolished and again it is not known what form of spinning machinery they were intended to house.

East Cheshire cotton-spinning mills of the mid 19th century continued to house heavier processes on their lower floors. At Bollin Mill in Macclesfield, for example, 'On the ground floor in the main building were the blowing room and the throstle room and a portion of the factory in which raw cotton was kept. The carding

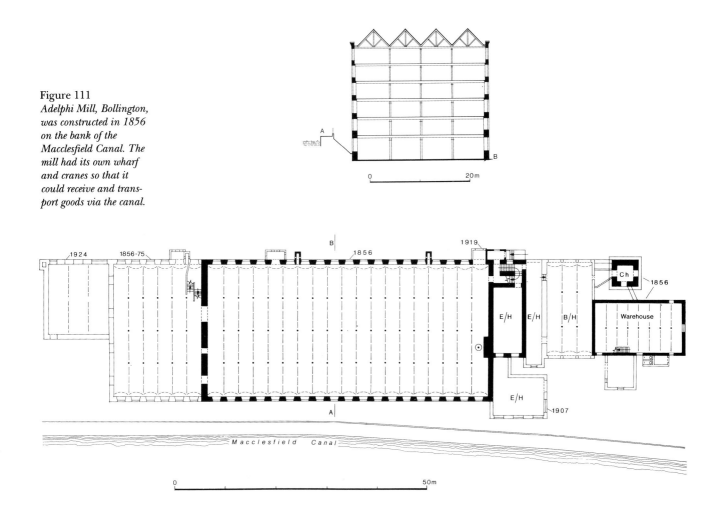

Figure 111
*Adelphi Mill, Bollington,
was constructed in 1856
on the bank of the
Macclesfield Canal. The
mill had its own wharf
and cranes so that it
could receive and trans-
port goods via the canal.*

room was on the second floor, and the third
and fourth consisted entirely of spinning rooms,
whilst the attic contained a spinning room and
reeling room.'[45]

At Clarence Mill the raw cotton was received
into a fireproof warehouse housed in a cellar
situated between the 1834–8 mill and its 1841
extension. This communicated with the rest of
the mill by a stone staircase. The ground floors
housed the processes of cotton mixing and
blowing, and because these processes produced
large amounts of inflammable dust they were
fireproof in construction. The carding machinery was housed at first-floor level, whilst the second, third and fourth floors, housed spinning.

After processing, the spun yarn was passed to a
delivery room situated between the two weaving
mills at the rear of the main mill, and after weaving the cloth was sent to an adjoining wing to be
checked and packed.

The warehousing of goods seems usually to
have been undertaken within the body of the
mill: at Clarence Mill in the cellar and at Bollin
Mill, Macclesfield, in a portion of the ground
floor. Those multi-storeyed mills constructed
with queen-post truss roofs, among them Higher
Mill, Bollington, and Lumbhole Mill, Kettleshulme, probably took advantage of the usable
attic space created by the truss for storage. A fire
which badly damaged Lowerhouse Mill in

Figure 112
*The warehouse at Quarry Bank Mill, Styal, was built of stone into a rock face which provided the cool, damp, conditions suitable for the storage of cotton.*

*Figure 113*
*Adelphi Mill, Bollington: a) the cotton warehouse erected in 1856; b) the roof of the cotton warehouse supported by fine iron trusses.*

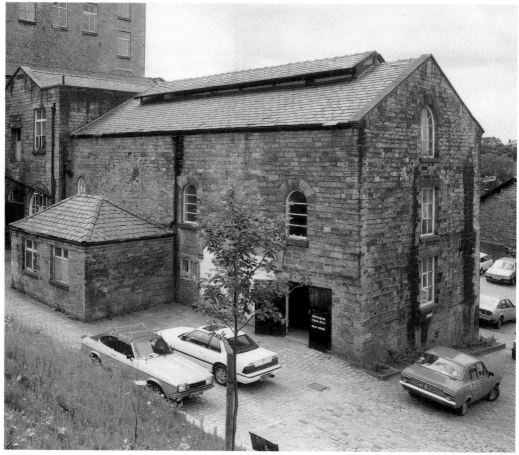

*a*

116

Bollington in 1835 began in raw cotton stored in the attic. During the building of Clarence Mill between 1834 and 1838 it was noted in the Swindells company minute book that 'in consequence of the great width of the spinning mill it has been thought advisable to have the roof made into an attic and 3 plans are to come in — 1 from Jno Revers — 1 from Jepson and 1 from Mr Lillie's man'.[46] Separate warehouses were sometimes built in order to house more substantial quantities of cotton, notably one at Quarry Bank Mill, Styal (Figure 112), and two which still stand at the Adelphi Mill, Bollington (Figure 113).

Generally, office accommodation was provided within the mill building, for example, offices in the weaving shed at Lower Heyes Mill,

*b*

Macclesfield, although for larger sites such accommodation was housed in a separate building, for example, the office lodge at Adelphi Mill, Bollington (Figure 114). Toilet blocks were generally of the dry shute type until the later part of the 19th century when water closets were first installed.

For all mills, delivery of raw cotton or despatch of finished goods before the introduction of the automobile was undertaken by horse and cart and the larger mills, Quarry Bank Mill (Figure 115) and Clarence Mill for example, had substantial stables on the site. For canal-side sites such as Adelphi Mill, Clarence Mill and the

short-lived Beehive Mill, in Bollington, goods could be moved by barge. Adelphi Mill in particular had a large wharf with cranes for loading and unloading (Figure 111).

Heating continued to be provided by steam-heated pipes, and lighting was by gas until electricity was introduced in the early decades of the 20th century. On a number of mill sites gas was produced from their own retorts, for use mainly for lighting. For example, a small retort survives at Lumbhole Mill, Kettleshulme. It was a gas light which caused the fire at Lowerhouse Mill in 1835. A Factories Inquiry Commission of 1834 was told that Quarry Bank Mill was at that time lit by Argand lamps. These were originally oil lamps with cylindrical wicks, but by 1834 the name was probably being used to describe gas lamps with cylindrical burners.[47] Lower and Higher Mill at Bollington shared a 'gas works' by 1832,[48] and at this time these two mills also had 'gasing machines',[49] a further use for gas on cotton mill sites. Gasing the cotton yarn involved passing the cotton thread through a gas flame to singe off superfluous ends not caught into the thread when the yarn was spun.

### Fireproofing

After the construction of Lowerhouse Mill, Bollington, in 1818 (see p 51), no other mill is known to have been built in east Cheshire with fireproof construction throughout until the Swindells built the 1854 extension to Clarence Mill, Bollington (Figure 116). The original Clarence Mill, built between 1834 and 1838 and demolished in 1877, had a fireproof ground floor like its twin, the 1841 extension, which is still standing. These floors were fireproofed in order to house the processes of mixing and blowing which produced large amounts of inflammable dust.[50] For the same reason the 1840s scutching rooms at Quarry Bank Mill, Styal, and at Lumbhole Mill, Kettleshulme, as well as the ground floor of the Adelphi Mill, Bollington, were of a fireproof construction.

The mid 19th-century fireproofing in east Cheshire did not differ markedly from that at Lowerhouse Mill. The mills' widths were generally spanned by three individual beams with parallel flanges, and joined at the column heads. There were therefore usually two rows of columns, but three at the Adelphi Mill where there were four spans of beams.[51] Generally the columns were either plain or with a simple moulding at the head, and slightly tapering.

It was not until 1877, when the original 1834–8 mill at Clarence Mill was demolished and replaced by one designed by the Lancashire firm of A H Stott and Sons, that a mill was built

Figure 116
*The 1854 extension to Clarence Mill, Bollington, is fireproof in construction.*

119

Figure 117
*The 1877 mill at Clarence Mill, Bollington, replaced the original 1834–8 mill. It was designed by A H Stott and Sons.*

Figure 118
*Clarence Mill, Bollington. a) The entrance hall of the 1877 mill is impressive, with the whole weight of the stair tower being carried on stone arches and substantial cast-iron columns.*

a

in east Cheshire using a more advanced form of fireproof construction (Figure 117). This, the last cotton mill to be built in east Cheshire, was perhaps the most imposing, embodying some fine decorative touches (Figure 118). It is the only mill in east Cheshire to have been constructed on the 'Oldham model', a design common in the great cotton-spinning areas of Lancashire.

The 1877 mill at Clarence Mill is 55 m long by 40 m wide (Figure 119). It is four storeys high with a basement and has a flat roof. Its walls are of yellow sandstone divided horizontally by continuous courses of red Accrington brick forming

*b*

*b) These stairs, which rise inside the tower of the 1877 mill, are of cast iron with stone treads.*

Figure 119
*This plan of the 1877 mill at Clarence Mill, Bollington, was drawn by the architects A H Stott and Sons. The mill was deeper than earlier mills in order to house long, late 19th-century spinning mules.*

**Figure 120**
*The brick arches and iron beams of the 1877 mill at Clarence Mill, Bollington, are supported by columns placed beneath the span of every other arch, a form of fireproof construction patented by Abraham Henthorn Stott in 1871.*

segmental arches over the windows on each floor, and at ground and first-floor levels projecting stone string-courses provide continuous sills. Three of the corners of the mill have clasping pilasters behind which are positioned urinals; the fourth corner has a projecting stair tower. This tower also served as a water tower, containing in its roof a water tank to feed a sprinkler system in case of fire, an arrangement similar to that at Adelphi Mill.

The internal structure of the mill (Figure 120) is of brick and cast iron and uses a form of fireproofing patented in 1871 by the Oldham millwright Abraham Henthorn Stott.[52] This involved the placing of columns beneath the span of every other brick arch instead of at the springing of each arch, as had been done previously, and giving each column bracketed capitals. These capitals supported not only I-section cross-beams at the extremity of each

bracket, but also longitudinal iron beams which followed the form of the arches between the columns, forming a boxed-beam arrangement. Placing the columns beneath the head of every second arch allowed greater distances between them and gave a less cluttered floor space. Even though these arches span 1.53 m, the distance allowed between the columns is 3·2 m, 0·5 m wider than those at Lowerhouse Mill built fifty years earlier. A plan of the No. 1 spinning room at Clarence Mill in 1915 shows how comfortably the mules were accommodated between the columns. There were sixteen mules equal in length to the width of the building and each containing 1,050 spindles. Seven individual cast-iron beams span the width of the mill, probably I-section, in line with Stott's patent design, and joining at the column brackets. The beam flanges are 150 mm in width and parallel.

By creating a rigid box frame of beams, this design of fireproofing was stronger than those formerly used and allowed the floors to be thinner and lighter, taking away much of the reliance on the exterior wall for loadbearing. The windows could therefore be larger than those in earlier mills and, when used in conjunction with a floor to ceiling height of 4·1 m at the highest point of the arch, allowed sufficient lighting to reach the centre of the mill.

### Housing powered weaving

With the development of the powerloom came the need to provide suitable housing for it. Initially, the small number of powerlooms which were first put into operation on east Cheshire cotton-mill sites could be housed on the lower floors of mill buildings. In 1826, for example, Watters and Lund housed 130 looms in Crompton Road Mill, Macclesfield.[53] However, by the 1850s and 1860s many Lancashire weaving establishments housed thousands of looms. Such large numbers could not be contained in traditional mill buildings and necessitated the building of weaving sheds.

From structural and documentary evidence it seems that owners of east Cheshire cotton mills sought to house their powerlooms as part of integrated sites, primarily in two or three-storeyed buildings rather than single-storeyed sheds. Several elements are common to these storeyed weaving mills. First, they are low, principally two-storeys high, thereby keeping the looms close to the ground in order to reduce the effect of vibration on the structure and on the woven cloth. Second, they are all additions to existing sites, and third, all date from the late 1830s and early 1840s, a time when integrated cotton firms were beginning to dominate the industry. Finally, they are all traditional in construction, using timber for cross-beams and trusses, and cast iron for columns for intermediate support. All but the weaving mills at Quarry Bank Mill, which are of brick, are stone-built, but the reasons for this are geographical rather than functional. There is no correlation between the dimensions of these weaving mills. They vary in length and width from 60 m by 11 m at Clarence Mill to 33 m by 6·5 m at Quarry Bank Mill. However, this is not surprising because the looms themselves did not make, by their individual size, any demands upon the length and width of a building, a shed's dimensions being determined, in relation to the looms, by their number and proposed arrangement.

At Waterside Mill, Disley, a two-storeyed wing, 31 m by 8 m, was added to the mill before 1851.[54] In 1834 the occupiers, Moseley and Howard, were described as 'manufacturers by power',[55] and it is therefore probable that the two-storeyed wing was built to house powerlooms and the associated processes. Robert Hyde Greg introduced powered weaving to Quarry Bank Mill, Styal (Figure 121), in 1836

Figure 121
*An illustration of Quarry Bank Mill, Styal, showing the site as it existed in 1990.*

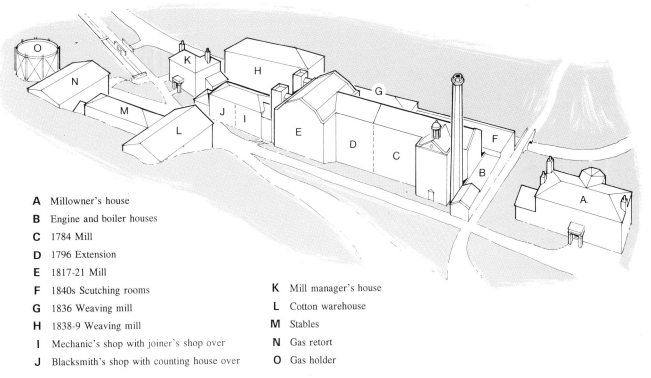

A  Millowner's house

B  Engine and boiler houses

C  1784 Mill

D  1796 Extension

E  1817-21 Mill

F  1840s Scutching rooms

G  1836 Weaving mill

H  1838-9 Weaving mill

I  Mechanic's shop with joiner's shop over

J  Blacksmith's shop with counting house over

K  Mill manager's house

L  Cotton warehouse

M  Stables

N  Gas retort

O  Gas holder

and built a weaving mill two storeys high with a cellar, and 33 m long by 6·5 m wide (this was reduced in height by one storey before 1870). Two years later a second two-storeyed weaving mill with a cellar was built adjacent to the first, 30 m long by 10 m wide, at a cost of £3,132. This was completed in 1838–9 but later, in 1842, at a cost of £1,185, it was increased in height by one floor (Figure 122). This extra floor was used for warping and beaming: the preparation of the warp ready for installation on the loom. Both weaving mills were built of brick with a traditional timber beam construction and lit from the side rather than by roof lights. The number of looms in the weaving mills at Quarry Bank Mill was increased gradually. From January to June 1836, forty-eight looms were purchased, followed by another fifty-four from July to

August. Between January and June 1842, fifty-one looms were installed, with a further sixty-five between September and December. Finally, in the first two months of 1843, twenty looms were added to bring the total at this time to 238.[56] Gradually increasing capacity in this way may simply have been the result of the time needed by the manufacturers to fill the order, but it also had the advantage of spreading the cost, and of allowing management the time to assess the new market and to allow them and their workforce to become familiar with the looms and with producing cloth.

When building Clarence Mill, Bollington, between 1834 and 1838 for the manufacture of cotton cloth, the Swindells decided to house their looms in a two-storeyed weaving mill which they built to the rear of the spinning mill

**Figure 122**
*Weaving mills were built at Quarry Bank Mill, Styal, in 1836 (centre of the riverside range) and 1838–9 (foreground).*

(Figure 123). It was demolished in 1877 but was 60 m long by 11 m wide, built of stone with traditional timber internal construction and a row of cast-iron columns running centrally down both the upper and lower floors. The building was double gabled, and the roof covered with slate. The floor was of timber but they appear to have had some difficulty in laying it. In the minutes of a meeting held in November 1834 it was recorded that 'the weaving mill we are aiming to complete but we find the floor beams badly laid in the walls — the joists too far apart — and the end joists far too weak'.[57] There was obviously concern that the building should be strong enough to withstand the weight and vibration of the looms on two floors. In this respect the arrangement of the 320 looms the building was to house was also of importance. It was decided to arrange them in rows of four

across the building. On the lower floor these rows were each composed of one 6/4 loom, 2·7 m wide, and three 9/8 looms, each 2·1 m wide. The remaining space was taken by a 0·9 m wide central alley and two 0·4 m wall alleys. The upper floor was similar except that each row was composed entirely of 9/8 looms and this allowed the central alley to be 1·2 m wide and the wall alleys to be 0·6 m wide. In 1841 Clarence Mill was extended and a new weaving mill built which was an exact copy of the first.

The most remarkable east Cheshire weaving shed is the second phase of weaving-shed development at Waterside Mill, Disley, which was built some time in the second half of the 19th century, after 1851.[58] It is the only one of its kind in the area, being 50 m by 52 m, dimensions more typical of single-storeyed sheds, but is two storeys in height, the lower storey being

Figure 123
*This two-storeyed weaving mill, erected at Clarence Mill, Bollington, in 1841, was an extension of a weaving mill erected in 1834–8, which was demolished in 1877.*

**Figure 124**
*The ground floor of the weaving mill at Waterside Mill, Disley, is fireproof in construction and was probably used for warehousing.*

fireproof in construction. Cast-iron columns support the brick arch vaulting at the springing of each arch, and at regular intervals along the length of each vault are square boxes, approximately 1·5 m square, let into the brickwork (Figure 124). These are now blocked, but may originally have been used for passing cotton up to and down from the weaving floor above. Being bordered on two sides by the mill and having a blind north elevation, the lower floor must have always been artificially lit, originally by gas light. The upper floor is lit from its north-light roof, and in this respect it is an amalgamation of the two-storeyed weaving mills described

above and the more extensive single-storeyed weaving sheds typical of the Lancashire cotton industry (Figure 125).

William Fairbairn, writing in 1863, commented that 'there is scarcely a cotton mill now in the kingdom where looms are employed that has not a shed attached to the lower storey on a level with the ground floor'.[59] He was referring to single-storeyed cotton-weaving sheds, built mainly in the mid 19th century. The dominant feature of these sheds was the roof construction which, by means of a series of saw-tooth-profile trusses, glazed generally on the north side and angled at about 60°, gave good

and even light to the whole floor area. The trusses were supported at the valleys by cast-iron beams which were in turn supported by columns. By lighting the building from above instead of from the walls, the shed could be of any length and width without leaving the central areas short of light.

In east Cheshire, the cotton industry seems generally not to have taken advantage of the saw-tooth-roofed weaving-shed design. By the time of its widespread use in the mid 19th century, the east Cheshire industry had shifted its concentration away from integrated manufacturing and back towards spinning. There are

therefore only two known developments of such single-storeyed, north-light sheds for cotton weaving in the area: two sheds built at Lowerhouse Mill in Bollington and three built at Lower Heyes Mill in Macclesfield.

The Greg family introduced powered weaving at Lowerhouse Mill four years before they introduced it at Quarry Bank Mill, Styal, but it is not known where the looms were housed. Whatever the arrangement, it was superseded by the building of two weaving sheds between the years 1849 and 1875. These sheds, forming extensions from the ground floor of the main mill on both its east and west sides, are of similar

Figure 125
*Aerial view of Waterside Mill, Disley, which shows the north-light roof of the two-storeyed weaving mill.*

Figure 126
*Single-storeyed north-light weaving sheds were erected at Lowerhouse Mill, Bollington, between 1849 and 1875.*

Figure 127
*The north-light trusses of the weaving sheds at Lowerhouse Mill, Bollington, are supported by cast-iron beams and columns.*

construction and were therefore probably built at about the same time (Figure 126). The support for the roof trusses is in the form of a single, central row of cylindrical cast-iron columns. Bracing the structure from column to column, at right angles to the main cast-iron tie-beams, are cast-iron tie-bars, I-shaped in section and with a web pierced by a pattern formed of crosses and rectangles (Figure 127). The walls of both sheds are of stone and contain no primary windows. In the shed to the west of the mill, two of the supporting columns at the centre of the row were cast with a mounting face and two boltholes where a shafting house would have been attached. In the walls opposite these particular columns are slots in which wheels could have turned. However, there are no other signs of the drive. In the shed to the east of the mill none of the columns was cast to carry shafting, but at each end of the shed, in line with the row of columns, there is a pier of stone with a corbel on each side. This may have carried shafting.

The main weaving shed at Lower Heyes Mill is by far the biggest single-storeyed north-light shed built in east Cheshire for either the cotton or the silk industry (Figure 128). The land on which it was built was leased from the Brocklehurst family in February 1867 by the Globe Cotton Spinning and Manufacturing Company Limited (see p 109), who occupied the site at the time and christened it the Globe Mill. The shed was built within a year of the date of the lease[60] and measures 90 m by 67 m. By 1903, a second, separate shed had been added to the site, 44 m by 27 m, and an extension to the main shed in 1905. By 1916, the company was working 1,560 looms, employing 550 weavers and producing 500,000 yards of calico per week.[61]

The main shed is brick-built and largely single-storeyed, except for a narrow basement, 7 m wide, which runs down its south-western side, the building of which was allowed by the fall in land down to the River Bollin. This lower floor, similar to the lower floor of the shed at Waterside Mill, is fireproof in construction and was, therefore, probably used as a warehouse. Each of the columns supporting the north-light roof of the main weaving floor was designed to carry drive shafting down the length of the building.

Externally, some concession to adornment in an otherwise plain building is displayed in the two main doorways. The access to the lower floor is in the west elevation and leads into a stone-flagged hallway where the timekeeping clocks stand and which has probably always been the workers' entrance. The doorway is central to the three bays of this elevation which break forward by one course of brick and are capped with a triangular pediment. The door itself is housed in the lower portion of a semicircular arch, the upper portion of which contains a loading-bay door and a semicircular light. This arch is flanked on either side at the upper floor level by semicircular-arched windows (Figure 129). The entrance to the offices, which are situated in the south corner of the shed at upper floor level, is in the south-east elevation. The existing doorway with its square light, concrete architrave and flat pediment, appears to be an early 20th-century alteration, but it is likely that there has always been a doorway at this point.

The shed was powered independently of the main spinning mill by an engine and boilers at

its north-west end. The size of the 1867 engine is not known but in 1903 a new steam-power plant was installed for the whole site. The main weaving shed was then driven by a triple-expansion horizontal engine of 750 horsepower, a type of engine rarely used in the cotton industry.

**Figure 128**
*The weaving shed at Lower Heyes Mill, Macclesfield, was built by the Globe Manufacturing and Cotton Spinning Company Limited in 1867.*

**Figure 129**
*The 1867 weaving shed at Lower Heyes Mill, Macclesfield, had an entrance for the workers (left) and another for office staff and management (right).*

## Power systems in relation to the design of mill building

All of the new cotton-spinning and manufacturing sites established in east Cheshire after 1826 — Adelphi Mill, Beehive Mill and Clarence Mill in Bollington, and Bollin Mill in Macclesfield — were built to be powered by steam. However, twenty-six water-powered sites established before 1826 continued, in varying degrees, to rely on and update their water-power systems even though most had steam power available. Examples vary from Lower Heyes Mill, Macclesfield, where, by 1843, only seven of the 67 horsepower it used came from its wheel,[62] to Quarry Bank Mill, Styal, where in 1845, of the 130 horsepower that could be generated on the site, 100 horsepower came from the waterwheel and only 30 from two Boulton and Watt steam engines.[63]

At the time of the installation of the 'great' wheel at Styal between 1817 and 1820 (see p 62) its power output was greater than that which could be produced by any contemporary steam engine, and as the wheel continued to satisfy the mill's power needs into the middle and later parts of the 19th century there was no need to replace it with steam. However, the reason why sites such as Lower Heyes, where steam came to dominate the power supply, chose to retain water power can only be surmised. Probably the fact that the water system was already in place and costing little encouraged the maintenance of the wheel even if it was only used to turn small amounts of machinery or as a backup to the steam-power system. The retaining of waterwheels may also have been encouraged further by legislation which excluded water-powered mills from the legal restrictions on working hours.

On sites such as Lower Mill, Higher Mill and Lowerhouse Mill at Bollington, and Ingersley Vale Mill at Rainow, water continued to play a prominent role in providing power, and developments in water-power technology enabled mills regularly to upgrade their water-power supply. In east Cheshire, cast iron was increasingly used in the construction of waterwheels. An iron suspension wheel was installed at Lumbhole Mill in about 1835 (see p 63), to work in tandem with a steam engine, and at Ingersley Vale Mill in the mid 19th century, where a single 17 m diameter wheel replaced a dual wheel system (Figure 130). By 1851, Sunnyside Mills, the Wood family's cotton mills at Sutton on the outskirts of Macclesfield, were being powered by two waterwheels made entirely of cast iron.[64] In 1828 William Fairbairn had built an iron, breast-shot, suspension wheel for the calico-printing

works at Handforth, near Wilmslow. The wheel was 5·5 m wide and 4·6 m in diameter and had 'ventilated buckets'. These were a Fairbairn invention which increased the efficiency of the wheel by allowing air caught in the bucket by the incoming water to escape.

In some cases wheels were moved to create space within the mill building. This was the case at the Higher and Lower Mill. In a notice of sale circulated to friends in 1859 the Swindells noted that: 'The power consists of both water and steam, there are two water wheels and three steam engines. The water wheels were formerly in the mills, but have been entirely removed and the space they occupied is made subservient to form the best part of the mills.'[65]

Upon taking up the lease of Higher and Lower Mill in 1832, Swindells and Oliver agreed with their landlords, John Harrop and Thomas Creswick, that: 'a new water wheel shall be put down with a proper cistern and other apparatus necessary to the Higher Mill in lieu of the present water wheel at the expense of the said John Harrop'.[66] In fact by the time the Swindells came to sell Higher and Lower Mill in 1859 the power systems of both mills had been completely upgraded. In the notice of sale the Swindells noted that: 'New wheel races formed of good "Ashlar stone" and two new water wheels are placed outside the mills, with gearing to connect them with the engines and are considered by the best judges to be very complete workmanship. One was done by Mr Lillie of Manchester and other by Messrs Gordon and Davies of Stockport'[67] (Figure 131). It would appear from this evidence that James Lillie worked on the gearing whilst Gordon and Davies installed the wheels. Lillie charged £300 for his work. The cost of installing one of the wheels, it is not clear at which mill, and building a 34·7 m long culvert was £1,503, of which the contract for the wheel itself cost £690.[68]

Figure 130 (*Opposite*)
*This 17 m diameter suspension wheel at Ingersley Vale Mill, Rainow, replaced a dual wheel system in the mid 19th century.*

Figure 131
*The wheel pit at Higher Mill, Bollington, is a good example of the ashlar masonry associated with water power. The penstock (left) is made of cast iron and timber.*

Figure 132
*Engine house, added to the rear of the 1841 and 1854 mills at Clarence Mill in 1877. The opening visible in the centre of the picture accommodated the rope race up to each floor of the mill to drive the machinery.*

Although in east Cheshire there was some advantage to be gained by the retention of water power, nationally the driving force behind the great expansion of the cotton industry was steam. Moreover, it was steam and not water power which was one of the factors in the expansion in mill size, following the continued advances in steam-power technology which enabled engines to drive ever greater amounts of machinery. Perhaps the most important of these developments was the use of 'compounding', most significantly by William McNaught in the mid 19th century. Compounding involved the use of high-pressure steam to drive a high pressure cylinder exhausting into a second cylinder working at a lower pressure. Initially, beam engines were compounded, but gradually the beam engine came to be largely replaced by either vertical engines or engines in which the cylinders were placed horizontally. It became more common during this period for engines to stand free and not rely on the

engine house for support. They were placed on cast-iron beds and, in the case of the vertical engines, were provided with a supporting cast-iron frame.

The transmission of the power from the engine to the machinery was performed more efficiently after the introduction of rope races in the latter half of the 19th century. These connected the shafting on each floor of the mill directly to the engine by means of a series of ropes and replaced the old system of vertical shafts. The ropes, made of cotton, manila or other fibres, were held in grooves around the circumference of a drum which acted as the flywheel. The individual ropes then passed up the height of the mill to turn around the main drive wheels on each floor (see Figure 132). These drums could be up to 12 m in diameter and carry thirty or more ropes.

By the late 19th century rope races were used in the larger east Cheshire cotton mills including Lower Heyes Mill (driven by an inverted vertical steam engine of 1,800 horse-power after 1903), Lowerhouse Mill, Adelphi Mill and Clarence Mill. When the Swindells demolished the original Clarence Mill in 1877 and built their Oldham-style extension they also installed a new power system for the whole site. They added two rope races, one for the new mill and the other for the 1841 and 1854 mills, positioned at the junction of the two (Figure 132). The machinery in the entire complex could be driven from either engine house.[69]

These engine and transmission developments, together with improvements in valve technology and boiler-making, dramatically increased power capacity so that by the end of the century engines were capable of generating over 4,000 horsepower for the large Lancashire and Yorkshire mills.[70] East Cheshire cotton mills did not develop to such a scale and in comparison their power requirements were more modest. The few cotton firms that had survived in Macclesfield town into the 1830s and 1840s were operating on a small scale and with relatively low power needs, requiring on average around 20 to 30 horsepower. Mr Ashness, at his cotton factory on Pickford Street in Macclesfield, was using a 20 horsepower engine in 1832,[71] while the Bollin Mill on George Street, was driving its machinery by a 36 horsepower condensing engine, built by Sherratts of Manchester, in 1845.[72]

The larger sites which came to be built outside the towns of Macclesfield and Congleton used correspondingly more power. Sunnyside Mill at Sutton, near Macclesfield, used two steam engines, one of 60 horsepower and the other of 40, as well as two waterwheels of 25 horsepower each. Lower Heyes Mill on the outskirts of Macclesfield contained 5,500 mule spindles, 536 throstle spindles and 223 powerlooms, and required the use of a 60 horsepower Sherratt engine as well as a 7 horsepower waterwheel.[73] When planning to build Clarence Mill in 1834, the Swindells calculated the amount of horsepower they would require to drive the machinery. The 320 looms they intended to house in the two-storeyed weaving mill to the rear of the main mill required 32 horsepower, whilst 6,400 throstle spindles required 25 and 8,640 mule spindles 17: a total of 74 horsepower. For the 1841 extension to this mill, which was in effect a copy of the original, they decided that 'the engine house be at the end of the spinning mill for two steam engines of forty horses power each'.[74] From this small amount of evidence, east Cheshire's larger cotton mills of the mid 19th century appear to have used from 70 to 100 horsepower. By 1882 power needs had increased to such an extent that Clarence Mill had a power capacity of 1,700 horsepower, com-

prising, 'pair of compound high and low pressure engines, by Galloway, new in 1877, of 700 horses power; and pair of condensing beam engines compounded with auxiliary high pressure engines of 1,000 power and Greens economiser to each'.[75] Lower Heyes Mill had 2,550 indicated horsepower by 1903.[76]

The engine and boiler houses of east Cheshire's cotton mills in the period after 1826 have little in common, since they vary in size and shape. However, some elements do stand out as typical. Arches become a feature of the power plant. The 1832 engine house built by Samuel Greg Junior at Lowerhouse Mill is lit by two tall and slender semicircular-arched windows (Figures 41, 133). The 1867 engine house at Lower Heyes Mill, unusual for mid to late 19th-century cotton mills in east Cheshire in

Figure 133
*The engine house at Lowerhouse Mill, Bollington, was erected in the early 1830s by Samuel Greg to house a double-beam engine which supplemented the waterwheel.*

**Figure 134**
*The power arrangements of Adelphi Mill, Bollington, developed in several phases. The boiler house with the triple-arched entrance (right) was erected in the mid to late 19th century whilst the tall engine house to the left was erected in 1907 and housed a large inverted vertical engine.*

cast-iron beams, as were the engine and boiler houses at Adelphi Mill. At Lowerhouse Mill not only the engine house but also the wheelhouse is fireproofed. The spans of these buildings are narrow enough not to require the use of columns, but in the boiler house at Adelphi Mill columns were needed to support the span. Tie-rods connecting the beams were visible below the level of the brick vaulting.

In general, chimneys of the mid 19th-century cotton mills in east Cheshire, like those at Quarry Bank Mill, Styal, and Adelphi Mill, Bollington (Figure 135), are octagonal, whilst those of the late 19th and early 20th centuries, the 1914 chimney at Clarence Mill for example, are circular in plan.

The last engine house built for an east Cheshire cotton mill was erected at the Adelphi Mill, Bollington, in 1907 and was built to house an inverted vertical steam engine (Figure 134). This stood on a bed of concrete 2·9 m thick and from the concrete engine bed the internal height of the building was 16·5 m. In plan it is 10 m by 7·6 m internally, allowing only 970 mm from the front of the engine bed to the north wall of the engine house and 200 mm between the 2·4 m broad rope drum and the south wall.

## Conclusion

The building of the 1877 extension to Clarence Mill in Bollington marked the end of cotton-mill building in east Cheshire. In terms of the number of mills, east Cheshire's contribution to the British cotton industry is minor. Only thirty-two of the total number of mills known to have been built in the area are believed to have been first used for cotton production. Nevertheless, these mills do reflect national developments in cotton-mill construction and amongst them are buildings of national importance. Lowerhouse Mill, Bollington, was the first fireproof mill in east Cheshire, and was built in 1818 at a time when fireproof construction nationally was still at an early and innovative stage. In contrast the 1877 mill at Clarence Mill was built at a time when fireproof building had become a highly developed method of construction. It was designed by a nationally important mill architect and engineer, A H Stott, to a design he had patented only six years before. Crompton Road Mill, Macclesfield, erected in 1823, may well have been the first cotton mill in east Cheshire to have been built specifically to house power-looms, at a time when powerloom weaving nationally was in its infancy. The two-storeyed weaving mills surviving at Quarry Bank Mill,

that it is built of brick instead of stone, has a semicircular-arched door to the engine house with two semicircular-arched windows on either side of it in a pattern which repeats the design of the main door to the weaving shed. The 1841 boiler house at Clarence Mill had three arches at ground-floor level, whilst the engine house erected in 1877 to the 1841 and 1854 mills at Clarence Mill was designed in its fenestration to be a series of tall arches resembling an arcade, typical of the 'Oldham type' mills. The use of arched, frequently tall, windows, although partly a design feature, was primarily intended to admit sufficient light to illuminate the engine. The use of wide arched doors, for example, those of the boiler house at Adelphi Mill, was intended to allow for the movement of engine parts and for the installation and removal of boilers, of which there could have been up to six, and also gave easier access for maintenance and repair (Figure 134).

Fireproofing (see p 51 and above) is also a feature of the mid to late 19th-century engine and boiler houses of the period. Both the 1841 and 1877 engine houses at Clarence Mill were constructed with brick vaulting supported by

Styal, and Clarence Mill, Bollington, are nationally significant standing examples of this particular response to the housing of powerlooms. The 1835 beam engine and waterwheel at Lumbhole Mill, Kettleshulme, designed to work in tandem, is a unique surviving example of the type of power arrangement which was so important to the water-powered textile industry of the early 19th century.

None of the surviving cotton mills of east Cheshire still produces cotton commercially. Indeed only two, Lower Heyes Mill, Macclesfield, and Higher Mill, Bollington, are used for a textile-related process: the weaving shed at Lower Heyes Mill is being used for screen printing, whilst Higher Mill is used for dyeing. One industry which has found that cotton mills suit its needs is the paper and card industry and both Lower Mill and Lowerhouse Mill in Bollington are occupied by coated paper and card manufacturers, whilst Waterside Mill, Disley, was at the time of the survey used for the manufacture of paper, predominantly for the sugar industry. Adelphi Mill and Lumbhole Mill are used by various light industries, and the Adelphi combines this with a new role as a hotel. The semi-rural location of cotton mills such as Adelphi Mill, as well as Clarence Mill, which is also currently being converted to a hotel, makes them ideal for use by the tourist and service sector. Quarry Bank Mill, Styal, became a thriving industrial museum in the early 1980s. As industrial buildings they are largely unsuitable for modern industrial requirements and are expensive to heat and maintain. In particular, it is the larger cotton mills in more rural locations for which it is most difficult to find new and successful uses. Demolition was a popular option in the 1950s,

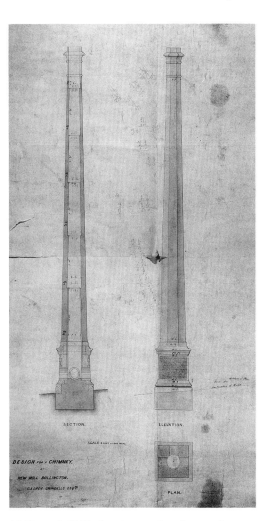

Figure 135
*The original drawings for the chimney erected at Adelphi Mill, Bollington, in 1856. Typical of mid to late 19th-century chimneys, it is octagonal in section.*

1960s and 1970s but is now less favoured as an option when reuse is possible. In the long term the survival of these buildings must be in some doubt, but in spite of this, their social, economic and architectural significance is undeniable.

# 6 THE MILL IN THE LANDSCAPE

Figure 136 *(Below)*
*This early 19th-century
view of Congleton shows
how the rural aspect of the
town was becoming inter-
rupted by industrial chimneys (Baines 1835, plate
10).*

Figure 137 *(Opposite)
James Cawley's 1838 map
of Macclesfield shows how
rapidly the town had
expanded, mainly to the
south and north east.*

At the beginning of the 18th century east Cheshire comprised several small communities, of which Macclesfield was the largest, whose economic basis was agricultural and whose cottage industries, including the making of buttons and the spinning of jersey wool, supplemented the low level of income provided by agriculture. Building stock, therefore, was largely domestic and agricultural. The process of industrialisation which took place from the mid 18th century onwards altered the face of these communities. The rural aspect of towns and villages was transformed by the introduction of the water-powered silk and later the cotton industry (Figure 136). This resulted in a movement of people into new urban centres to work in the textile mills and a substantial phase of building which expanded the small communities and their communication systems in order to serve the needs of an industrial society.

The 1804 Enclosure Award Map of Macclesfield shows that some 18th-century industrial development had taken place already between the River Bollin and the Dams Brook, around Park Green (then known as Parsonage Green) and Sunderland Street (then known as Pickford Street).[1] However, the town was still at that time largely centred around its medieval core, focused on the church and market place.[2] Yet, by the time of the publication of James Cawley's map of Macclesfield in 1838 (Figure 137) the town had almost doubled in size.[3] Congleton also expanded throughout the 19th century (Figure 138) to be almost unrecognisable from the small, predominantly agricultural town it had been at the end of the 18th century.[4]

The mills themselves had a tremendous impact on the landscape. By the middle of the 19th century they dominated almost every major

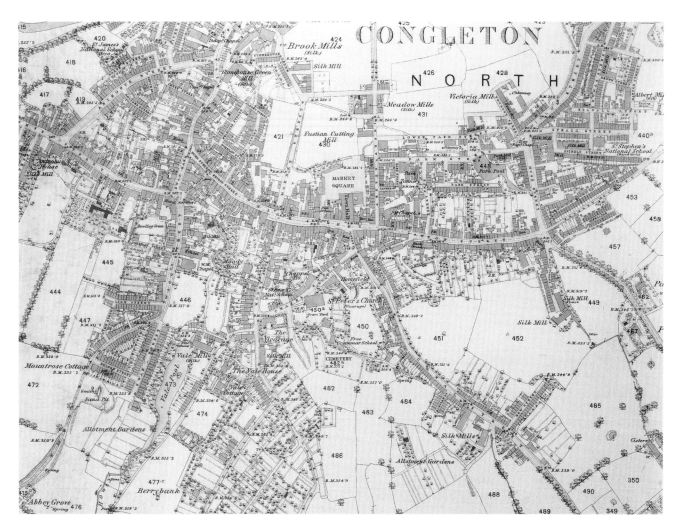

**Figure 138**
*By the time of the publication of the 1873 Ordnance Survey map, Congleton had expanded from the predominantly rural town it had been at the beginning of the century, centred upon High Street and Wagg Street, to one of mills and workers' housing. During the 19th century the town expanded westwards around West Street and Swan Street, and eastwards around Spragg Street and Thomas Street.*

**Figure 139**
*By the 1870s the streets of east Cheshire towns were dominated by mills. Here Meadow Mill (right), Fair Mill (centre) and Brook Mills (left) form a group in Congleton.*

street in Macclesfield (Figure 4), Congleton (Figure 139) and Bollington (Figure 140). The earliest mills occupied water-side sites, so that streams and rivers, particularly in the centres of Macclesfield and Congleton, were dammed and diverted and came to be enclosed in alleyways of mill walls and housing. The Dams Brook in Macclesfield and the Howty Brook in Congleton are now mostly culverted and rarely seen above

ground. In the Pennines mills were erected to take advantage of the streams and rivers. By the beginning of the 18th century the flow of the water, particularly of those streams descending from Rainow into Bollington, was interrupted by a series of dams, reservoirs and leats which serviced the mills on their banks. Their water was needed for the finishing and dyeing processes, but was most valuable as a source of power, initially turning waterwheels but later providing steam for engines (Figures 141, 142).

In the towns the increase in population brought about by industrialisation created a demand for housing which the existing stock could not accommodate. In Macclesfield the population increased from 8,743 in 1801 to 23,129 by 1831,[5] whilst in Congleton (including Buglawton) the increase was from 4,378 to 11,439 over the same period.[6] This prompted new housing developments in both towns. In Macclesfield one of these was to the south of the town and involved the building of those streets bordered by Park Lane and Mill Lane, including High Street, James Street and St George's

Figure 140
*Mid 19th-century drawing of Higher and Lower Mills, Bollington, showing mills erected along watercourses in greenfield sites.*

Figure 141
*The 1801 weir at Ingersley Vale Mill, Rainow, is an example of how water-courses were harnessed to provide water power.*

Street. To the north east new housing grew up around Buxton Road and Hurdsfield Road and included Waterloo Street, Arbourhay Street and Daybrook Street. In Congleton comparable developments took place to the west of the town around the area of West Road and to the east around Moor Street and Bromley Road.[7] These new areas of housing altered the pattern of urban development in east Cheshire which had hitherto respected the local topography and ancient land boundaries and whose growth had represented an organic development of the medieval settlements. Industrial housing, for the sake of compactness, convenience and cheapness, was built in rows of terraces in streets laid to a uniform grid pattern. Such large amounts of new housing required large areas of land which were only available some distance away from the medieval centres.

Most of this housing was built speculatively, in order to provide income from rent. Thomas Bullock, for example, a Macclesfield silk manufacturer of the early 19th century and the owner of St George's Street Mill until 1852,[8] expanded

Figure 142
*Rivers were dammed to form mill pools. The water from this pool, at Daneinshaw Mill, Congleton, turned a waterwheel which was situated centrally within the mill.*

his business into property in the mid 19th century. By 1850 he owned and let large amounts of workers' and weavers' housing (for garret houses see p 54) on Bond Street, Newton Street and Brown Street to the east of the town and in the area already noted bordered by Park Lane, to the south of the town centre.[9]

Sometimes, however, it is clear that houses were intended for the work-force of a particular mill, or that they at least formed part of a mill development, as at Victoria Mills, Macclesfield (Figure 143). A terrace of two-storeyed brick cottages which formed a rectangular development between Crown Street West and Parr

Street, Macclesfield, provides a distinctive example (Figure 144). James Cawley's map of 1838 (Figure 137) clearly shows that these cottages and the neighbouring Crompton Road Mill were at the time an isolated development, on the western edge of the town. They all date from the 1820s, and it is likely that the housing was intended to accommodate the mill's work-force. In 1834 Joseph Watters, builder of Crompton Road Mill, had 'eight or ten families living in houses which we leased with the old factory; we exercise no superintendence farther than to require them to keep their houses clean and orderly'.[10] Not all owners subscribed to this

Figure 143
*This archway forms an access through a terrace of housing into the mill yard of Victoria Mills, Macclesfield.*

practice: the Brocklehurst family for example did not lease houses to employees as 'it tends to infringe the independence of both parties'.[11]

The tied-house arrangement was probably more common away from the towns. The existence of housing close to the mill was particularly important for the more rural sites, such as Crag Mill at Wildboarclough or Lumbhole Mill at Kettleshulme, to which it would have been almost impossible for workers living in the towns to travel each day. Both of these sites have neighbouring workers' housing. By 1813 the Crag Mill site contained alongside the cotton mill 'twelve cottages for work people [and] a very good and convenient house for the overlooker of the works'.[12] As a further example, in 1824 a newly erected silk mill in Cranage, near Congleton, was advertised for sale together with 'five cottage houses'.[13] The Tithe Map for Buglawton, near Congleton, shows how housing came to be clustered around the mills which as a result became almost self-sufficient communities. John Johnson, a Congleton silk manufacturer and owner of Throstles Nest Mill, Buglawton, in 1840 also owned forty-eight cottages in the streets neighbouring the mill (Figures 145 and 146).[14]

The workers' housing which was erected in east Cheshire during the late 18th century and throughout the 19th century was of a type which

**Figure 144**
*A group of houses on Crown Street West and Parr Street, Macclesfield, built in the early 19th century, was probably owned by the builders of Crompton Road Mill to provide accommodation for their work-force.*

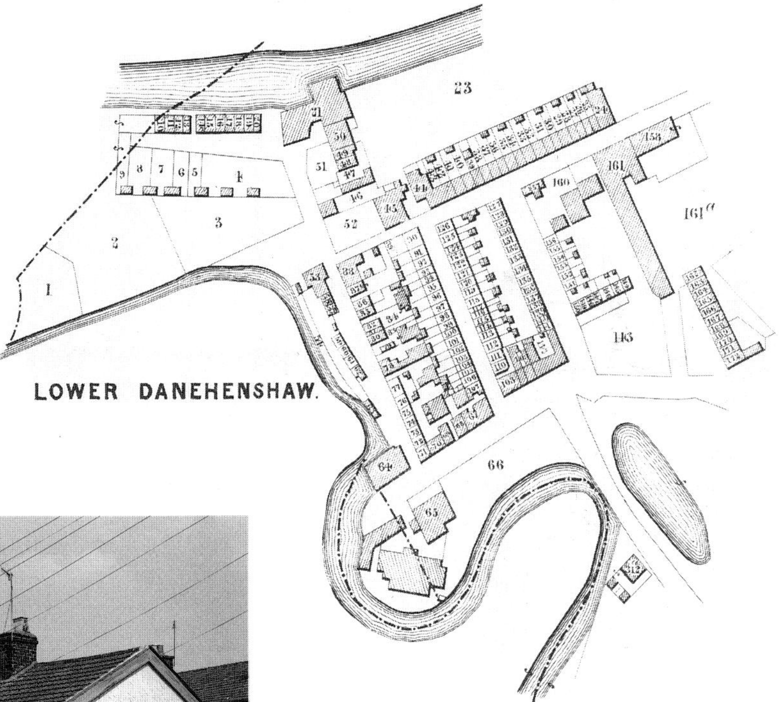

**Figure 145**
*This map of Buglawton in 1840 shows workers' housing situated between Throstles Nest Mill (right), Lower Daneinshaw Mill (below) and Flint Mill (above).*

LOWER DANEHENSHAW.

**Figure 146**
*1–8 Bridge Row, Lower Daneinshaw, Buglawton.*

Figure 147
*Workers' housing on St George's Street, Macclesfield. The ginnel gave access to the yard at the rear and enabled the privies to be emptied.*

Figure 148
*Pear Tree House, Jordangate, Macclesfield, was built in 1728 for the Glovers, a family of silk merchants.*

can be seen in industrial areas throughout the country. The typical house was of two storeys, of either brick or stone, with stone-flag or slate roof covering. The houses were generally built in terraced rows (Figure 147) and were simple two-up, two-down cottages, heated by an open fire in each room. The privies were situated in a yard to the rear and were often shared. One group of houses in Silk Street, Congleton, shared their 'necessary houses' with the neighbouring mill.[15]

New houses were also being built for the increasing wealthy, middle-class section of the east Cheshire population. In the 17th and early 18th centuries town houses were built close to the town centre, the more central the better. The Glovers, for example, a wealthy family of silk merchants who later became involved in the mid 18th-century silk-throwing industry, built Pear Tree House in Macclesfield in 1728 (Figure 148).[16] Its position, close to the centre of town on one of the main streets, and its elegant architecture reflect the prominent status of the family, as does a late house of c1700 on Chestergate, Macclesfield (Figure 149). However, as the town centres became more overcrowded and unpleasant the middle class found it more desirable to live on the outskirts of the town. Ormerod, the Cheshire historian, recorded in 1819 that manufacturers had spoilt the town centre of Macclesfield so that it was 'no longer fitted to be the residence of a gentleman'.[17] Examples of substantial 19th-century villas can therefore be seen on the edges of towns, such as those erected along Byrons Lane, Macclesfield, and Park Lane, Congleton.

Figure 149
*A c1700 house situated on Chestergate, Macclesfield, and traditionally said to have been the home of Charles Roe.*

Figure 150
*The millowner's house at Gin Clough Mill, Rainow.*

Figure 151
*Limefield House at Clarence Mill, Bollington, was built for the Swindells family c 1830.*

For millowners with rural mills there was a tendency to build their houses close to the mill. At Gin Clough Mill, Rainow, the millowner's house abuts the mill (Figure 150), whilst at Quarry Bank Mill, Styal, the millowner's house is adjacent. Clarence Mill, Bollington, has two associated millowners' houses, Limefield House and Rock Bank House (Figures 151, 152). The house at Gin Clough Mill is a modest, two-storeyed dwelling in keeping with a small rural

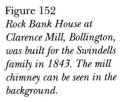

Figure 152
*Rock Bank House at Clarence Mill, Bollington, was built for the Swindells family in 1843. The mill chimney can be seen in the background.*

Figure 153
*This furniture store was built c 1883 for Arighi, Bianchi and Co Ltd. Its façade is made up of decorated panels of cast-iron windows separated by brick pilasters.*

mill, whereas the houses at Quarry Bank Mill and Clarence Mill are far grander in both scale and architecture, reflecting the mills with which they were associated.

Along with the increase in housing there was a corresponding increase in building for the service sector. Between 1825 and 1850 the number of retail shops in Macclesfield increased from 236 to 801[18] and in Congleton the number of alehouses increased from thirty in 1828 to fifty-two by 1848.[19] These buildings were generally functional, brick buildings, two or three storeys high, which formed part of terraced rows. Apart from the shop windows, their overall appearance was not greatly different from much of the contemporary housing. Occasionally a shop was built with a degree of architectural style, and a good example of this is the showroom of Arighi, Bianchi and Co Ltd. This striking, late 19th-century furniture showroom (Figure 153), erected after the arrival of the railway from Bollington in 1872 had led to the demolition of Mr Arighi's previous shop, has decorated panels of cast-iron windows separated by brick pilasters.

Mills, particularly in rural areas, occasionally had shops and public houses close to their sites. These were sometimes in the ownership of the millowner and whilst being convenient for his work-force they were also a way in which he could recoup some of the wages he had paid his employees. Furthermore, difficulties in obtaining small change led, in the late 18th and early 19th centuries, to some millowners paying their work-force in tokens or credit slips which could

be exchanged for goods in the millowners' 'truck' or 'tally' shops and public houses. This practice was made illegal in the early 19th century, but the Truck Acts were very difficult to enforce.[20] Fernley and Swindells owned a shop close to their Ingersley Vale Mill in Rainow. In 1829 they were accused in the local petty sessions court of paying one of their employees, John Bell, 'the sum of £10 as wages, partly in silver and partly in cheques of 10 shillings each'.[21] These cheques could be exchanged for goods at the provisions shop adjacent to the mill, but the court decided that as they could also be cashed the millowners had not broken the law.

Work in the mills was hard, with long hours and low rates of pay. In the early and mid 19th century a normal working day was between twelve and thirteen hours. At the Brocklehurst family mills in 1834 the usual hours worked were:

*Two hours before breakfast (twenty minutes allowed for breakfast) three hours and forty minutes to dinner (one hour allowed for dinner), four hours from dinner to tea (twenty minutes allowed for tea), forty minutes more complete the day; and the people, except those from a distance and the youngest, work two hours longer [overtime]; except on a Saturday, [when] they all leave off at five o'clock.[22]*

**Figure 154**
*The schoolhouse close to Waterside Mill, Disley.*

*a*

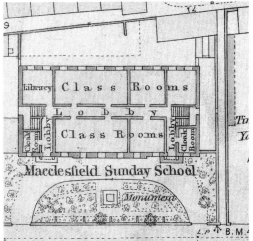

Figure 155
*Large Sunday School, Roe
Street, Macclesfield.*
*a) The school was erected
in 1813 and taught
2,451 pupils in its first
year.*

*b) The 1871 Ordnance
Survey map shows how it
was subdivided at that
date.*

*b*

The youngest operatives were as young as six years old. The hours they worked were less than the adults but still could be up to eleven hours a day during the week, leaving little time for education.[23] Although schools were provided close to some mills, among them one at Waterside Mill, Disley (Figure 154), this was not usually the case. A Parliamentary Return of 1819 stated that in Congleton 'the children of the poor are very generally employed in the mills or cotton manufactories, but they avail themselves of the Sunday Schools being their only means of obtaining instruction'.[24]

Sunday schools began to be established towards the end of the 18th century. The first one in Macclesfield was founded by the Reverend David Simpson in 1778, and there was a Sunday school in Astbury, near Congleton, by 1789. The Large Sunday School on Roe Street, Macclesfield (Figure 155), was built in 1813 and was paid for with funds raised by a committee headed by John Whittaker. In the first year the school taught 2,451 pupils and had 200 voluntary teachers.[25] Later in the 19th century, charitable and religious societies established Sunday schools in east Cheshire, among them the National School in Duke Street, Macclesfield, and St Stephen's National School on Spragg Street, Congleton. In addition to these, many of the nonconformist churches and chapels which were built in the 18th and 19th centuries had associated Sunday schools.

In 1858 an Industrial and Ragged School was started in Macclesfield by the Reverend Henry Briant in order to house, educate and train poor, orphaned and homeless children. After the passing of the Industrial Schools Act in 1865 the school opened new premises on Brooke Street with 130 beds, a dining room, schoolrooms, workshops and a gymnasium (Figure 156).[26]

Both Macclesfield and Congleton were centres of nonconformism from the mid 18th century and throughout the 19th century: the established church initially found it difficult to communicate with the new urban populations. Methodist teaching, on the other hand, struck a chord with the textile workers and was also popular with the millowners and manufacturers who appreciated its emphasis on hard work and self-discipline. Chapel building was financed by the congregation involved, although millowners often donated large amounts of money and paid to have the best pews reserved for them.

Figure 156
*The Industrial and Ragged School, Brook Street, Macclesfield, was built in 1865 and had 130 beds.*

Figure 157
*The Wesleyan Chapel, Sunderland Street, Macclesfield, was erected in 1779 on land donated by John Ryle, silk throwster and cotton spinner.*

Methodist meetings began in Macclesfield in the 1740s and were attended by worshippers who travelled from as far as Astbury, near Congleton. In 1750 Elizabeth Clulow and George Pearson, father of George Pearson the silk manufacturer and builder of Sunderland Street Mill, rented a meeting house on Buxton Road. Later 18th-century meeting houses in Macclesfield, on Commercial Road in 1764 and Sunderland Street in 1779 (Figure 157), were provided by John Ryle, a silk and cotton manu-facturer who with Michael Daintry built Park Green Mill in the town. By 1760 several members of the Manchester Methodist Circuit were from Congleton and were all employed in the silk industry.[27] They worshipped in a small chapel behind Troutbeck's Shop, probably near Victoria Street,[28] until a chapel was built on Wagg Street in 1766–7. Christ Church in Macclesfield (Figure 158), paid for by Charles Roe, one of the town's silk manufacturers, was built in 1775–6. Roe was opposed to Methodism

Figure 158
*Christ Church, Macclesfield, was paid for by Charles Roe and erected in 1775. Roe opposed Methodism but supported an evangelical movement within the Church of England. A monument to him was erected in the church after his death in 1781 (Figure 17).*

Figure 159
*St George's Church, St George's Street, Macclesfield, was erected as a Congregationalist chapel in 1824.*

Figure 160
*Holy Trinity Church, Hurdsfield, Macclesfield, was erected in 1858. It is not a Commissioners' church although its architect, William Hayley, had designed churches for the Commissioners.*

but supported a nonconformist movement within the Church of England. John Ryle Junior, another silk manufacturer, donated the land on which St George's Church, Macclesfield (Figure 159), was erected in 1822–4. Methodism in east Cheshire reached a peak in the 1830s but Methodist and other nonconformist chapels continued to be built throughout the 19th century.

During the early to mid 19th century a number of churches were erected in areas where the Commissioners of the Church of England deemed that their existing buildings did not serve the needs of the growing population. These Commissioners' Churches, conformed to the simple, gothic, architectural style exemplified by St Paul's Church (1843–5) and St Peter's Church (1849), Macclesfield, and Holy Trinity Church, Hurdsfield (Figure 160), of 1837–9. In Congleton in the early 19th century the need for new churches to accommodate the 11,000 Church of England worshippers was great. At that time they only had St Peter's Church, Congleton (Figure 161), in which to worship, but by 1861 four more churches had been built: Holy Trinity, St John's, St James's and St Stephen's.[29]

## Mill communities

Two basic forms of mill community existed in the late 18th and 19th centuries, those which had sprung up in existing agricultural communities and had gradually altered and changed them in a largely unplanned way, and those which came about because of the erection of a factory building which needed a place for its work-force to reside. The development of Langley, a small community situated to the south east of Macclesfield, may be taken as an example of how an essentially rural settlement was changed into an industrial community by the introduction of textile manufacture, whereas two other mill communities, Styal and Lowerhouse, were deliberately fostered by paternalistic millowners.

Figure 161
*St Peter's Church, Chapel Street, Congleton, built in 1740–2.*

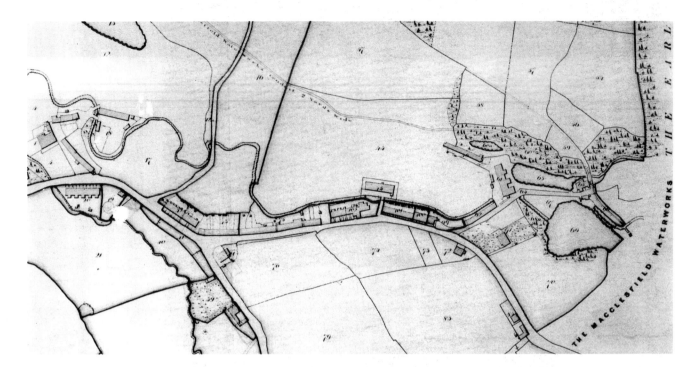

Figure 162
*Plan of Langley, surveyed by Cawley and Firth of Macclesfield, 1851 (CRO D2817/49).*

Figure 163
*44–53 Main Road, Langley, were built in the early 19th century to house the millworkers of the village.*

## Langley

Although Langley had a history of textile working, specifically bleaching, which went back into the 18th century or earlier, it was with the purchase of Langley Hall Estate by David Yates, a Manchester silk throwster, some time between 1798 and 1808 that a textile industry of significance was established there.[30] It was probably Yates who built the Bollinhead group of mills at the end of the 18th and beginning of the 19th century, possibly initially for silk throwing (Figure 162). Little is known about the site, the buildings of which are now demolished, but it consisted of three mills, two of three storeys and one of two storeys, which, according to an advertisement of 1815, were driven by two 4·5 m waterwheels and were used for bleaching and spinning.[31] This would imply that cotton was being produced, perhaps cotton tape which it is known was manufactured in Langley by around 1825. The most northerly of the three mills in fact came to be known as the Tape Works, and subsequently as Albert Mill. However, by 1831 one of the three-storeyed mills was being used as a silk factory and powerloom shop.[32]

At some time between 1815 and 1818 Isaac Smith, who is thought to have been a Nottingham cotton bleacher,[33] moved to Langley and leased part of the Bollinhead site, initially for bleaching[34] but later for smallware manufacture.[35] He prospered and bought the Langley Estate in 1831. Smith was one of the financiers of the first chapel in Langley which was built in 1818 and was Wesleyan.[36] Methodists had been active in the village since the late 18th century and Wesleyanism remained the dominant religious force in the settlement, supported by most of the Langley manufacturers with their wives and children. The chapel contained a schoolroom which was used as a Sunday school.[37]

Until about 1825 the industrial development of Langley seems to have centred on the Bollinhead group of mills. A number of two-storeyed terraced cottages, Wards Cottages and St Dunstans Cottages on Main Road, and probably 44 to 53 Main Road (Figure 163), were built to accommodate the mills' employees. Over the same period — according to local tradition, in 1810 — six garret houses were also built, numbers 5 to 10 Main Road (Figure 164). Varey's

Figure 164
*5–10 Main Road, Langley, are weavers' garret houses said to have been built in 1810.*

Figure 165
*Langley Methodist Chapel replaced a chapel of 1818 and was built in 1858. It contained a schoolroom.*

Figure 166
*The Langley Institute was sponsored by William Whiston, a local printer and dyer, and was erected in 1883.*

Trade Directory of 1825 lists five silk weavers in Langley 'who have looms in their own homes'.[38] They were presumably weaving silk thrown at one of the Bollinhead mills, although silk could have been brought from Macclesfield. The St Dunstan public house was also added to Main Road at this time and was licensed in 1825.[39]

The period after 1825 saw the development of the printing works off Cock Hall Lane and the dyeworks near Langley Hall. This seems to have stimulated more housing, including additions to Main Road, but most notably terraces at Hall Yard, next to Langley Hall, and Red Row terrace. These terraces extended the development away from the central group around Bollinhead and spread the village lengthways along Main Road. The first Wesleyan Chapel stood for only thirty years before dry rot and structural inadequacies made the building unsafe.[40] Isaac Smith died in 1850, but his children headed the fundraising for the new chapel which opened in 1858 and, like the old chapel, contained a schoolroom (Figure 165).

A Mechanics' Institute was established in Langley in 1849[41] offering classes and recreational facilities for the Langley mill workers, but seems not to have survived very long. By 1874 the Langley Working Men's Club and Reading Room had been established but this too closed quickly.[42] By this time more housing had been erected. Four houses had been added to the garrets and Langley Hall Farm had been demolished to be replaced by a terraced row of ten cottages known as Smith's Row. Although it may seem that these and other similar small numbers of dwellings at mill sites in east Cheshire could not house the amount of workers needed for the mills, there was little control over the way in which they were occupied. The census of 1861 recorded that the ten cottages in Smith's Row contained eleven households totalling fifty-one people. The year 1883 saw the erection of the Langley Institute (Figure 166), sponsored by William Whiston. Its aims were much the same as the Mechanics' Institute but were aimed at the whole village. Whistons had come to own the print works at Langley and were in partnership with the Macclesfield silk firm of Brocklehursts.

There was little development in Langley after the 1870s and as the 19th century drew to a close the Bollinhead group of mills fell into decline and disuse. There was no need for the village to expand further. Nevertheless, it developed during its brief periods of expansion through the early and mid 19th century into a mixture of factory, housing, religious and recreational buildings. Some industrialists believed that it was possible and neccessary to imitate this type of development and mixture of buildings in planned mill communities.

## Styal

The growth in population in east Cheshire was part of a nationwide increase. The population of Great Britain, which had been increasing since the mid 18th century, grew from 10.69 million to 24.14 million in the years between 1801 and 1831.[43] This led to concern, voiced most notably by Thomas Malthus in 1798,[44] that a continuing increase would lead to food shortages and mass poverty. Moreover, changes in the organisation of society brought about by the industrial revolution, namely the movement of large sections of the population into towns and cities to work in the mills, led some to believe that this decline in living standards would be accompanied by a similar one in morals. They argued that, deprived of the ordered and familiar life of the country village, society would tend to break down. As a consequence of this view industrialists such as Robert Owen, the New Lanark cotton spinner, and Samuel Greg, owner of Quarry Bank Mill, Styal, concluded that the solution was to bring the structured life of the country villages to the industrial towns by constructing 'village' communities in which their workers could live.

The growth of Styal village, developed by Samuel Greg, mirrored the expansion of the Quarry Bank Mill site. As has already been noted, a mill in a rural location was dependent upon bringing the work-force to the site and housing them. For his apprentices, Greg built an apprentice house in 1790 and housed up to 100 there at the beginning of the 19th century (Figure 167). Some came from as far afield as Hackney and Chelsea.[45] By 1834 they came 'mostly from the Liverpool poor-house, a few from the neighbouring parishes. Some are orphans [and] are visited by the overseers and

Figure 167
*The apprentice house at Quarry Bank Mill, Styal, was built in 1790 and housed up to 100 apprentices at the beginning of the 19th century.*

parents, generally once a year, from Liverpool.'[46] The apprentices were educated by members of the Greg family or by a hired tutor, and a superintendent and his wife lived with them in the apprentice house.

The older members of the work-force lived in the village (Figure 168) and many were housed in cottages owned by the Greg family

Figure 168
*Styal village and Quarry Bank Mill as shown on an Ordnance Survey map of 1875.*

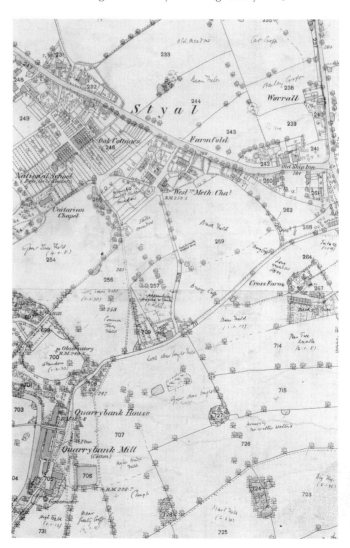

Figure 169
*Workers' housing at Styal;*
*a) Oak Cottages;*
*b) houses with outside*
*privies at the rear.*

Figure 170
*Oak School at Styal was*
*built by the Greg family in*
*the 1820s.*

(Figure 169a). The rent was deducted from their wages. Each house had a parlour, a back kitchen and two bedrooms, a small garden and an outside privy at the rear[47] (Figure 169b). Greg also built Oak School for the village children in the 1820s (Figure 170) and, at about the same time, Norcliffe Chapel where the villagers could worship and their children attend Sunday school (Figure 171).

Samuel Greg and the later Gregs at Quarry Bank Mill developed Styal village to ensure that they attracted employees and that once employed they were happy enough to work well.

They realised that to some extent loyalty could be engendered in the work-force by ensuring their dependence on their employers for many of their basic needs, for example housing and health care.

### Lowerhouse

In 1832, when Samuel Greg Junior took over Lowerhouse Mill, Bollington, and its associated settlement (Figure 41), he determined to take his father's approach one step further in an attempt to create a utopian community. In a more altruistic vein than that adopted at Styal,

Figure 171
*Norcliffe Chapel and Sunday School at Styal was built in the 1820s.*

157

Figure 172
*The mill manager's house, Lowerhouse, was built by Philip Antrobus c1818.*

Figure 173
*The workers' housing at Lowerhouse, Bollington, was built by Philip Antrobus c1818 and was refurbished by Samuel Greg in the early 1830s.*

Greg wanted to convert his work-force to the moral outlook and attitude of his own class, which he saw as improving them. Lowerhouse Mill had become vacant in 1830, after the death of its builder Philip Antrobus, but because of legal complications concerning the will it could not be let until the passing of a private Act of Parliament. The property included not only the mill (Figure 41), but also 'a handsome dwelling house and an excellent garden behind the same, well stocked with fruit trees', a manager's house (Figure 172) 'stone built, which will be found very convenient for the work people', fifty cottages (Figure 173) and 100 acres of meadow and pasture land.[48] Greg refurbished the fifty cottages which were 'well built and of pretty good size, but in extremely bad repair and wanting many little accomodations, such as water, coal sheds, cupboards &c ... There were only three or

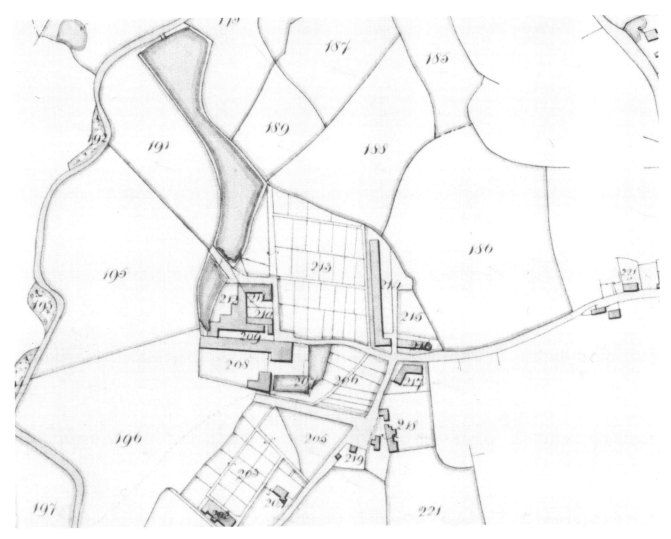

four families at this time on the spot, and my first care was to get rid of these aborigines and start entirely "de novo".'[49] He divided some of the meadow and pasture land into allotments so that his employees could grow their own fruit and vegetables (Figure 174), and he provided a Sunday school and a library (Figure 175).

All this had, more or less, been provided for the work-force at Quarry Bank Mill, but Greg went further by providing lessons in singing, drawing and natural history, a sports field, and hot baths heated by steam from the mill. He also held tea parties to improve etiquette and manners, and instituted the Order of the Silver Cross for well-mannered and behaved girls. Foul language was forbidden and the mixing of sexes was limited. Greg commented, 'I put those on any list whose manners and characteristic mark them out as in some degree superior to their fellows, or those who, I think with a little notice and encouragement, and the advantage of good society, may gradually become civilised and polished.'[50] It is not known whether Greg's experiment was a success.

For him personally its ending was disastrous. Faced with mounting debts and a strike he suffered a nervous breakdown and, in 1847, retired from the family business leaving his brother William to pick up the pieces. According to Samuel Greg's wife, 'From the day he was taken ill ... to the day of his death in 1876, he never went near the mill again, though it was only ten minutes walk from the house, and, with very few exceptions, he had no more intercourse with the people there.'[5]

Figure 174
*The Bollington Tithe Award Map shows Lowerhouse as it was in 1849. The mill pond supplied water to the water-wheel at the end of the mill. To the right of the mill site itself are the small allotments provided by Samuel Greg for the mill-workers which are adjacent to the long terrace of workers' cottages.*

Figure 175
*Lowerhouse Library was built c1832 and extended in 1862.*

# Conclusion

The architectural legacy of the industrial revolution in east Cheshire's textile industry does not include many buildings of outstanding quality. There are no mills, for example, with ironwork like that of Stanley Mill at King's Stanley, Gloucestershire, or with an elevation as daring as the Egyptian façade of Marshall's Temple Mill in Leeds. There are few mill sites as extensive as those of the Lancashire cotton industry, or warehouses as fine as those in Manchester. Neither does the landscape allow as dramatic a setting as that of Cressbrook Mill or Litton Mills in Derbyshire. Nevertheless there is no doubt that those buildings which have survived in east Cheshire are of great importance. Among them are some of the earliest factory buildings in Britain, and the study of them has revealed not only the development of early mill architecture from 1744 onwards, but also, in their use, the economics and logistics of industrialised textile production.

The earliest form of factory building which has been identified for the textile industry seems to have been the throwing 'shade', in which was performed a simple but time-consuming method of throwing silk. Nationally, this was an industry of significance which pre-dated both powered silk-throwing and cotton spinning. Nevertheless it was the introduction of water-powered Italian throwing machinery into Britain which marked a watershed in British industrial history. It is interesting to note that research for the survey has highlighted the fact that it was not so much the new machine which inspired the boom in the British powered silk-throwing industry — there were relatively few mills built to house the Italian, circular throwing machine — but rather the system of production in which it was used. It was the powered cotton-spinning industry which first exploited this system to the full.

Between about 1785, when powered cotton spinning was established in east Cheshire, and the slump of 1826, both the silk and cotton industries enjoyed a period of general prosperity and expansion. It was during this time that the greater proportion of the area's mills were built. The design of mills erected during this period was that first developed for the powered silk-throwing industry. In Macclesfield the first mill for this purpose was built in 1744, and in Congleton in 1753. This form of multi-storeyed mill building continued as adaptable and functional accommodation for both the silk-throwing and the cotton-spinning industries until such time as the demands of new technology and means of production necessitated a change in architectural response.

Recovery after the slump of 1826 was dependent upon the adoption of advances in spinning and weaving technology, and this resulted in new forms of factory building. Significant progress was made in the silk industry with the introduction of the Jacquard loom, the greater head-height of which required increased floor to ceiling heights. Developments in silk and cotton spinning also necessitated more sophisticated factory organisation and expanded premises. Similarly, the introduction of powered weaving, for which the traditional narrow multi-storeyed mills were neither strong enough nor of sufficient capacity, also required changes in the design of factory buildings.

Early responses to these demands survive in east Cheshire: multi-storeyed mills, built during the 1830s, of increased loadbearing capacity and scale, reliant upon the support of intermediate cast-iron columns to house heavy machinery and vibrating looms at ground and first-floor levels; two-storeyed mills built from the 1830s for housing powered weaving; and single-storeyed north-light sheds for a variety of heavy mechanised processes.

Whilst increased mill capacity was ultimately achievable by means of steam power, power systems in themselves did not initially define the size of mills, since it has been shown that mills of similar dimensions were built to be powered by either horse, water or steam. The greater energy resources of steam which enabled larger mills to be erected for the cotton industry were not required for relatively small-scale production in the silk industry.

East Cheshire mills were characterised by the pragmatic approach of the millowners for whom they were built. The organisation and scale of the silk industry, its vulnerability to economic depression, and the construction of mills for both silk and cotton processing on a speculative basis, led to the construction of mills of generally small-scale structure. Pragmatism is also apparent in the generally functional and unadorned exterior elevations which demonstrate neither the desire nor the need, nor possibly the resources, to essay a commanding appearance. The functionalism displayed by the majority of east Cheshire mills is reflected in the buildings that were erected around them. The workers' and garret housing is simple in design, intended to serve a basic need and no more. Chapels and Sunday schools generally have little architectural pretensions. The Large Sunday School on Roe Street, Macclesfield (Figure 155), with its ranks of windows and rectangular plan, is extremely mill like, as is, to provide a different example, the Industrial and Ragged School on Brook Street in the same town (Figure 156). The reasons for this may be several but perhaps foremost was the desire to build quickly and cheaply and the fact that the entrepreneurs who were building the mills were also the people who were promoting the expansion of the towns and neighbouring communities.

In this context those few mills which were erected with an eye to architectural effect stand out prominently. Such mills appear to have been built by entrepreneurs who were venturing into a new area of production and wished to impress. John Clayton and Nathaniel Pattison, builders of the Old Mill, Congleton, were breaking new ground, not only by utilising silk-throwing machinery but also by building one of the first textile mills in the country. Similarly, there is evidence to show that the silk manufacturers who erected pedimented mills in Macclesfield in the early 19th century were amongst the first to house powered silk weaving on site, and that the intention of the builders of the fine Clarence Mill, Bollington, of 1877, was to communicate the advantages and virtues of joint-stock companies.

Only three out of a possible eight mills from 1744 to c1780 remained standing at the time of survey. From the period c1780 to 1826, there were twenty-one out of sixty-four, from mills built between 1826 and the 1870s nine out of twenty-five, and from the 1880s to the 1930s thirteen out of seventeen. The greatest losses occurred during the 1960s during an intensive period of public and private redevelopment. Of those mills which remain, the majority at the time of survey were used for light industrial workshops for a variety of trades, particularly printing, carpentry and light engineering. About a quarter were still in textile-related use, either for the production of yarn and/or cloth, for the making-up of garments, or for finishing in the form of embroidery. Only one mill, Sutton Mill, is entirely used for the processing of silk, and only Quarry Bank Mill at Styal, still spins and weaves cotton, albeit as a by-product of a museum's service. Other surviving mills are used for warehousing, both wholesale and retail.

Although many buildings have been lost, four Macclesfield mills of architectural interest, have been listed as a result of the findings of the survey: Little Street Mill, an extremely rare example of a horse-powered mill, Park Mill, a two-storeyed weaving mill and the two London Road mills as a mid 19th-century group of distinction. It is hoped that others will be considered as representative examples of a group of buildings of national importance.

# GAZETTEER

This gazetteer lists all sites, both standing and demolished, for which files were created during the survey of textile mills in east Cheshire by the East Cheshire Textile Mill Survey, the aims and scope of which are explained in the Introduction.

The gazetteer is arranged alphabetically by parish, and then by mill name. Individual entries contain the following information: file number; mill name; national grid reference.

The archive which results from this survey is available for consultation at the Macclesfield Museums Trust, The Heritage Centre, Roe Street, Macclesfield, Cheshire SK11 6UT. Negatives and prints of photographs taken by the Royal Commission on the Historical Monuments of England are held at the National Buildings Record at the Royal Commission on the Historical Monuments of England, Fortress House, 23 Savile Row, London W1X 2JQ.

## BOLLINGTON

| | | |
|---|---|---|
| ECTMS 133 | Adelphi Mill | SJ 9296 7716 |
| ECTMS 217 | Beehive Mill | SJ 9304 7703 |
| ECTMS 134 | Clarence Mill | SJ 9344 7809 |
| ECTMS 135 | Defiance Mill | SJ 9373 7798 |
| ECTMS 137 | Higher Mill | SJ 9390 7762 |
| ECTMS 136 | Lower Mill | SJ 9377 7768 |
| ECTMS 131 | Lowerhouse Mill | SJ 9217 7763 |
| ECTMS 218 | Oak Bank Print Works | SJ 9380 7790 |
| ECTMS 139 | Sowcar Mill | SJ 9425 7803 |
| ECTMS 219 | Turner Heath Mill | SJ 928 768 |
| ECTMS 132 | Waterhouse Mill | SJ 9293 7785 |

## BOSLEY

| | | |
|---|---|---|
| ECTMS 213 | Dane Mills | SJ 9134 6479 |
| ECTMS 242 | Lower Works | SJ 9125 6504 |

## CONGLETON

| | | |
|---|---|---|
| ECTMS 196 | Albany Mill | SJ 8614 6255 |
| ECTMS 237 | Albert Mill | SJ 8644 6305 |
| ECTMS 208 | Bank Mill | SJ 8689 6343 |
| ECTMS 210 | Bath Vale Mill | SJ 8726 6330 |
| ECTMS 163 | Booth Street Mill | SJ 8543 6295 |
| ECTMS 164 | Booth Street Mill (2) | SJ 8544 6298 |
| ECTMS 176 | Bridge Mill | SJ 8578 6331 |
| ECTMS 170 | Bridge Street Mill | SJ 8578 6287 |
| ECTMS 246 | Bromley Road Mill | SJ 8651 6305 |

| | | |
|---|---|---|
| ECTMS 181 | Brook Mills | SJ 8583 6313 |
| ECTMS 200 | Canal Street Mill | SJ 8652 6212 |
| ECTMS 174 | Cross Street Mill | SJ 8573 6308 |
| ECTMS 175 | Danebridge Mill | SJ 8582 6238 |
| ECTMS 211 | Daneinshaw Mill | SJ 8823 6187 |
| ECTMS 161 | Dane Mill | SJ 8540 6340 |
| ECTMS 245 | Dane Mill (Slate's) | SJ 8565 6321 |
| ECTMS 167 | Daneside Mill | SJ 8575 6325 |
| ECTMS 162 | Dane Street Mill | SJ 8535 6312 |
| ECTMS 203 | Davenshaw Mill | SJ 8660 6349 |
| ECTMS 206 | Eaton Bank Mill | SJ 8674 6386 |
| ECTMS 195 | Edward Mill | SJ 8646 6305 |
| ECTMS 184 | Fair Mill | SJ 8597 6308 |
| ECTMS 202 | Flint Mill | SJ 8652 6362 |
| ECTMS 160 | Forge Mill | SJ 8490 6360 |
| ECTMS 238 | Highbank Mill | SJ 8627 6281 |
| ECTMS 205 | Higher Washford Mill | SJ 8668 6376 |
| ECTMS 187 | Kinsey Street Mill | SJ 8605 6301 |
| ECTMS 188 | Lower Park Street Mill | SJ 8614 6301 |
| ECTMS 191 | Lower Spragg Street Mill | SJ 8630 6300 |
| ECTMS 186 | Meadow Mill | SJ 8604 6305 |
| ECTMS 173 | Moody Street Mill | SJ 8587 6266 |
| ECTMS 179 | Old Mill | SJ 8585 6336 |
| ECTMS 190 | Park Mill | SJ 8625 6296 |
| ECTMS 220 | Pool Bank Mill | SJ 895 266 |
| ECTMS 209 | Primrose Vale Mill | SJ 8717 6341 |
| ECTMS 239 | Prospect Mill | SJ 8521 6291 |
| ECTMS 168 | Providence Mill | SJ 8577 6322 |
| ECTMS 183 | Riverside Mill | SJ 8595 6311 |
| ECTMS 178 | Roldane Mill | SJ 8592 6345 |
| ECTMS 166 | Royle Street Mill | SJ 8572 6327 |
| ECTMS 236 | Royle Street Mill (2) | SJ 8579 6335 |
| ECTMS 177 | Salford Mill | SJ 8581 6339 |
| ECTMS 185 | Shepherd Mills | SJ 8608 6308 |
| ECTMS 199 | Shop Lane Mill | SJ 8650 6250 |
| ECTMS 165 | Silk Street Mill | SJ 8549 6295 |
| ECTMS 212 | Silver Springs Mills | SJ 895 627 |
| ECTMS 193 | Spindle Street Mill | SJ 8634 6299 |
| ECTMS 192 | Spragg Street Mill | SJ 8632 6295 |
| ECTMS 180 | Stonehouse Green Mill | SJ 8579 6301 |
| ECTMS 197 | Sunnyside Mill | SJ 8620 6254 |
| ECTMS 169 | Swan Bank Mill | SJ 8541 6311 |
| ECTMS 182 | Square Mill | SJ 8591 6311 |
| ECTMS 194 | Thomas Street Mill | SJ 8641 6311 |
| ECTMS 204 | Throstles Nest Mill | SJ 8664 6358 |
| ECTMS 172 | Vale Mill | SJ 8576 6270 |
| ECTMS 189 | Victoria Mill | SJ 8627 6303 |
| ECTMS 241 | Victoria Street Mill | SJ 858 629 |
| ECTMS 171 | Wagg Street Mill | SJ 8576 6286 |

| | | | |
|---|---|---|---|
| ECTMS | 198 | Wallworth Bank Mill | SJ 8632 6273 |
| ECTMS | 201 | Washford Mill | SJ 8642 6357 |
| ECTMS | 240 | Westfield Mill | SJ 8522 6284 |

**DISLEY**

| | | | |
|---|---|---|---|
| ECTMS | 157 | Waterside Mill | SJ 9810 8532 |
| ECTMS | 158 | Woodend Mill | SJ 979  869 |

**EATON**

| | | | |
|---|---|---|---|
| ECTMS | 207 | Havannah Mills | SJ 869  646 |

**HOLMES CHAPEL**

| | | | |
|---|---|---|---|
| ECTMS | 234 | Cranage Mill | unsited |

**KETTLESHULME**

| | | | |
|---|---|---|---|
| ECTMS | 159 | Lumbhole Mill | SJ 9882 8038 |

**KNUTSFORD**

| | | | |
|---|---|---|---|
| ECTMS | 233 | Silk Street Mill | SJ 752  787 |

**MACCLESFIELD**

| | | | |
|---|---|---|---|
| MACSM | 11 | 19 Charles Street | SJ 916  734 |
| MACSM | 18 | 11 Duke Street | SJ 916  734 |
| MACSM | 119 | 30a King Edward Street | SJ 7383 9154 |
| MACSM | 107 | 3 St George's Street | SJ 9180 7310 |
| MACSM | 60 | 5 Short Street | SJ 9184 7365 |
| MACSM | 58 | 47 Sunderland Street | SJ 9189 7347 |
| MACSM | 2 | Albert Mill | SJ 9224 7399 |
| MACSM | 71 | Albion Mill | SJ 9201 7247 |
| MACSM | 72 | Alma Mill, Crompton Road | SJ 9106 7357 |
| MACSM | 65 | Alma Mill, Pickford Street | SJ 9198 7338 |
| MACSM | 54 | Arbourhay Street Mill | SJ 9220 7403 |
| MACSM | 98 | Athey Street Mill | SJ 9126 7347 |
| MACSM | 3 | Bank Street Works | SJ 9200 7315 |
| MACSM | 4 | Bank Top Mill | SJ 9223 7319 |
| MACSM | 100 | Barn Street Mill | unsited |
| MACSM | 5 | Bollinside Mill | SJ 9197 7331 |
| MACSM | 73 | Bond Street Mill | SJ 9233 7346 |
| MACSM | 74 | Bridge Street Mills | SJ 9142 7334 |
| MACSM | 94 | Broken Banks Workshop | SJ 9193 7312 |
| MACSM | 76 | Brookside Mill | SJ 9200 7332 |
| MACSM | 78 | Brook Street Mill | SJ 9220 7328 |
| MACSM | 67 | Brown Street Mill | SJ 9145 7311 |
| MACSM | 6 | Brunswick Street Mill | SJ 918  738 |
| MACSM | 125 | Buckley Street Mill | SJ 9152 7305 |
| MACSM | 8 | Catherine Street Mill | SJ 9133 7367 |
| MACSM | 9 | Chapel Mill | SJ 9196 7320 |
| MACSM | 10 | Charles Street Mill | SJ 9165 7334 |
| MACSM | 70 | Charlotte Street Mill | SJ 9185 7336 |
| MACSM | 15 | Chestergate Mill | SJ 9135 7387 |
| MACSM | 14 | Chester Road Mill | SJ 9089 7362 |
| MACSM | 112 | Clough Mill | SJ 9212 7306 |
| MACSM | 12 | Commercial Road Mill | SJ 9195 7377 |

| | | | |
|---|---|---|---|
| MACSM | 68 | Commercial Road/ Queen Street Mill | SJ 9195 7377 |
| MACSM | 83 | Commongate Mill | SJ 9210 7364 |
| MACSM | 85 | Croft Mill | SJ 9153 7353 |
| MACSM | 81 | Crompton Road Mill | SJ 9105 7354 |
| MACSM | 123 | Cuckstool Pit Hill Mill | SJ 920  736 |
| MACSM | 120 | Dale Street Mill | SJ 9230 7349 |
| MACSM | 121 | Davenport Street Silk Machinery Factory | SJ 9205 7345 |
| MACSM | 17 | Depot Mill | SJ 9176 7334 |
| MACSM | 82 | Dog Lane Mill | SJ 9165 7368 |
| MACSM | 106 | Duke Street Mill | SJ 9173 7331 |
| MACSM | 86 | Elizabeth Street Mill | SJ 9152 7332 |
| MACSM | 19 | Exchange Mill | SJ 916  735 |
| MACSM | 126 | Fud Shop | SJ 9205 7394 |
| MACSM | 63 | George Street Mill | SJ 9196 7334 |
| MACSM | 64 | George Street New Mill | SJ 9195 7336 |
| MACSM | 87 | Goodall Street Mill | SJ 9228 7326 |
| MACSM | 77 | Gosling's Mill, Pickford Street | SJ 9180 7342 |
| MACSM | 124 | Great King Street Mill | SJ 9150 7357 |
| MACSM | 88 | Green Street Mill | SJ 9208 7343 |
| MACSM | 20 | Grosvenor Street Mills | SJ 913  738 |
| MACSM | 21 | Gutters Mill | SJ 9183 7373 |
| MACSM | 90 | Henderson Street Mill | SJ 9135 7338 |
| MACSM | 91 | Hibel Road Mill | SJ 9205 7398 |
| MACSM | 111 | Hine's Factory | SJ 920  730 |
| MACSM | 93 | Hope Mill 'A' | SJ 9157 7327 |
| MACSM | 127 | Hope Mill 'B' | SJ 9155 7329 |
| MACSM | 22 | Hurdsfield Road Mills | SJ 9220 7403 |
| MACSM | 247 | Johnson's Mill | unsited |
| MACSM | 235 | Jordangate Mill | unsited |
| MACSM | 24 | King Edward Street Mill | SJ 9142 7382 |
| MACSM | 23 | King Street Mill | SJ 9202 7379 |
| MACSM | 95 | Knight's Mill | SJ 922  731 |
| MACSM | 25 | Knight Street Mill | SJ 922  731 |
| MACSM | 56 | Lansdowne Street Mills | SJ 9220 7403 |
| MACSM | 26 | Little Street Mill | SJ 9148 7383 |
| MACSM | 115 | London Road Mill | SJ 9197 7239 |
| MACSM | 96 | Lowe Street Mill | SJ 9194 7304 |
| MACSM | 99 | Lower Beech Mill | unsited |
| MACSM | 28 | Lower Exchange Street 'B' Mill | SJ 9179 7347 |
| MACSM | 29 | Lower Exchange Street 'F' Mill | SJ 9180 7348 |
| MACSM | 97 | Lower Heyes Mill | SJ 9194 7425 |
| MACSM | 80 | Mill Street Mill | unsited |
| MACSM | 32 | Newgate Mill | SJ 916  734 |
| MACSM | 101 | Oxford Road Mill | SJ 9093 7353 |
| MACSM | 102 | Paradise Mills | SJ 9177 7319 |
| MACSM | 30 | Park Green Mill | SJ 9195 7315 |
| MACSM | 31 | Park Lane Mill | SJ 9176 7322 |
| MACSM | 92 | Park Mill | SJ 9165 7279 |
| MACSM | 122 | Parr Street Shirt Mill | SJ 9113 7349 |
| MACSM | 103 | Peel Street Mill | SJ 9170 7273 |
| MACSM | 35 | Pickford Street 'A' Mill | SJ 9187 7340 |
| MACSM | 33 | Pickford Street 'B' Mill | SJ 9185 7340 |
| MACSM | 57 | Pickford Street Mill | SJ 9176 7339 |
| MACSM | 34 | Pickford Street New Mill 'B' | SJ 9185 7340 |

| | | |
|---|---|---|
| MACSM 75 | Pioneer Mill | SJ 9188 7336 |
| MACSM 104 | Pitt Street Mill | SJ 9194 7270 |
| MACSM 36 | Pleasant Street Mill | SJ 9250 7425 |
| MACSM 105 | Pool Street Mill | SJ 9204 7289 |
| MACSM 37 | Roe's Button Mill | SJ 9178 7336 |
| MACSM 129 | Rowbothams Mill | SJ 9203 7394 |
| MACSM 38 | Royal George Mills | SJ 9134 7378 |
| MACSM 79 | Royal Silk Warehouse | SJ 9188 7375 |
| MACSM 117 | Ryle Street Mill | SJ 9209 7348 |
| MACSM 43 | St George's Street Mill | SJ 9193 7285 |
| MACSM 84 | Samuel Street Mill | SJ 9173 7326 |
| MACSM 41 | Short Street Mill | SJ 9184 7365 |
| MACSM 39 | Silk Street Mill | SJ 916 734 |
| MACSM 40 | Soho Mill | SJ 922 728 |
| MACSM 89 | Spring Gardens Mill | SJ 916 745 |
| MACSM 42 | Stanley Street Mill | SJ 9159 7373 |
| MACSM 69 | Sunderland Street Mill | SJ 9192 7348 |
| MACSM 44 | Sunderland Street 'Slipper' Mill | SJ 9192 7352 |
| MACSM 1 | Sunnyside Mill | SJ 9215 7352 |
| MACSM 108 | Sutton Mill | SJ 9198 7276 |
| MACSM 61 | Thorp Street Gas Mill | SJ 9198 7387 |
| MACSM 62 | Thorp Street Leather Mill | SJ 9194 7395 |
| MACSM 66 | Thorp Street Stoneley's Mill | SJ 9196 7389 |
| MACSM 116 | Townley Street Mill | SJ 9195 7336 |
| MACSM 55 | Victoria Mill | SJ 9220 7403 |
| MACSM 59 | Victoria Mills | SJ 9205 7300 |
| MACSM 109 | Vincent Street Mill | SJ 9167 7315 |
| MACSM 110 | Vincent Street New Mill | SJ 9311 9162 |
| MACSM 46 | Wardle Street Mill | SJ 9170 7321 |
| MACSM 47 | Waterloo Street Mill | SJ 919 737 |
| MACSM 51 | Waters Green (Hadfields) Mill | SJ 9202 7379 |
| MACSM 48 | Waters Green Mill | SJ 9187 7356 |
| MACSM 50 | Waters Green Mill 'A' | SJ 9194 7376 |
| MACSM 49 | Waters Green Mill 'B' | SJ 9194 7376 |
| MACSM 113 | Waters Green New Mill | SJ 9194 7368 |
| MACSM 52 | Waterside Mill | SJ 9205 7305 |
| MACSM 53 | Wellington Mill | SJ 9185 7354 |
| MACSM 114 | Whiston Street Mill | SJ 9118 7338 |
| MACSM 128 | Whitening Croft Mill | SJ 9304 7383 |
| MACSM 118 | Wood Street Mill | SJ 9175 7337 |

**PRESTBURY**

| | | |
|---|---|---|
| ECTMS 130 | Butley Mill | SJ 899 774 |

**RAINOW**

| | | |
|---|---|---|
| ECTMS 148 | Brookhouse Clough Mill | SJ 9476 7512 |
| ECTMS 147 | Brookhouse Mill | SJ 9461 7523 |
| ECTMS 142 | Cow Lane Mill | SJ 9457 7580 |
| ECTMS 144 | Gin Clough Mill | SJ 9584 7644 |
| ECTMS 141 | Hough Hole Mill | SJ 9444 7647 |
| ECTMS 140 | Ingersley Vale Mill | SJ 9423 7732 |
| ECTMS 143 | Lowerhouse Mill | SJ 9538 7656 |
| ECTMS 145 | Millbrook Mill | SJ 9489 7575 |
| ECTMS 138 | Rainow Mill | SJ 9412 7749 |
| ECTMS 146 | Springbank Mill | SJ 9451 7518 |

**SANDBACH**

| | | |
|---|---|---|
| ECTMS 230 | Brook Mill | SJ 7588 6049 |
| ECTMS 244 | Drakeford's Mill | unsited |
| ECTMS 229 | Newfield Mill | SJ 7590 6105 |
| ECTMS 231 | Town Mill | SJ 7581 6075 |
| ECTMS 243 | Wheelock Heath Mill | unsited |
| ECTMS 232 | Wheelock Mill | SJ 7513 5928 |

**SUTTON**

| | | |
|---|---|---|
| ECTMS 153 | Albert Mill | SJ 9422 7164 |
| ECTMS 154 | Bollinhead Mill | SJ 9438 7166 |
| ECTMS 151 | Langley Manufacturing Co | SJ 9394 7155 |
| ECTMS 152 | Langley Print Works | SJ 9409 7125 |
| ECTMS 150 | Riverside Mill | SJ 9389 7163 |
| ECTMS 149 | Sutton Lane Ends Mill | SJ 9285 7115 |

**WILDBOARCLOUGH**

| | | |
|---|---|---|
| ECTMS 215 | Crag Mill | SJ 9835 6875 |
| ECTMS 216 | Higher Mill | |
| ECTMS 214 | Lower Mill | SJ 9828 6862 |

**WILMSLOW**

| | | |
|---|---|---|
| ECTMS 227 | Bollin Walk Mill | SJ 8505 8130 |
| ECTMS 156 | Carrs Mill | SJ 843 817 |
| ECTMS 223 | Dean Row Mill | SJ 877 815 |
| ECTMS 225 | Folly Holes Mill | SJ 847 815 |
| ECTMS 221 | Handforth Bleach Works | SJ 857 831 |
| ECTMS 222 | Handforth Print Works | SJ 866 828 |
| ECTMS 228 | Hawthorn Street Mill | SJ 8425 8092 |
| ECTMS 226 | Manchester Road Mill | SJ 8485 8128 |
| ECTMS 224 | Mill Street Mill | SJ 848 814 |
| ECTMS 155 | Quarry Bank Mill | SJ 8345 8290 |

# NOTES

## 1 HISTORICAL BACKGROUND OF THE SILK AND COTTON INDUSTRIES IN EAST CHESHIRE

1 Pigot and Co 1834.
2 Kerridge 1985, 20.
3 Everett 1840.
4 Hodson 1978, 145.
5 Hills 1970, 6; Kerridge 1985, 125.
6 Hodson 1978, 145.
7 Roberts 1970, 8.
8 Finney 1785; Radcliffe 1828.
9 Kerridge 1985, 79.
10 The strongest and best kind of silk thread, formed of several strands twisted together in the contrary direction to that in which their component filaments are twisted (*Oxford English Dictionary*, Compact Edition, 1980, 2008).
11 Silk thread consisting of two or more single strands loosely twisted together; used for the weft or cross threads of the best silk goods (*Oxford English Dictionary*, Compact Edition, 1980, 3376).
12 Kerridge 1985, 141–2.
13 Warner 1921, 630.
14 An Act to Right the Trade of Silk Throwing, 1667–8, quoted in Warner 921, 627.
15 Warner 1921, Appendix C, 633.
16 In 1704 Thomas Cotchett leased water rights on the River Derwent (Chapman 1987, 14).
17 Hutton 1817, 161.
18 For a more detailed account see Chaloner 1963, 8–20.
19 *Journal of the House of Commons*, vol 30, 1765, 213.
20 Corry 1817, 64.
21 *Journal of the House of Commons*, vol 30, 1765, 213.
22 Deeds, Old Mill, Congleton, in the possession of the owners.
23 *Journal of the House of Commons*, vol 30, 1765, 213.
24 Hertz 1909, 711.
25 Cheshire County Records Office, WS 1758, Lankford, Samuel.
26 *Journal of the House of Commons*, vol 30, 1765, 208.
27 Ure 1861, 13.
28 Chaloner 1963, 43.
29 Corry 1817, 85.
30 *Macclesfield Courier and Herald*, 8 October 1825.
31 The production of fine silks never recovered.
32 Mathias 1983, 116–17.
33 Catling 1978, 35–57.
34 Mathias 1983, 352.
35 For a more detailed discussion see Farnie 1979, 209–76.
36 Farnie 1979, 318–23.
37 Mathias 1983, 380–3, 434.
38 The Thorp Street Leather Mill in Macclesfield was used for the storage of sugar and in Congleton a number of mills were taken over for the billeting of Dutch and American troops.

## 2 HOUSING THE SILK INDUSTRY *c*1700–*c*1780

1 Cheshire County Records Office, Macclesfield Corporation Minute Books. LBM.
2 Davies 1961, 43.
3 Cheshire County Records Office, WS 1631, Turton, R.
4 Cheshire County Records Office, Macclesfield Borough Council Minutes, April 1619–September 1744, LBM/1/1–2.
5 Cheshire County Records Office, WS 1617, Rowe, Stephen, quoted in *Origins of the Silk Industry*, Source Books on Silk, Cheshire Museums and Archives Education Project, 1989.
6 Cheshire County Records Office, WS 1828, Street, Joseph
7 Finney 1785, 6. The cover date of 1785 appears to be the date of a first edition and the edition held by Wilmslow Public Library contains some later revision.
8 Birkenhead Public Library, Macclesfield Stallage Court, 1735, B/II/13.
9 Cheshire County Records Office, WS 1739, Pownall, Richard.
10 Cheshire County Records Office, WS 1738, Braddock, Samuel
11 Crozier 1947, 10.
12 Malmgreen 1985, 9–10.
13 Cheshire County Records Office, Macclesfield Borough Council Minutes, April 1619–September 1744, LBM/1/1–2.
14 Cheshire County Records Office, WS 1741, Wood, Samuel. The names Dubourg and Van Nypens are an indication of earlier French and Flemish influences in the London market.
15 Cheshire County Records Office, WS 1681, Massey, J, also, WS 1631, Turton, R.
16 Birkenhead Public Library, Macclesfield Stallage Court, 1732, B/II/12.
17 Warner 1921, 149.
18 Kerridge 1985, 79.
19 Yates 1822, 100.
20 John Rylands Library, Manchester, Methodist Archive, A List of Names of the Societies in the Manchester Circuit, May 1759. This document contains two lists relating to Congleton, the first dated May 1759 and the second, on the next page, undated.

21  *The Directory and Guide for the City and County of Chester*, 1789, 90–2.

22  *Origins of the Silk Industry*, Source Books on Silk, Cheshire Museums and Archives Education Project, 1989.

23  A richly coloured and patterned silk cloth originating from India which was often used for gowns or handkerchiefs.

24  Prout 1829.

25  Lardner 1831, 201; Crippa 1990, 169–212.

26  *Journal of the House of Commons*. Parliamentary Committee of Inquiry into children's working conditions, 1841.

27  *Journal of the House of Commons*, 1863.

28  *Journal of the House of Commons*. Parliamentary Committee of Inquiry into children's working conditions, 1841.

29  Cheshire County Records Office, WS 1727, Mottershead, E.

30  Deeds, 14–18, Jordangate, Macclesfield, in the possession of the owner.

31  Guildhall Library, Sun Fire Insurance Records, MS 11936/190–211.

32  Eadwine Psalter, Trinity College, Cambridge, MS R.17.1, f263.

33  *Origins of the Silk Industry*, Source Books on Silk, Cheshire Museums and Archives Education Project, 1989.

34  Chapelot and Fossier 1985, 119.

35  Cheshire County Records Office, Enclosure Award Map and Schedule, 1804, QDE2/10.

36  Chaloner 1950–1, 136–7.

37  Cheshire County Records Office 1771, LRE239.

38  Byng, J. *The Torrington Diaries: A Selection from the Tours of the Hon. John Byng (Later 5th Viscount Torrington) Between the Years 1781 and 1794*. Andrews, B (ed), abridged into one vol by Andrews, F 1954.

39  This seems, however, to have been a technique more commonly applied to domestic rather than industrial architecture.

40  Sales notices of 1831 and 1841 show that Chestergate Mill was subsequently used as 'a warehouse with the winding and weaving rooms over it' (*Macclesfield Courier and Herald*, 30 April 1831 and 14 August 1841).

41  Cheshire County Records Office, Enclosure Award Map and Schedule, 1804, QDE2/10.

42  Williamson 1936, 63–4.

43  Ibid, 59–64.

44  Stockport is now in Greater Manchester.

45  *Journal of the House of Commons*, vol 30, 1765, 213–14. The word mill here must mean the factory building and not the machine since multiples of the organzine machines were housed within one building.

46  This calculation assumes that each of the seven major silk-throwing firms occupied separate mill buildings.

47  *Journal of the House of Commons*, vol 30, 1765, 208.

48  Corry 1817, 56. Corry believed that Roe's Button Mill was built in 1756.

49  Cheshire County Records Office, Macclesfield Land Tax Assessment, 1743.

50  Cheshire County Records Office, WS 1726, Hall, Jonah.

51  Cheshire County Records Office, WS 1738, Braddock, Samuel.

52  Cheshire County Records Office, WS 1758, Bradock, James.

53  Indenture of lease 1750, Gutters Mill, deeds in the possession of Macclesfield Borough Council.

54  Malmgreen 1985, 208.

55  Chaloner 1953, 781.

56  Chaloner 1950–1, 134.

57  Davies 1961, 114.

58  Cheshire County Records Office, WS 1723, Roe, Thomas.

59  Deeds, Sunderland Street Mill, Macclesfield, in the possession of the owners.

60  Hegginbotham 1882, 317–18.

61  An indenture of 1758 records that this figure was short of what the premises cost but gives no actual cost for the building of the mill. Deeds, Old Mill, Congleton, in the possession of the owners.

62  Chaloner 1950–1, 138.

63  Chaloner 1953, 781.

64  Ibid.

65  Defoe 1971, 458.

66  Williamson 1936, 62.

67  English 1971, 65.

68  Chaloner 1963, 14–15.

69  Cossons 1972, 468.

70  Yates 1822, 95.

71  Staffordshire County Record Office, A Survey Valuation and an Assessment of the Poors Rate on all the Lands and Houses in the Township of Congleton, Taken in the Month of March 1775, D(W)1909/D/2/1.

72  *Macclesfield Courier and Herald*, 4 July 1812.

73  Deeds, Old Mill, Congleton, in the possession of the owners.

74  Evidence given by Nathaniel Pattison to the House of Commons in 1765 (*Journal of the House of Commons*, vol 30, 1765, 213).

75  Yates 1822, 95.

76  *Journal of the House of Commons*, vol 30, 1765, 213.

77  Yates 1822, 95.

78  Cheshire County Records Office, Notice of Sale, 25 October 1811, DCB/1595/11/2.

79  *Journal of the House of Commons*, vol 30, 1765, 215.

80  Yates 1822, 95; Cossons 1972, 468.

81  Plans of the Mill Street wing were drawn in 1945. In 1959, immediately prior to its

demolition, the remains of the rear wing of the mill were described by J Massey (Massey 1959). These sources, together with the representation of the mill on Roe's monument in Christ Church, Macclesfield, comprise a valuable record of the building.

82  Deeds, Sunderland Street Mill, Macclesfield, in the possession of the owners.
83  Ibid.
84  *Journal of the House of Commons*, vol 30, 1765, 215.
85  Cheshire County Records Office, Enclosure Award Map and Schedule, 1804, QDE2/10.
86  Ibid.
87  Cheshire County Records Office, Cawley, J. Map of Macclesfield, 1838.
88  Ordnance Survey 1875, 1:500.
89  Corry 1817, 56.
90  *Macclesfield Courier and Herald*, 4 July 1812.
91  Crippa 1990, 186.
92  Zonca 1607.
93  Negri 1831.
94  Chaloner 1953, 781.
95  Chaloner 1950–1, 136.
96  Deeds, Park Green Mill, Macclesfield, in the possession of the owners.
97  Deeds, Sunderland Street Mill, Macclesfield, in the possession of the owners.
98  Ibid.
99  Ibid.
100  Ordnance Survey 1871, 1:500.
101  Deeds, Old Mill, Congleton, in the possession of the owners.
102  The annual rent was £150, plus 30 shillings in lieu of 'mill dust', forty bushels of malt and seventy-two pecks of barley. The latter was for giving to poor people nominated by the Mayor. They were also to lay down '2000 piles in kiln or any lesser quantity' and mill for the townspeople taking a toll of 1/24th for malt, and 1/16th for corn. Deeds, Old Mill, Congleton, in the possession of the owners.
103  Yates 1822, 96–7.
104  Deeds, Old Mill, Congleton, in the possession of the owners.
105  Sketch plan in the possession of *Congleton Chronicle.*
106  English 1971, 74.
107  Phillips 1792, 103–4. Brindley's involvement with the construction of machinery in Old Mill, Congleton, is also discussed in Smiles 1904, 175–8.

### 3  HOUSING THE SILK AND COTTON INDUSTRIES *c*1780–1826

1  Corry 1817, 66.
2  The figures in this analysis are not absolute, owing to the nature of some of the dating evidence.
3  *Journal of the House of Commons.* Select Committee of Inquiry into the State of the Silk Trade, 1832.
4  Cheshire County Records Office, deeds to Gin Clough Mill, Rainow, DDX 47.
5  Deeds, Lower Heyes Mill, Macclesfield, in the possession of the owners.
6  Davies 1961, 239.
7  Jenny spinning survived in Stockport into the 1820s. Ex. inf. Dr D A Farnie.
8  Finney 1785, 7–8. The mill described by Finney seems to have been Folly Holes Mill, now demolished.
9  Rose 1978, 8.
10  Finney 1785, 7–8.
11  Tunnicliffe 1789, 67. 'Checks were plain weaves with warp and weft stripes intersecting to form large ... squares.' Kerridge 1985, 125.
12  Unwin 1924, 45–6.
13  *Macclesfield Courier and Herald*, 18 February 1815.
14  Finney 1785, 7–8.
15  Yates 1822, 100; Cheshire County Records Office, Articles of Partnership, DCB 1595/27/14, DCB 1595/8/6, DCB 1595/2/5.
16  Cheshire County Records Office, Articles of Partnership, DCB 1595/27/14.
17  Guildhall Ms 11936/347 No. 536457.
18  Rose 1978, 8.
19  Corry 1817, 66–7.
20  Ibid, 71.
21  The broadloom allowed the weaving of a wide piece of silk cloth, rather than narrow tape or ribbon.
22  *Journal of the House of Commons.* Select Committee of Inquiry into the State of the Silk Trade, 1832. Brocklehurst's definition could also be applied to cotton.
23  *Macclesfield Courier and Herald*, 30 June 1821. The author was exaggerating the effect of these weaving establishments on the Spitalfields industry.
24  Pigot and Co 1822–3.
25  *Macclesfield Courier and Herald*, 14 June 1817.
26  *Macclesfield Courier and Herald*, 8 February 1827.
27  Yates 1822, 100.
28  Cheshire County Records Office, Particulars of Estates and Rents Late the Inheritance of Mr John Booth deceased 26 February 1820, DCB/1595/16/3.
29  Staffordshire Records Office, A Survey Valuation and an Assessment of the Poors Rate on all the Lands and Houses in the Township of Congleton, Taken in the Month of March 1775, D(W)1909/D/2/1.
30  Cheshire County Records Office, Notice of sale, 25 October 1811, DCB/1595/11/2.
31  *Macclesfield Courier and Herald*, 30 January 1813 and 8 March 1817.

32 *Journal of the House of Commons*. Select Committee of Inquiry into the State of the Silk Trade, 1832.
33 Hills 1970, 32.
34 Ibid, 64.
35 Plan of mill in Quarry Bank Mill, Styal, archives.
36 *Macclesfield Courier and Herald*, 14 April 1821.
37 Hills 1970, 73–87.
38 For a detailed analysis of the mechanisation of cotton production see Hills 1970, 33–88.
39 Chapman 1981–2.
40 Lancashire County Museums Service, Helmshore Textile Museum.
41 Hills 1970, 68.
42 Corry 1817, 67.
43 Deeds, Stonehouse Green Mill, Congleton, in the possession of the owners.
44 Deeds, Higher Mill, Bollington, in the possession of the owners.
45 Guildhall MS 7253/32A No 160151.
46 *The Universal British Directory*, 1790–8.
47 Yates 1822, 99.
48 *Macclesfield Courier and Herald*, 8 June 1811.
49 Deeds, Lower Heyes Mill, Macclesfield, in the possession of the owner.
50 Deeds, Park Mill, Congleton, in the possession of the owners.
51 Deeds, Pickford Street 'A' Mill, Macclesfield, in the possession of Macclesfield Borough Council.
52 *Macclesfield Courier and Herald*, 1 January 1825.
53 Deeds, Pickford Street 'A' Mill, Macclesfield, in the possession of Macclesfield Borough Council.
54 Guildhall MS 11937/11 No. 649233.
55 Guildhall MS 11936/347 No. 536457.
56 Ibid.
57 Chapman 1974, 474.
58 *Journal of the House of Commons*. Select Committee of Inquiry into the State of the Silk Trade, 1832.
59 Examples from the 18th century are: Quarry Bank Mill in Styal; Park Green Mill, 47 Sunderland Street Mill, Pickford Street Mill and Little Street Mill in Macclesfield; Gin Clough Mill in Rainow; and the early phase of Brook Mills in Congleton. Standing examples from the periods of building expansion in the early 19th century are: Ingersley Vale Mill, Bollington; Thorp Street Leather Mill, Catherine Street Mill and Lowe Street Mill in Macclesfield; Throstles Nest Mill, Vale Mill and Park Mill in Congleton; Town Mill in Sandbach and Wheelock Mill, Wheelock.
60 Deeds, Bollin Mill, in the possession of Macclesfield Museums Trust.
61 *Macclesfield Courier and Herald*, 24 June 1820.
62 Tann 1970, 123.
63 *Macclesfield Courier and Herald*, 29 November 1817.
64 Stephens 1970, 103.
65 Although there are three standing pedimented mills in Congleton, one, Salford Mill, was built about 1850, whilst Dane Mill and Daneinshaw Mill, have pediments as part of a secondary phase of development.
66 *Journal of the House of Commons*, Select Committee of Inquiry into the State of the Silk Trade, 1832.
67 Rathbone, C, *Macclesfield Times*, 5 March 1953.
68 *Macclesfield Courier and Herald*, 11 November 1826.
69 *Macclesfield Courier and Herald*, 27 May 1826.
70 For a full discussion of fireproofing in mill building see Skempton and Johnson 1962; Fitzgerald 1987–8, 127–45.
71 Evidence for the building date comes from a datestone carved on the keystone of the lunette in the engine house gable, and a lease, dated 1818, details of which are contained in an abstract of title held by the owners.
72 Each cross-beam is composed of three individual beams spanning 4.38 m. They are joined at the columns by side-mounted shrink rings. These circular rings hold together two semicircular spigots, one of which is cast into the end of each beam. In this way adjoining beams are held together across the width of the room.
73 In a fire at Lowerhouse Mill, Bollington, in 1835, the heat was so intense that some of these sheets melted.
74 Massey 1959, 34, 40.
75 Deeds, Pickford Street 'A' Mill, Macclesfield, in the possession of Macclesfield Borough Council.
76 Deeds, Crompton Road Mill, Macclesfield, in the possession of the owner.
77 Massey 1959, 41.
78 Ibid, 41, 99.
79 *Macclesfield Courier and Herald*, 24 May 1823.
80 *Macclesfield Courier and Herald*, 19 May 1821.
81 *Macclesfield Courier and Herald*, 6 May 1826.
82 Select Committee Report on the Ribbon Weavers of Coventry and Leek and the Silk Weavers of Macclesfield, 1818, vol 9.
83 Corry 1817, 121.
84 Cheshire County Records Office, Enclosure Award Map and Schedule, 1804, QDE2/10.
85 Cheshire County Records Office, Particulars of Estates and Rents Late the Inheritance of Mr John Booth deceased, 26 February 1820, DCB/1595/16/3.
86 Survey of Macclesfield garret houses, 1984–6, Macclesfield Museums Trust.

87  Aspin 1972.

88  Wootton 1866.

89  *Macclesfield Courier and Herald*, 15 May 1821. This site was historically in east Cheshire, prior to the re-drawing of county boundaries.

90  *Macclesfield Courier and Herald*, 13 April 1812.

91  Cheshire County Records Office, Enclosure Award Map, 1804, QDE2/10.

92  *Macclesfield Courier and Herald*, 20 April 1811.

93  *Macclesfield Courier and Herald*, 20 April 1811 and 22 October 1814. The rooms have been shortened by about 1·8 m, by the addition of a warehouse in 1909.

94  *Macclesfield Courier and Herald*, 22 October 1814.

95  *Macclesfield Courier and Herald*, 5 August 1826.

96  Ordnance Survey 1871–5, 1:500.

97  47 Sunderland Street Mill, Macclesfield, is the closest of these mills to a watercourse, but there is no evidence, structural or documentary, that it was water powered.

98  Deeds, Pickford Street Mill, in possession of the owners; Cheshire County Records Office, Enclosure Award Map and Schedule, 1804, QDE2/10.

99  A 999 year lease, advertised in *Macclesfield Courier and Herald*, 17 September 1814 and 25 May 1844.

100  Cheshire County Records Office, Enclosure Award Map and Schedule, 1804, QDE2/10. This is a rare example of female ownership of a mill.

101  Hills 1970, 99.

102  For a more detailed discussion of the development of waterwheels see Hills 1970, 93–115.

103  *Macclesfield Courier and Herald*, 29 July 1820.

104  The evidence for the primary process of Park Green Mill, Macclesfield, is not clear.

105  Farey 1827.

106  Cheshire County Records Office, Enclosure Award Map of Macclesfield, 1804, QDE2/10.

107  A row of closers running up the Park Green elevation seems to indicate that they once formed a corner of the Mill Lane wing.

108  It is recorded that James Brindley repaired machinery at a mill on this site in 1733 (Smiles 1904, 307–33).

109  Massey 1959, 56.

110  Deeds, Stonehouse Green Mill, Congleton, in the possession of the owner.

111  Ibid.

112  *Macclesfield Courier and Herald*, 21 April 1821. The site description, ownership and the lease date of 12 May 1785 ascribe this advertisement to the Brook Mills, Congleton, site.

113  Deeds map of 1839, estate map of 1853, in the possession of the owner.

114  The background information on Quarry Bank Mill, Styal, is derived from Quarry Bank Mill Museum archives and publications, and also Rose 1978.

115  Adlington Hall Estate MSS. Chancery Court case Deposition, 1806.

116  *Macclesfield Courier and Herald*, 17 August 1822.

117  *Macclesfield Courier and Herald*, 17 January 1827.

118  The wheel was still operational in the 1950s, although a steam engine was installed during the late 19th century, and subsequently a gas engine, during the mill's use as a saw-mill.

119  Adlington Hall Estate MSS, Chancery Court case Deposition, 1806.

120  The mill caught fire again in the 1960s and suffered considerable interior damage.

121  *Macclesfield Courier and Herald*, 24 February 1816. The width of this secondary phase of building is similar to the four largest mills in east Cheshire of this period, but wider by 2 m than other contemporary mills.

122  *Macclesfield Courier and Herald*, 18 December 1822.

123  *Macclesfield Courier and Herald*, 10 February 1816.

124  The engine is a double-action condensing engine, four-stroke cylinder with slide valve, which may have been built by Sherratts of Salford.

125  The earliest reference to Boulton and Watt's activities in east Cheshire comes in a letter of 1775 from Boulton and Watt responding to an inquiry from Samuel Roe of Macclesfield, probably concerning Macclesfield copper works: Birmingham Public Library, Boulton and Watt Papers, Letter Book 1. Matthew Boulton to Samuel Roe, 29 June 1775.

126  *Macclesfield Courier and Herald*, 28 September 1811.

127  Although it is known that the sun and planet gearing tended to be unreliable, it is not known whether the second of Daintry and Ryle's engines replaced the first, or whether Daintry and Ryle owned two cotton mills at this time. It is possible that one or both of these engines was for their Park Green Mill, Macclesfield.

128  This mill was probably Sunnyside Mill, Macclesfield.

129  Chaloner 1951, 121–36.

130  Hills 1970, 190–207.

131  Ibid, 147–8.

132  *Macclesfield Courier and Herald*, 26 June 1826.

133  This capacity may be explained by Pearson's intention to expand into cotton spinning at

their Sunderland Street Mill site, Macclesfield, in a new mill building.

| Date of Advertisement | Mill | HP | Silk or Cotton | Size (yds) | Storeys |
|---|---|---|---|---|---|
| 8 Jun 1811 | Commongate Mill | 14 | S or C | 25 x 8 | |
| 18 Jan 1812 | Pickford Street 'A' Mill | 20 | C | 25 x 11½ | 5 |
| 27 Mar 1813 | Waters Green | 8 | S | 27 x 8 | 4 |
| 17 Mar 1818 | Waterside | 6 | S | 12 x 8 | 4 |
| | | | | 16 x 6 | 3 |
| | | | | 16 x 8 | 4 |
| 6 Jan 1821 | Lowerhouse Mill (Rainow) | 20 | C | 10 x 11 | 3 |
| 24 May 1823 | Depot Mill | 28 | S & C | 25 x 11 | 6 |
| | | | | 27 x 10 | 4 |
| | | | | 49 x 7/8 | 4 |
| 9 Aug 1826 | Park Lane Mill | 8 | S | c32 x 9 | |
| 19 Dec 1829 | Royle Street Mill | 3 | S | 21 x 9 | 2 |

All except Royle Street Mill, Congleton, and Lowerhouse Mill, Rainow, are Macclesfield sites. Lowerhouse Mill, Rainow, was built as a water-powered cotton factory in 1792 but by 1821 had converted to steam. More than one set of dimensions indicates more than one mill building on the site. It can also be seen from the above list that power could be shared between a group of mills, although the ratio of hand-powered to mechanised processes and the working capacity of the mills are not known, therefore the use and power requirements of the individual mills cannot be estimated (*Macclesfield Courier and Herald*).

134   Below is a list of mills built during the early 19th century, with specifications. Taken from advertisements in *Macclesfield Courier and Herald*.

| Mill | Dimensions (ft) | Storeys |
|---|---|---|
| Bank Top Mill, Macclesfield | 94 x 26 | 4 |
| Charles Street Mill, Macclesfield | 94 x 24 | 3 |
| Exchange Street Mill, Macclesfield | 100 x 24 | 4 |
| King Street Mill, Macclesfield | 97 x 24 | 4 |
| King Edward Street Mill, Macclesfield | 86 x 24 | 4 |
| Moody Street Mill, Congleton | 84 x 26 | |
| Pioneer Mill, Macclesfield | 113 x 24 | 3 |
| Prospect Mill, Congleton | 76 x 27 | |
| Silk Street Mill, Macclesfield | 89 x 26 | |
| Spragg Street Mill (Upper), Congleton | 62 x 29 | 2 |
| Union Mill, Macclesfield | 78 x 26 | |
| Westfield Mill, Congleton | 123 x 26 | |
| Wheelock Heath Mill, Wheelock | 78 x 26 | |

135   It is possible to identify the outline of the engine houses of many of these mills on James Cawley's map of Macclesfield, published in 1838 (Cheshire County Records Office, Cawley, J. Map of Macclesfield, 1838).

136   No absolute date can be given for the steam-power systems on any of these sites, although evidence implies a pre-1826 date.

## 4   HOUSING THE SILK INDUSTRY 1826–1990

1   Only one firm, Adamley Textiles Ltd, now throws and weaves silk in Macclesfield. Its branch at Langley Park also dyes and prints silk.
2   Wootton 1866.
3   Davies 1961, 136.
4   Varey 1825; Crozier 1947.
5   *Journal of the House of Commons*. Select Committee of Inquiry into the State of the Silk Trade, 1832.
6   In the late 1980s Brocklehursts were taken over by a multi-national company, Bodicote, who sold the business in 1991 to J Whiston. The business trades under Brocklehurst Whiston. Production has ceased at Hurdsfield Road Mills, Macclesfield, which are to be sold in mid 1992.
7   Holden 1805, 1806, 1807.
8   Select Committee Report on the Ribbon Weavers of Coventry and Leek and the Silk Weavers of Macclesfield, 1818, vol 9.
9   Cheshire County Records Office, Cawley, J. Map of Macclesfield, 1838.
10   Wootton 1866.
11   Worrall 1872.
12   Post Office, 1878.
13   *Macclesfield Courier and Herald*, 7 March 1840.
14   *Macclesfield Courier and Herald*, 13 December 1851.
15   *Macclesfield Courier and Herald*, 12 May 1838.
16   Smales closed during 1991, however, when Tootal transferred the production to Failsworth.
17   Cheshire County Records Office, 1784 Macclesfield tax assessment. Enclosure Award Schedule, 1804, QDE 2/10.
18   Davies 1961, 137.
19   Morris and Co 1864.
20   Prout 1829, 47, 59.
21   Aspin 1972.
22   *Journal of the House of Commons*, vol 30, 1765.
23   Warner 1921, 415.
24   Singer *et al* 1958, 322.
25   Iredale and Townhill 1973.
26   Warner 1921, 407.
27   Silk spinning in Congleton finally ceased in 1952 with the relocation of Peter Wild and Co to Leek.
28   *Macclesfield Courier and Herald*, 15 April 1848.
29   Cheshire County Records Office, Cawley, J. Map of Macclesfield, 1838. Ordnance Survey 1871, 1:500.

30  Cheshire County Records Office, DCB/2114/MP5.

31  Cheshire County Records Office, Tithe Map of Congleton, 1845.

32  Edgar 1987. For a detailed account of the establishment of the Jacquard industry in Britain, see Rothstein 1977.

33  *Macclesfield Courier and Herald,* 24 November 1821.

34  Lords Committee on the Silk Manufacturers Bill, 1823.

35  *Macclesfield Courier and Herald,* 9 August 1828.

36  *Macclesfield Courier and Herald,* 5 January 1850.

37  *Macclesfield Courier and Herald,* 23 January 1850.

38  Lardner 1831.

39  Factories Inquiry Commission 1836.

40  Parliamentary Papers. Reports from Assistant Hand-Loom Weavers' Commissioners, 1840, 490.

41  Aspin 1972.

42  The looms remain in place in Paradise Mills, Macclesfield, which is now a working silk museum.

43  The primary phase of Victoria Mill, Congleton, was demolished in 1988.

44  Cheshire County Records Office, Congleton Tithe Award Map, 1845.

45  Deeds, Victoria Mills, Macclesfield, in the possession of the owners.

46  The average diameter of columns used in Macclesfield mills was 120mm.

47  It is important to note that in the silk industry the term 'shed' is used as loosely at this time as when the first records were made of throwing 'shades', or sheds. The word appears to have meant the room in which the looms were housed, but came locally to be applied to the whole building.

48  White & Co 1860.

49  Cheshire County Records Office, Plan no. 902, Macclesfield Borough Council.

50  The Jacquard mechanisms were replaced *c*1975.

51  Cheshire County Records Office, Plan no. 94, Macclesfield Borough Council.

52  Ordnance Survey 1871, 1:500.

53  Cheshire County Records Office, Plan no. 782, Macclesfield Borough Council.

54  Cheshire County Records Office, Plan no. 660, Macclesfield Borough Council.

55  The vaulted roof was removed in the 1980s and replaced with the present pyramidal roof.

56  *Macclesfield Courier and Herald,* 13 April 1833.

57  *Macclesfield Courier and Herald,* 26 February 1842.

58  *Macclesfield Courier and Herald,* 15 December 1848.

59  *Macclesfield Courier and Herald,* 30 May 1835.

60  *Macclesfield Courier and Herald,* 23 August 1828.

61  Indenture of lease, 24 April 1893.

62  Friends of Macclesfield Silk Heritage Silk History Group, *Bridge Street,* 1984.

63  Minute Books 1889–1934, Macclesfield Silk Manufacturing Society.

64  Photograph in the James Arnold collection, Macclesfield Silk Museum.

65  Cheshire County Records Office, Plan no. 1497, Macclesfield Borough Council.

66  *Macclesfield Courier and Herald,* 23 September 1916.

67  Head 1887, 158–9.

68  Morris and Co 1874, 442.

69  Head 1887, 159.

## 5  HOUSING THE COTTON INDUSTRY 1826–1950

1  Fairbairn 1863, 12.

2  The thirteen firms were Woods, Birchenough and Goodall, Whitmore and Berisford, Critchley and Widdall, Roberts, Watters, Eaton, Whitney, Mason, Roberts and Battey, Samuel Hall, Gosling and Ashness, and Downes. Wootton 1866. Printed in parts in *Macclesfield Courier and Herald,* 1880. The three surviving were John Ashness, Joseph Watters and Co, and Charles Wood and Brother.

3  The six firms were Richard Martin, the Whitfield brothers (Martin and the Whitfields became partners in 1788), the Reade brothers, Vaudrey, Booth, and Drakeford. The one surviving firm by 1834 was William and Charles Vaudrey. Pigot and Co 1834.

4  Chapman 1987, 39.

5  Cheshire County Records Office, Swindells Papers, SWC 29 and 31.

6  Chapman 1987, 39.

7  Rose 1978.

8  Ibid.

9  *Macclesfield Courier and Herald,* 22 July 1848.

10  *Macclesfield Courier and Herald,* 21 October 1882.

11  Deeds, Paradise Mills, Macclesfield, in the possession of Macclesfield Museums Trust.

12  In planning to build Clarence Mill, Bollington, in 1834 the Swindells were able to draw upon their own considerable funds as a large company as well as borrowing from a bank. The partnership of Swindells and Brooke provided £5,000, Swindells and Oliver £3,000, and a bank the final £3,000 of the building cost. Cheshire County Records Office, Swindells Papers, Minute Book, 1834–42, SWM.

13  For the advantages of smaller firms in the cotton industry see Farnie 1979, 209–15. Evidence that the Swindells both made their

own machinery and purchased it secondhand comes from Cheshire County Records Office, Swindells Papers, Minute Book, 1834–42, SWM.

14 Cheshire County Records Office, Swindells Papers, Minute Book, 1834–42, SWM.

15 For a more detailed study of the reorganisation of the cotton industry in the second half of the 19th century see Farnie 1979, 277–323.

16 Mathias 1983, 352–4.

17 Deeds, Beehive Mill, Bollington, in the possession of the landowner.

18 Farnie 1979, 237.

19 *Macclesfield Courier and Herald*, 22 February 1896.

20 Recruitment brochure published by the Fine Spinners and Doublers Ltd undated, c1950.

21 Farnie 1979, 194.

22 Rose 1978, 37.

23 *Macclesfield Courier and Herald*, 19 August 1916.

24 Deeds, Lower Heyes Mill, Macclesfield, in the possession of the owners.

25 Deeds, Clarence Mill, Bollington, in the possession of the owners.

26 Catling 1978, 41–2.

27 The evolution of the self-acting mule is fully discussed in Catling 1978, 35–57, and Mann 1958, 288–9, Figures 158–9.

28 Cheshire County Records Office, Swindells Papers, SWB.

29 *Macclesfield Courier and Herald*, 31 August 1857.

30 *Macclesfield Courier and Herald*, 6 May 1882.

31 Benson 1983.

32 Hills 1970, 208–29.

33 Parliamentary Papers, Reports from Assistant Hand-Loom Weavers' Commissioners, 1840, 490.

34 Pigot and Co 1834.

35 Parliamentary Papers (House of Commons) 1834 (167), *Employment of Children in Factories*, xx, C1, Part 2.

36 *Macclesfield Courier and Herald*, 6 May 1826.

37 Cheshire County Records Office, Swindells Papers, Minute Book, 1834–42, SWM.

38 Cheshire County Records Office, Swindells Papers, Minute Book, 1834–42, SWM.

39 Farnie 1985.

40 When the Swindells family decided to build the 1841 extension to Clarence Mill, Bollington, it was resolved 'that the stone be got as much as possible from the quarry belonging to M Swindells Snr'. Cheshire County Records Office, Swindells Papers, Minute Book 1834–42, SWM.

41 *Macclesfield Courier and Herald*, 6 May 1843 and 31 August 1857.

42 Cheshire County Records Office, Swindells Papers, Minute Book, 1834–42, SWM.

43 Cheshire County Records Office, Swindells Papers, Minute Book, 1834–42, SWM.

44 Ordnance Survey 1871, 1:2500.

45 *Macclesfield Courier and Herald*, 19 April 1845. The floor referred to here as the second floor was the second storey, i.e. the first floor.

46 Cheshire County Records Office, Swindells Papers, Minute Book, 1834–42, SWM.

47 Parliamentary Papers (House of Commons) 1834 (167), *Employment of Children in Factories*, xx, C1, Part 2.

48 Cheshire County Records Office, Swindells Papers, SWB 1–37.

49 Cheshire County Records Office, Swindells Papers, SWB 1–37.

50 Cheshire County Records Office, Plan and schedule of Clarence Mill, Bollington, 1841–54, SWB.

51 No parabolically flanged beams have been observed in east Cheshire's fireproof mills, and no evidence, apart from Lowerhouse Mill, Bollington, of side-mounted shrink rings.

52 Gurr and Hunt 1985, 21.

53 *Macclesfield Courier and Herald*, 6 May 1826.

54 Cheshire County Records Office, Disley Tithe Award Map, 1851.

55 Pigot and Co 1834.

56 Quarry Bank Mill Archives. Mill memoranda.

57 Cheshire County Records Office, Swindells Papers, Minute Book 1834–42, SWM.

58 Cheshire County Records Office, Disley Tithe Award Map, 1851.

59 Fairbairn 1863, 172.

60 Deeds, Lower Heyes Mill, Macclesfield, in the possession of the owners.

61 *Macclesfield Courier and Herald*, 19 August 1916.

62 *Macclesfield Courier and Herald*, 6 May 1843.

63 Quarry Bank Mill, Styal, Literature.

64 *Macclesfield Courier and Herald*, 20 September 1851.

65 Cheshire County Records Office, Swindells Papers, SWB.

66 Ibid.

67 Ibid.

68 Ibid.

69 *Macclesfield Courier and Herald*, 6 May 1882.

70 For a more detailed discussion of steam-engine development see Hills 1970.

71 *Macclesfield Courier and Herald*, 24 March 1832.

72 *Macclesfield Courier and Herald*, 23 August 1845.

73 *Macclesfield Courier and Herald*, 6 May 1843.

74 Cheshire County Records Office, Swindells Papers, Minute Book, 1834–42, SWM.

75 Macclesfield Courier and Herald, 6 May 1882.

76 Prospectus of sale, 1903, held with Lower Heyes Mill, Macclesfield, deeds in the possession of the owner.

## 6 THE MILL IN THE LANDSCAPE

1 In 1804 what is now Sunderland Street was known as Pickford Street, after the landowner Joseph Pickford, and what is now Pickford Street was known as Sugar Street.
2 Cheshire County Records Office, Enclosure Award Map, 1804, QDE 2/10.
3 Cheshire County Records Office, Cawley, J. Map of Macclesfield, 1838.
4 Ordnance Survey Map of Congleton, 1:2500, 1871–2.
5 Davies 1961, 374.
6 Stephens 1970, 345.
7 Ibid, 122.
8 *Macclesfield Courier and Herald,* 11 June 1852.
9 Bills, letters and receipts of Thomas Bullock in the possession of Macclesfield Museums Trust.
10 Parliamentary Papers (House of Commons) 1834 (167), *Employment of Children in Factories,* xx, C1, Part 2.
11 Ibid.
12 *Macclesfield Courier and Herald,* 20 February 1813.
13 *Macclesfield Courier and Herald,* 5 June 1824.
14 Cheshire County Records Office, Buglawton Tithe Award Map and Schedule, EDT/75/2.
15 Cheshire County Records Office, Particulars of Estates and Rents Late in the Inheritance of Mr John Booth deceased 26 February 1820, DCB/1595/16/3.
16 Malmgreen 1985, 208.
17 Ormerod 1819, quoted in Davies 1961, 146.
18 Davies 1961, 231.
19 Stephens 1970, 160.
20 Mathias 1983, 140.
21 *Macclesfield Courier and Herald,* 8 August 1829.
22 Parliamentary Papers (House of Commons) 1834 (167), *Employment of Children in Factories,* xx, C1, Part 2.
23 Ibid.
24 Parliamentary Papers, Digest of Parochial Returns to Select Committee on the Education of the Poor 1819, ix,73. Quoted in Stephens 1970, 275.
25 Davies 1961, 218–19.
26 For a more detailed view of education in Macclesfield and Congleton see Davies 1961, 210–28, and Stephens 1970, 272–308.
27 John Rylands Library, Manchester, Methodist Archive. A List of Names of the Societies in the Manchester Circuit, May 1759. This document contains two lists relating to Congleton, the first dated May 1759 and the second, on the next page, undated.
28 Stephens 1970, 243.
29 For a more detailed study of religion in Macclesfield and Congleton see Stephens 1970, 201–71, and Davies 1961, 299–360.
30 Dawson 1973; CRO Land Tax Assessments for Langley End; Hanshall 1823, 524.
31 *Macclesfield Courier and Herald,* 22 April 1815.
32 *Macclesfield Courier and Herald,* 20 July 1831.
33 Dawson 1973.
34 Pigot and Co 1822–3.
35 Varey 1825.
36 Smith 1875, 320.
37 *Macclesfield Courier and Herald,* 16 September 1911.
38 Varey 1825.
39 Dawson 1973.
40 Smith 1875, 321.
41 Bagshaw 1850.
42 Morris and Co 1874.
43 Mathias 1983, 415.
44 Malthus 1798.
45 Rose 1978, 22.
46 Parliamentary Papers (House of Commons) 1834 (167), *Employment of Children in Factories,* xx, C1, Part 2.
47 Rose 1978, 27.
48 *Macclesfield Courier and Herald,* 13 March 1830.
49 Letter dated January 1835 written by Samuel Greg to the Factory Inspector Leonard Horner. Greg wrote two letters to Horner, the second dated March 1838. Both letters are reproduced in Greg 1875.
50 Letter dated January 1835 written by Samuel Greg to the Factory Inspector Leonard Horner, reproduced in Greg 1875.
51 Greg 1875.

# BIBLIOGRAPHY

Aspin C (ed) 1972. *Angus Bethune Reach. Manchester and the Textile Districts in 1849*

Bagshaw, S 1850. *Trade Directory*

Benson, A P 1983. *Textile Machines*

Buchanan, R A 1980. *Industrial Archaeology in Britain*

Catling, H 1978. The development of the spinning mule. *J Textile Hist* **9**, 35–57

Chaloner, W H 1950–1. Charles Roe of Macclesfield (1715–81): an eighteenth century industrialist. *Trans Lancashire Cheshire Antiq Soc* **62**, 133–56

1951. The Cheshire activities of Matthew Boulton and James Watt of Soho, nr Birmingham, 1776–1817. *Trans Lancashire Cheshire Antiq Soc* **61**, 121–36

1953. Sir Thomas Lombe 1685–1739 and the British silk industry. *History Today* **3**, 778–85

1963. *People and Industries*

Chapelot, J and Fossier, R 1985. *The Village and House in the Middle Ages*

Chapman, S D 1974. The textile factory before Arkwright: a typology of factory development. *Business Hist Rev* **48**, 451–78

1981–2. The Arkwright mills — Colquhoun's Census of 1788 and archaeological evidence. *Ind Archaeol Rev* **6**, 5–27

1987. *The Cotton Industry in the Industrial Revolution*

Corry, J 1817. *The History of Macclesfield*

Cossons, N (ed) 1972. *Rees's Manufacturing Industry (1819–20)*. 5 vols

Crippa, F 1990. Il torcitoio circolare da seta: evoluzione, macchine superstiti, restauri. *Quaderni Storici* **73**, 169–212

Crozier, M 1947. *An Old Silk Family*

Davies, C S 1961 (ed). *A History of Macclesfield*

Dawson, C 1973. *Langley*

Defoe, D 1971. *A Tour Through The Whole Island Of Great Britain, 1724–6*

Edgar, J 1987. *Report concerning Application for Listed Building Consent for Demolition of the Former Silk Mill, Streatham*

English, W 1971. A study of the driving mechanisms in the early circular throwing machines. *Textile Hist* **2**, 65–75

Everett 1840. *Manchester Guide*

Fairbairn, W 1863. *Treatise on Mills and Millwork. Part 2. On Machinery of Transmission and the Construction and Arrangement of Mills*

Farey, J 1827. *A Treatise on the Steam Engine*

Farnie, D A 1979. *The English Cotton Industry and the World Market 1815–1896*

1985. The metropolis of cotton spinning, machine making and mill building. In Gurr and Hunt 1985

Finney, S 1785. *Survey of the Parish of Wilmslow*

Fitzgerald, R 1987–8. The development of the cast iron frame in textile mills to 1850. *Ind Archaeol Rev* **10**, 127–45

Giles, C P and Goodall, I H 1992. *Yorkshire Textile Mills 1770–1930*

Greg, S 1875. *A Layman's Legacy*

Gurr, D and Hunt, J 1985. *The Cotton Mills of Oldham*

Hanshall, J H 1823. *History of Cheshire*

Head, R 1887. *Congleton Past and Present*

Hegginbotham, H 1882. *Stockport Ancient and Modern*

Hertz, G B 1909. The English silk industry in the eighteenth century. *Engl Hist Rev* **24**, 710–25

Hills, R L 1970. *Power in the Industrial Revolution*

Hodson, H 1978. *Cheshire, 1660–1780: Restoration to Industrial Revolution*

Holden 1805. *Directory*

1806. *Directory*

1807. *Directory*

Hutton, W 1817. *History of Derby*

Iredale, J A and Townhill, P A 1973. Silk spinning in England: the end of an epoch. *Textile Hist* **4**, 100–108

Kerridge E 1985. *Textile Manufactures in Early Modern England*

Lardner, Rev D (ed) 1831. *A Treatise on the Origin, Progressive Improvement and Present State of the Silk Manufacture. Cabinet Cyclopaedia*

Malmgreen, G 1985. *Silk Town: Industry and Culture in Macclesfield, 1750–1835*

Malthus, T 1798. *An Essay on the Principle of Population as it Affects the Future Improvement of Society*

Mann, J de L 1958. The textile industry: machinery for cotton, flax, wool, 1760–1850. In Singer *et al* 1958, 277–307

Massey, J 1959. The silk mills of Macclesfield. Unpub RIBA thesis, Manchester University School of Architecture

Mathias, P 1983. *The First Industrial Nation: an Economic History of Britain 1700–1914*

Morris and Co 1864. *Commercial Directory and Gazetteer of Cheshire*
  1874. *Trade Directory*

Negri, P 1831. *Manuale pratico per la stima delle case e degli opifici industriali*

Ormerod, C S (ed) 1819. *History of the County Palatine and City of Chester*

Phillips, J 1792. *Phillips' Inland Navigation*

Pigot and Co 1822–3. *Commercial Directory for the County of Cheshire*
  1834. *Commercial Directory for the County of Cheshire*

Post Office 1878. *Directory of Cheshire*

Prout, J A 1829. *A Practical View of the Silk Trade*

Radcliffe, W 1828. *Origin of the New System of Manufacture Commonly Called Power Loom Weaving*

Roberts, L 1970. *Treasure of Trafficke, 1641*. In Hills 1970, 8

Rose, M B 1978. *The Gregs of Styal*

Rothstein, N 1977. *The Introduction of the Jacquard Loom to Great Britain*

RCHME 1991. *Recording Historic Buildings: a Descriptive Specification*. 2nd edn

Singer, C *et al* (eds) 1958. *A History of Technology. Vol IV. The Industrial Revolution c1750 to c1850*

Skempton, A W and Johnson, H R 1962. The first iron frames. *Architect Rev* **131**, 175–86

Smiles, S 1904. *Lives of the Engineers*

Smith, B 1875. *Methodism in Macclesfield*

Stephens, W B 1970 (ed). *History of Congleton*

Tann, J 1970. *Development of the Factory*

Tunnicliffe 1789. *Directory of the Principal Merchants &c. in Cheshire*

Unwin, G 1924. *Samuel Oldknow and the Arkwrights*

Ure, A 1861. *The Philosophy of Manufactures*

Varey, P 1825. *The History and Directory of Macclesfield and its Vicinity*

Warner, F 1921. *The Silk Industry of the United Kingdom — Its Origins and Development*

White and Co 1860. *Macclesfield Directory*

Williams, M and Farnie, D A 1992. *Cotton Mills in Greater Manchester*

Williamson, F 1936. George Sorocold of Derby. *Journal of the Derbyshire Archaeological and National History Society* **57**, 43–93

Wootton, J 1866. *Macclesfield Past*

Worrall 1872. *Directory of Stockport*

Yates, S 1822. *History of Congleton*

Zonca, V 1607. *Novo teatro de machine et edificii*

# INDEX